FRENCH HUMANIST TRAGEDY

For Odette, Dorothy and Grahame

FRENCH HUMANIST TRAGEDY
A REASSESSMENT

Donald Stone, Jr.

Manchester University Press

Rowman and Littlefield

Published by Manchester University Press
Oxford Road, Manchester M13 9PL

ISBN 0 7190 0567 1

First published in the United States 1974
by Rowman and Littlefield, Totowa, N.J.

ISBN 0 87471 537 7

c e

Printed and bound by
T. & A. Constable Ltd., Edinburgh

CONTENTS

PREFACE

It was Jacques Guicharnaud who long ago suggested that I should explore this subject and to him first I express my thanks. In the intervening years a summer Canaday grant from Harvard and a Guggenheim Fellowship (1968-9) provided that indispensable financial support which permitted me to complete my basic research.

Numerous individuals have given me of their valuable time and advice. To Mme Basanoff of the Bibliothèque Nationale, Miss Jakeman and Miss Shaw of the Houghton Library, Loretta Freiling and Friedrich Solmsen of Wisconsin's Institute for Research in the Humanities I am especially grateful. Professors Harold Gotoff and Glen Bowersock kindly reviewed my Latin translations.

Looking back over the period during which this book was being prepared, I must single out one moment above all as the summit of a personal as well as professional experience: my stay at Gonville and Caius College, Cambridge. To the Master and Fellows of that most hospitable institution, I cannot say enough in gratitude. It is only just that this book should be dedicated to two present and one past member of the Modern Languages Faculty of Cambridge, for without the warmth of their friendship and the stimulus of their insights, this volume might not have been.

D. S., Jr.

ABBREVIATIONS

The following abbreviations are used in the notes and bibliography:

A.U.M.L.A.—*Journal of the Australasian Universities Language and Literature Association*

B.A.—La Bibliothèque de l'Arsenal

B.H.R.—*Bibliothèque d'humanisme et renaissance*

B.M.—The British Museum

B.N.—La Bibliothèque Nationale

H.L.—The Houghton Library, Harvard University

M.L.N.—*Modern Language Notes*

M.L.R.—*Modern Language Review*

P.M.L.A.—*Publications of the Modern Language Association*

R.C.C.—*La Revue des cours et conférences*

R.D.M.—*La Revue des deux mondes*

R.H.L.F.—*La Revue d'histoire littéraire de la France*

R.S.H.—*La Revue des sciences humaines*

R.S.S.—*La Revue du seizième siècle*

Y.F.S.—*Yale French Studies*

Attention is also called to the fact that in discussion of the French plays characters' names are reproduced as they appear in the original French. As a result, the spelling of certain names which appear in more than one play will vary slightly within the text.

INTRODUCTION

From the outset my principal aim in studying French tragedy before the coming of Classicism[1] was to uncover those factors which determined its nature and function. If there was never a time when I felt that such a study might be used to rehabilitate this literature as a series of misunderstood masterpieces, the realization that even the most sympathetic modern reader would probably squirm with discomfort at a staging of any of these plays offered the very real challenge to understand what this literature—far more extensive and far more varied than the manuals suggest—meant for the society that produced it. As the years passed, I saw that to explain the factors involved and to know the essentials of the function that tragedy fulfilled only led to the larger problem of the relationship between the sixteenth century and the periods that came before and after it.

Here in a century where greater contact with antiquity is said to have brought poetry, ideas, and institutions to disassociate themselves from their medieval heritage flourished a genre in which not only the medieval element refused to die but also dramatists, using on occasion the same subject, the same form as Corneille and Racine, produced a body of plays quite different from their seventeenth-century counterparts. Again and again the evidence suggested that a significant break with the past came in the seventeenth century, not the sixteenth, but this idea ran counter to the basic tenets of French literary history. I have pursued it, nonetheless, and the pages to follow offer my conclusions.

The fact that previous work on French tragedy before Corneille often proved disappointing and prejudiced provided no little encouragement for a reassessment of the genre. Elliott Forsyth's Sorbonne thesis, entitled *La Tragédie française de Jodelle à Corneille (1553-1640), le thème de la vengeance,* if compared with M. C. Bradbrook's *Themes and Conventions of Elizabethan Tragedy,* Madeleine Doran's *Endeavors of Art* or J. M. R. Margeson's *The Origins of English Tragedy* demonstrates in yet another area Bernard Weinberg's remark that French sixteenth-century studies have much to learn from the work of their English colleagues.[2] Richard Griffiths' 'The Influence of Formulary Rhetoric upon French Renaissance Tragedy', published in 1964, is the first example I can find in French studies of the sort of analysis done by Bradbrook, Doran, and Margeson, who have described in detail the importance of medieval drama, rhetorical traditions, and theatrical conventions for any interpretation of Elizabethan tragedy.

To date no book has attempted to do as much for French humanist drama. Instead, most critics have preferred to work within the perspective on French tragedy dominant in the eighteenth century. In that period appeared two histories of French theatre, one by the Parfaict brothers (1745-9), the other by Corneille's nephew Fontenelle (1758). For each, the story of tragedy is itself a minor drama in which the forces of regularity and good taste win out over the forces of boredom and coarseness. The Parfaict brothers accentuate the differences between the medieval genres ('ennuyeux à l'excès', with a 'plan ridiculement construit' and 'grossieretés sans nombre', I, xiv)[3] and the humanist drama ('une forme plus raisonnable', I, xxiii). They consider Garnier superior to his predecessors and find in Hardy's plays, despite gross neglect of the bienséances, 'une marche de Théatre assez réguliere' (IV, ii). Fontenelle's discussion, limited to the stages of development in theatre after 1552, traces a nearly identical evolution. Of Jodelle's *Cléopâtre captive* he writes: 'Point d'action, point de jeu, grands & mauvais discours partout' (p. 53). If Garnier reveals 'plus de noblesse, d'élévation, de force que Jodelle, . . . la constitution de ses Piéces n'est pas meilleure. Elles sont toutes aussi dénuées d'action, aussi languissantes, aussi simples, & conduites avec aussi peu d'art' (p. 71). Hardy, for all his faults ('nul scrupule sur les mœurs ni sur les bienséances', p. 72), produced plays that broke with the boredom of earlier tragedies. Then, as both histories state, Corneille brought tragedy to the majesty it had lacked for so long.

Later critics of French tragedy kept this perspective alive through a similar tendency to associate irregularity with the medieval theatre, to criticize those traits of sixteenth-century drama that did not conform to the traits of Classical tragedy, and to search out in the same works signs of the coming of French Classicism. Rigal, Faguet, and Lancaster never doubted that the origins of the irregular tragicomedy lay in medieval theatre. Faguet and Rigal also devoted many pages to a discussion of the lack of unities (or their near presence) in early tragedies and set a significant precedent for more recent studies.

Because in Garnier's *Les Juives* (1583) 'la fable est d'une simplicité extrême, l'action encore lente est cependant bien liée', Loukovitch does not hesitate to remark that the play signals 'le premier pas dans l'évolution de la tragédie religieuse vers le classicisme' (p. 60). In analysing the *Tragédie de Sainte Agnès*, he finds another thread—psychology. That we are dealing with a mere glimmer is no deterrent to Loukovitch: 'Par sa psychologie encore rudimentaire, *Sainte Agnès* fait entrevoir un peu la tragédie chrétienne classique. C'est la première lueur de l'aube: le grand jour est encore loin' (p. 122). Lebègue's remarks on Des Masures reveal a totally similar scale of values: 'L'auteur sacrifie trop l'art à l'édification: le héros a le défaut d'être continuellement parfait, et l'action est retardée par des cantiques et de pieuses effusions. Mais Des Masures observe l'unité de temps, et il a su dessiner quelques caractères avec une finesse qui fait penser à Térence' (*La Tragédie française*, pp. 30-1). By the same token, the inability to find any psychology or movement in Jodelle has produced endless repetition of Fontenelle's criticisms. Chamard (1940): 'Je ne vois guère, pour ma part, en quoi *Didon* est supérieure à *Cleopatre*. L'œuvre est aussi vide d'action. . . . *Didon* n'est, comme *Cleopatre*, qu'une longue élégie en cinq actes' (*Histoire*, III, 218). Lebègue (1944): 'La *Didon* . . . ne se distingue guère de la *Cléopâtre* que par un délayage encore plus intempérant: les vers parlés y sont deux fois plus nombreux, bien qu'il n'y ait aucune incertitude dans l'action' (*La Tragédie française*, p. 34, n.). Forsyth (1962): 'Comme la *Cléopâtre*, la *Didon* reste une pièce élégiaque, sans action' (p. 149).

The limitations of this traditional perspective are many. Surely there is a difference between observation and explanation. To repeat continually that sixteenth-century tragedy was elegiac or devoid of psychology will not tell us why this is so and I see no reason to believe that a search for the why is a less necessary pursuit. Also, our analyses must lose much of their value as accurate accounts of the past if we accept *a priori* the notion that France in the sixteenth century broke with the Middle Ages to accomplish a Renaissance (as if we all agreed on the meaning of that word), which in turn prepared French Classicism. Can we be sure that the traits of French Classical drama, so carefully tracked down in the early tragedies, were of any consequence to those authors who seem to have used them very sparingly? To state the same objection another way, can we feel free to make absolute judgments and to use absolute criteria when we are also concerned with the particular quality of a period's thinking?

In a chapter entitled 'La Tradition antique', Forsyth defines the tragic in Seneca as 'le simple spectacle des souffrances qu'infligeaient à l'homme les ravages des passions et les changements de la fortune'. The ensuing paragraph begins, 'Les gens de la *Renaissance*, qui, à certains égards, étaient restés fidèles à la pensée du *moyen âge*, trouvèrent à leur gré une littérature qui prêchait ainsi la fragilité des choses humaines, la maîtrise des passions, la punition du pécheur par les puissances célestes et l'acceptation résignée des décrets de la volonté divine' (p. 101, my italics). Despite the chapter heading and the insertion of the word 'Renaissance', the author realizes that the attraction to Seneca cannot be correctly explained except by the addition of a phrase about the Middle Ages. When, after noting the overlap between Senecan and Christian ethics and Seneca's sermon-like tone 'qui caractérise tant d'ouvrages du moyen âge et de la Renaissance', the critic tells us, 'Ainsi Sénèque offrit aux hommes du XVIe siècle une tragédie dont le caractère s'accordait parfaitement avec l'esprit de la Renaissance' (p. 102), the muddle is complete. Because of a lingering medieval cast of mind, the men of the sixteenth century appreciated in Seneca the spirit of the Renaissance. Lebègue creates a similar problem in *La Tragédie française de la Renaissance* when he writes, 'Il n'y a pas eu, en France, de coupure brusque entre les anciens genres et la tragédie du XVIe siècle; mais, en fait, les auteurs des tragédies régulières les ont dédaignés et ont cherché ailleurs des modèles' (p. 10). In both cases the authors are too competent to neglect the long medieval shadow that falls on France in the sixteenth century; yet one is certain of change in models and the other of a period (and a spirit) called the Renaissance.

There is perhaps a subtlety to Forsyth's reasoning that escapes me but it does seem hard to avoid noticing a parallel here with the traditionalist approach of Fontenelle, Rigal, and others. It becomes blatant when Forsyth, who has so cogently noted that the nexus between these dramatists and Seneca lies in their common preference for a drama centred on 'la fragilité des choses humaines', writes that if the earliest French dramatists 'choisissent le plus souvent leur modèle dans le théâtre ancien, ils se contentent d'en imiter la forme extérieure sans en saisir véritablement le dynamisme interne' (pp. 145-6). But why must a dramatist interested primarily in conveying a moral lesson create any 'dynamisme interne' unless the *critic* feels that this should be so, that tragedy is somehow not tragedy without such internal conflict? The second clause brings us, I think, even closer to the heart of our problem. Critics cannot have it both ways. We cannot be told to recognize the medieval cast of thought directing our dramatists and yet judge their works by standards set in the seventeenth century that continue to appear valid to us.

By giving to this study the subtitle 'A Reassessment', I wished to emphasize that the principal work which remained to be done on French humanist tragedy concerned its interpretation, not its history. Those interested in a catalogue of the pertinent dates and titles associated with the genre will find them in the numerous studies of Lebègue and Lanson. Moreover, as with the development of any literary phenomenon, all manifestations of interest in tragedy during the sixteenth century do not bear equally on an interpretation of its origins and evolution. If the pages to follow make no mention of the Latin dramas of Stoa and Barthélemy de Loches, yet do refer to Buchanan's *Jephthes sive votum*, it is not only because the plays of Stoa and de Loches are in style and subject matter quite unlike the majority of humanist tragedies but also because they cannot be compared in influence to Buchanan's Latin play which had several contemporary translations and is known to have been played decades after its composition.

In the case of the Italian theatre, discussion has been omitted for lack of evidence. The strong ties between France and Italy in the sixteenth century, the general tendency to turn toward Italy for artistic inspiration would make it seem unthinkable to analyse a genre's evolution in France during this period without reference to its Italian counterpart. However, to date, extensive proof of Italian influence on French humanist tragedy has been difficult to find. Lanson once attempted to define Italy's role in the establishment of tragedy in France and with the exception of the presentation of a play by Alamanni in 1555 and of a translation of Trissino's *Sofonisba* in 1556 was obliged to admit that what he had discovered was 'peu considérable et peu précis' ('L'Idée de la tragédie', p. 57). My own soundings have proved no more successful.

Certain basic tenets of Giraldi's views on tragedy—the division into five acts, the use of a chorus at the end of acts, of messengers and soliloquies—the French could find easily in Horace or Seneca; others—a happy ending, many characters, and a hero that is neither too good nor too evil—do not correspond at all to standard French practice.

When French dramatists treated subjects already used by Italians, comparison reveals fundamental differences, not striking similarities. In a study of three Dido plays, J. Friedrich demonstrated that Jodelle owes nothing to the Italian Dolce. Rucellai's handling of the Rosemund story bears no resemblance to the spirit or the composition of Chrétien des Croix' *Albouin*. Trissino's *Sofonisba* was twice translated into French before Montreux, Montchrétien, and Mairet wrote their versions of the story; yet only Montchrétien's structure parallels that of Trissino and all three Frenchmen offer substantially different portraits of the fated couple.

There is a distinctly international aspect to French humanist tragedy and Italy has its contribution to make but it is a peculiarity of this drama and an essential element to the reassessment proposed here that decisive non-French influences are not always to be found in the world of the theatre. For the same reason, a charting of its fortunes must take us far from dramatic theory. On the other hand, there is no discounting the direct influence of French medieval dramas and of certain plays by Euripides and Seneca which will be studied in some detail. An unnecessary digression, some may say. However, if we are to understand fully French humanist tragedy, we must understand fully what the vagaries of history and of the transmission of texts determined the sixteenth century should know of serious drama and how the period interpreted this material. Providing such an understanding necessitated frequent quotation since many of the crucial texts are extremely rare. To those readers who would have accepted my conclusion without such proof, I am grateful, but in that these texts create the perspective on tragedy we need to know, they are more than proof; they are the stuff awareness is made of.

Before concluding this Introduction, I wish to acknowledge my debt to those who have not seen fit to tread the path of tradition. In addition to the studies on English tragedy already mentioned, special note must be taken of the work done recently at Cambridge University. I have cited Richard Griffiths' article (reworked from his Cambridge thesis); Gillian Jondorf's book on Garnier was originally a Cambridge thesis also. They have established with H. B. Charlton, H. W. Lawton, and Bernard Weinberg an openmindedness about sixteenth-century tragedy that I hope my own study will not betray.

NOTES TO THE INTRODUCTION

[1] To avoid any possible confusion, I have used the word 'classical' throughout to describe the works of antiquity or any imitation thereof and 'Classical' to designate works and views produced by the French Classicism of the seventeenth century.

[2] See Weinberg's review of Marc Whitney's edition of Olivier de Magny, *Les Odes amoureuses de* 1559, in *Romance Philology*, 20 (1966-7), 126-30.

[3] Whenever possible, references will be given in the text and the reader is referred to the bibliography for a full description of the work quoted. In the event that more than one work by the same author appears in the bibliography an abbreviated title will appear in the text with the page reference.

I CONCEPTS AND CONTEXTS

I SIXTEENTH-CENTURY VIEWS

The strongest reason for rejecting Fontenelle's perspective on French tragedy before Corneille is the absence of any such perspective in contemporary material related to the genre and abundant evidence from this same material that tragedy was conceived in terms quite removed from the theories of drama of the seventeenth century. Although there is no dearth at this time of *arts poétiques* or remarks by the dramatists themselves on their genre, René Bray felt obliged to declare, 'Le XVIIᵉ siècle tout entier se détourne de devanciers qui, malgré leur bonne volonté, n'ont pas su créer la méthode et la doctrine dont on sent impérieusement le besoin' (p. 27). Other scholars are no more positive in evaluating what was written by the sixteenth century.

Bernard Weinberg, commenting on Grévin's ideas on tragedy, writes, 'Essentially, there is no theory of the dramatic art in Grévin's preface; there is merely a re-echoing of the standard tradition relating to the origins and histories of the genres and to the etymologies of the names and other words. This is strictly medieval.' The few ideas taken from Aristotle 'remain secondary and incidental. They do not lead to any total theory of poetics or the dramatic art; they do not lead to any reinterpretation of the traditional concepts; they do not lead to any reorientation of thinking about comedy and tragedy' ('The Sources of Grévin's Ideas', p. 53). H. W. Lawton, after a study of all the various contemporary documents which mention tragedy and Aristotle, concludes that 'while there was a growing knowledge of the *Poetics*, a real understanding of the treatise was lacking to the sixteenth century' ('Sixteenth Century French Tragedy', p. 175). The almost casual manner in which the *Deffence* deals with tragedy—offering no theory, only a hint at models and tone—has prompted Banachévitch to hypothesize that if the Coqueret band had known that Jodelle and La Péruse would soon take up the genre, more would have been said about tragedy (p. 87). Perhaps, but there is every reason to believe that their extended remarks would have differed little from those analysed by Weinberg and Lawton.

The uniformity throughout the sixteenth century among those who attempt to define the matter of tragedy is remarkable. In a pioneering article published in 1904, Gustave Lanson established that the humanists derived their definition of tragedy from two Latin grammarians, Donatus and Diomedes, who had written that tragedy showed the fragility of human things through a reversal of fortune in the lives of the great. It is not surprising to find Lazare de Baïf stating in 1537 in his translation of Sophocles' *Electra*, 'Tragedie est vne moralite composee des grandes calamitez, meurtres & aduersitez suruenues aux nobles & excellentz person-naiges' (sig. A2ʳ) or Bochetel, in 1544, translating Euripides' *Hecuba*, 'ce ne sont que pleurs, captivitez, ruines et desolations de grans princes, et quelquefois des plus uertueux' (p. 4) or to find the words of Donatus and Diomedes appended to a 1544 Paris edition of Erasmus' translation of *Hecuba*, but here is Peletier's list of tragic subjects published in 1555: 'occisions, exiz, maleureus defin¢mans d¢ fortun¢s, d'anfans e d¢ parans' (p. 72) and La Taille's dated 1572, 'Son vray subiect ne traicte que de piteuses ruines des grands Seigneurs, que des inconstances de Fortune, que bannissements, guerres, pestes, famines, captiuitez, execrables cruautez des Tyrans' (*De l'art de la tragédie*, p. 10). Although Scaliger included Aristotle's definition of tragedy in his *Poetices libri septem* (1561), he felt obliged to add his own and offered this familiar portrait of the genre: 'The events of tragedy are grand, terrible, [such as] the commands of kings, murders, laments, suicides by hanging, exiles, bereavements, parricides, incests, conflagrations, battles, blindings, wailings, shriekings, complaints, funerals, eulogies, and dirges' (III, 96). Laudun's list of 1597 is practically a translation of Scaliger's ('les commandements des Roys, les batailles, meurtres, viollement de filles & de femmes, trahisons, exils, plaintes, pleurs, cris, faussetez' p. 282), and reinforces the conclusion that thought on tragic subjects did not change significantly throughout the century.

A similar uniformity could be traced with respect to the style required by tragedy (lofty) and the characters (great). There was little more said and little to imply that dramatic action or human psychology ever mattered. This is not to minimize the presence in the sixteenth century of remarks on Aristotle or technique in general. The simple fact is that the writers themselves minimized their discussions by deriving them from diverse sources, stopping far short of any analysis, and serving up detached comments in lieu of any connected theory.

When Grévin declares near the beginning of his 'Brief Discours' that he has yet to see 'Tragédies et Comédies Françoises, excepté celles de Médée et d'Hécuba, lesquelles ont été faictes vulgaires, et prises du Grec d'Euripide' (p. 5), the reader is given to suspect that Grévin possesses a more sophisticated view of tragedy than that displayed by his contemporaries. He even paraphrases Aristotle. 'La Tragédie donc (comme dit Aristote en son art poëtique) est une imitation ou représentation de quelque faict illustre et grand de soymesme, comme est celuy touchant la mort de Jules César' (p. 6). Unfortunately, from this point on, all is disappointment. Grévin touches on the etymology of the word 'tragédie', the great names of Greek drama, how his own play is not imitated from Muret's *Julius Caesar*, and why he does not use choruses. The 'Discours' then passes to comedy.

Weinberg has shown that Grévin's ideas are all second-hand. More crucial, and equally characteristic of the period, is the lack of desire on Grévin's part to explore the exact meaning of such words as 'imitation' or 'représentation'. One is led to believe that the resemblance between 'faict illustre' and the list of tragic subjects provided by the Latin grammarians has completely reassured Grévin that he is not dealing with any new concepts.

Similarly, how characteristic of the century for Rivaudeau to state in the dedicatory poem accompanying *Aman* that he will try to avoid the failings of Euripides as censured by Aristotle and then to abandon the discussion. The reasons behind Aristotle's judgment—and his particular concept of tragedy—seem in no way pertinent. One could well argue that Rivaudeau's announcement derives more from a humanist's desire to follow the dictates of an authority than from a dramatist's inquiry into the nature of tragedy. Rivaudeau's humanist bent is openly referred to in the dedicatory poem when he states that now he would like to undertake a commentary of Euri-

pides, now an explication of 'les grans thesors des Grœcs' and 'des
liures saintz les plus rares secrets' (p. 41). The projects recall
Toutain's pleasure at publishing his translation of Seneca's
Agamemnon as a work 'auiourd'hui entre les doctes desiré' (sig. *4ʳ)
or Erasmus' decision to translate Euripides in order to perfect his
knowledge of Greek and his ability to deal with early sacred texts.
Erasmus once called his translations 'an exercise in Greek'[1] and at
the time he was working on the Euripidean texts, described his task
in these terms: 'to make good Latin out of good Greek requires a
remarkable artist who is not only very well provided with a copious,
ready store of words in both languages, but also most quick-sighted
and careful'.[2] The linguistic (versus literary) emphasis here is worth
remembering. It reveals in the present context to what degree
sixteenth-century humanists' interest in tragedy often fitted into
a larger preoccupation with language that, to say the least, was not
concerned with dramatic theory.

Rivaudeau's *Avant-Parler* to *Aman* is no less disparate in content
although it is slightly more concerned with technique than the dedication. He speaks at some length about how to use a messenger
correctly and how to arrange for the telling of events preceding the
drama's opening. He speaks against machines (one of Aristotle's
criticisms of Euripides), licentious material (noting that Horace has
already condemned this in Plautus), and plays that last beyond
twenty-four hours. The approach is elementary. Rivaudeau brings
together a number of 'don't's' in writing plays culled from the
authorities, who are now fully recognized as such. About Aristotle
he writes, 'Vray est que ceux qui auront bien leu le petit traité
d'Aristote n'auront pas grand besoin ni de tout ce que j'ay escript
en mon liure [on Electra, which does not seem to have survived] ni
de ce que ie sçauroy enseigner icy' (p. 44). With Horace, where
Rivaudeau also sends 'ceux qui voudront lire quelque chose de la
tragedie' (p. 46), appears the name of Scaliger, whose volume is
recommended by Rivaudeau although he admits to knowing only
its title.

The book in question is Scaliger's *Poetices libri septem*, mentioned
above. Once considered responsible for the reign of Aristotle over
dramatic theory, Scaliger has become the object of stringent
criticism and has been revealed as a poor interpreter of the *Poetics*.[3]
Edith Kern and Spingarn even doubt that Scaliger's influence as
a theorist was very great. What is certain is that if this book (printed

only in Lyons, Heidelberg, and Leyden) was well studied by the French, they found a discussion of tragedy surrounded primarily by didactic, not dramatic considerations: 'Now a poet teaches, he does not merely delight, as some think. . . . And indeed, is there not one and only one end in philosophical exposition, in oratory, and in the drama? Indeed there is. All have one and the same end: persuasion' (I, 1).

Such a mixture of views runs no less through Jean de La Taille's *De l'art de la tragédie*. Although his list of subjects, already quoted, has the same origin as Scaliger's, La Taille also attempts to discuss tragedy in terms of its effect. In a particularly Aristotelian development, he establishes that since tragedy's aim is to move, its subject must be exceptional in nature and its characters neither too evil nor too good. If this is not the case, our emotions will not be those desired. Beyond this point, the treatise is as discursive as any other. La Taille clearly understands why the tragic hero may be neither a criminal nor a saint but why does he state that the action must be presented 'en vn mesme iour, en vn mesme temps, et en vn mesme lieu' (p. 11)? He definitely does not relate this concept to his point about the aim of tragedy. When he is clear, we find concerns and distinctions far removed from those of the *Poetics*. La Taille proudly assures his reader: 'ie n'ay des histoires fabuleuses mendié icy les fureurs d'vn Athamant, d'vn Hercules, ny d'vn Roland, mais celles que la Verité mesme a dictees' (p. 14). Truth here has a specifically religious sense and La Taille joins Théodore de Bèze in equating 'true' subjects with those taken from the Bible. In condemning the life of courtiers and medieval genres, the treatise offers additional evidence of its wide-ranging material and its involvement with questions of the day.

I accentuate the disjointed quality of the remarks because, ultimately, in this form they could be and probably were of limited inspirational value. We respond with enthusiasm when La Taille writes, 'Qu'il n'y ait rien d'oisif, d'inutile, ny rien qui soit mal à propos' (p. 11), filling out his observations with what we know about the success of a unified Racinian plot. La Taille's treatise describes plot in rather different terms, however: 'Qu'elle soit bien entrelassee, meslee, entrecouppee, reprise, et sur tout à la fin rapportee à quelque resolution et but de ce qu'on auoit entrepris d'y traicter' (p. 11). This is no picture of a concatenation of interlocking events from which, as Aristotle states, no element can be withdrawn. I shall presently propose that La Taille had something quite different from unity of action in mind when he wrote 'Qu'il n'y ait rien d'oisif. . .'

It is similarly tempting to find a feeling for dramatic action in these words by La Taille regarding plot, 'qu'elle change, transforme, manie, et tourne l'esprit des escoutans de çà de là' (p. 11), or these by Scaliger, 'And that tragedy which is able to fill the spectator and send him away satisfied, must have one or many changes of fortune' (III, 96). Both statements must be carefully scrutinized, however. Placed in context, they show that movement in the plot, far from participating (as it does for Aristotle) in the creation of tragedy's proper effects, simply insures that the play has lived up to tragedy's definition. Witness Scaliger's description of the situation that prevails at the close of a good tragedy: 'joy of the wicked [changed] to grief, sadness of the good [changed] to joy, but only after danger or the suffering of exile, judgment, murder, vengeance' (III, 96). Scaliger does not suggest in the least that the satisfaction of which he spoke earlier is related to the manipulation of emotions effected by peripeteia. Satisfaction seems to derive from recognizing that the appropriate fate has been meted out to the main characters— something that requires changes of fortune because the passage from sadness to joy or the reverse cannot otherwise be depicted. The entire perspective is moral, not aesthetic, quite in keeping with Scaliger's view that drama, like oratory, must persuade.

La Taille's ensuing statements point to a comparable mentality. The spectator is to be subjected to this movement in order to see 'vne ioye tournee tout soudain en tristesse, et maintenant au rebours, à l'exemple des choses humaines' (p. 11). Again structure relates to matter in such a way as to show that while the author may sound as if he is talking about a means to create dramatic effects, he is in fact describing a plot which best renders the traditional subject of a reversal of fortune and its tacit commentary on human existence.

Against these pseudo treatises it is interesting to place remarks by playwrights like Théodore de Bèze and Louis Des Masures. Although patently serious about their dramas, they not only have little to say about the technique of writing tragedy, but treat the genre with utmost vagueness. Bèze scores those who use their talent on worldly subjects instead of God's praise. When he arrives at a discussion of his own subject, he says that 'il tient de la Tragedie & de la Comedie' and as a consequence he has separated the prologue and divided the play into pauses 'à la façon des actes des Comedies' (p. 48). Yet, because the work contains more of the tragic form than of the comic, he preferred to call the play a tragedy. The remaining portion of the preface accentuates Bèze's effort to use a language, orthography, and poetic form comprehensible to 'les simples gens' (p. 50).

Bèze is appreciably more concerned with separating his present literary enterprise from the genres and style of his contemporaries than with explaining his ideas on tragedy. The few sentences on the genre are matter of fact. He seems in no way disturbed by the dual quality of his play although the grammarians defined tragedy and comedy in such a way as to distinguish between them, not confuse them. He feels no need to explain his choice of the title of tragedy for *Abraham sacrifiant* and his comments suggest that the only criterion involved was the proportion between sombre and happy events. Although he calls the sentiments expressed 'des plus grandes' (p. 49), he does not even follow the grammarians in insisting that such must be the style of tragedy. The only specific association between the play and the genres mentioned is one of form. The prologue and a division into pauses are acknowledged borrowings from comedy.

The 236 verse *epistre* written by Louis Des Masures to introduce his *Tragédies saintes*, a trilogy on David and Saul, shares many traits with Bèze's preface. He, too, prefers the 'saincte Parole' to 'la lire Latine, ou la Françoise Muse' (vs. 66) and eschews a learned style. Above all, he is far more precise (and long winded) about the value of David as an example to teach how God protects his own in time of oppression than about the genre he has selected to transmit this lesson. We must content ourselves with the assurance that he is presenting 'à l'ancienne mode, / Quelques tragiques traits' (vv. 194-5). Des Masures recognizes that some may object to his using the word 'tragedie' since his conclusion is not a piteous spectacle, but justifies himself as Bèze had done: through the long threat of tragedy. David must live an agitated life throughout the trilogy before his triumph. The 'ancienne mode', the 'tragiques traits' are never defined and the one phenomenon Des Masures clearly associates with tragedy is an element he admits is absent from his trilogy (the final piteous spectacle).

However convenient it might be to dismiss Bèze and Des Masures as religious militants, ready to sacrifice serious thinking about their chosen genre to their propaganda, the fact is that these dramatists share more with their contemporaries than one might think. I have already pointed out the continuity from *Abraham sacrifiant* to *Saül le furieux* over true versus 'feints' subjects. A further link between Bèze and La Taille appears in the latter's declaration that through the story of Saul and David he can show 'vn des plus merueilleux secrets de toute la Bible, vn des plus estranges mysteres de ce grand Seigneur du monde' (p. 9). Bèze had already written, 'je trouve trois personnages, ausquels il me semble que le Seigneur a voulu representer ses plusgrandes merveilles, à scavoir Abraham, Moyse, et David' (p. 46). Thus, although Bèze devotes the majority of his preface to demonstrating his piety whereas La Taille discusses theory, these quotations show that the poets had a common inspiration which was scarcely literary in nature or short-lived in their own century. Marcé's dedication to *Achab* (published in 1601) repeats much that Bèze had stated in 1550. The subject is taken, he says, from 'des pancartes sacrées, recongnoissant le debuoir d'vn Chrestien estre d'employer ses hõnestes loisirs, à traicter de la Sainte Escripture, plustost que s'amuser & perdre le temps a representer des fables, & histoires profanes' (sig. ã2ᵛ).

Thus, in addition to possessing diverse interests and intents, French sixteenth-century writers of tragedy repeatedly demonstrate that the genre was associated with considerations quite unrelated to action, characterization or *bienséances*. They also show to what degree Lanson's assertions about the importance of Donatus and Diomedes over Aristotle have very limited value in explaining the range of attitudes toward tragedy, for what appears to be of consequence to the dramatists and translators does not always derive from the grammarians. Jodelle, speaking of himself, states that he wrote plays to 'apporter l'ancien / Miroir Tragic, Comic, qui Rois, & peuple dresse'.[4] Donatus had said and Badius had repeated in his edition of Terence that in Cicero's words, 'Comedy is an imitation of life, a mirror of custom, an image of truth' (sig. [a6ʳ]). Gradually, the metaphor is developed in unexpected ways. Jean Behourt, prefacing his *Hypsicratée* (1604), speaks of epics, tragedies, and comedies as depicting 'comme en vn miroir' the excellence and reward of virtue and the ugliness and punishment of vice (p. 6). Bochetel, too, equated tragedy with teaching about vice and both he and Antoine de Baïf considered tragedy important for the education of princes. Bochetel's association of tragic style with 'grãdeur d'argumens, &

grauité de sentences' (p. 4) is still being heard in 1606, when on the title page of his *Céciliade* Soret calls attention to the play's 'beaux exemples Moraux, graues Sentences, naïues allegories & comparaisons familiers [*sic*]'. Roland Brisset believed that tragedy, like music, could 'ranger [les mœurs] à la raison' (sig. ã2ᵛ) and Jean Heudon hoped that his *S. Clouaud* would interest the man eager to 'regler droictement la course de sa vie' (p. 11). Pierre Matthieu states specifically that *Aman* shows the bad effects of ambition and envy; Montchrétien, that *Sophonisbe* will attest to virtue's immortality.

When M. Philone, author of *Adonias* (1586) called the play 'Vray Miroir . . . de l'Estat des choses presentes' (sig. A1ʳ), he used the mirror image to point out yet another side of tragedy important to the sixteenth century. Garnier's description of his own theatre mentions none of the qualities for which he appeals to modern critics but only a lament for 'les desastres Romains, & les malheurs Gregeois, / Pleurant nos propres maux sous feintes etrangeres' (Courtin, *Hymnes*, f. [4ʳ]). Jean de La Taille, in introducing his brother Jacques' play *Daire*, presented this association in a more positive light and points out that through watching the misfortune of Darius, one will be better able to sustain France's misfortunes.

Even the *arts poétiques* can contain surprises. Few traits of humanist tragedy have won for it more abuse than its tendency to describe rather than depict an action. Yet Vauquelin de la Fresnaye boldly maintained that just as it is more beautiful to see a dragon or a hideous face done by an artist than the real object,

> Il est aussi plus beau voir d'vn pinceau parlant
> Dépeinte dans les vers la fureur de Roland,
> Et l'amour forcené de la pauure Climene,
> Que de voir tout au vray la rage qui les mene.

(p. 15)

This reversal of Horace's observation that we are less stirred by what we hear than by what we see with our own eyes (vv. 180-2) provides one of the most valuable clues to the aesthetics of French humanist tragedy and helps us to bring our thinking in line with that of the sixteenth century.

It is singularly instructive for the modern critic to note that contemporary readers of humanist tragedy give no signs of having regretted a lack of dramatic action, psychology, or 'dynamisme interne'. In the main the liminary poems single out for comment the poet's erudition, the power of his verse, and the play's moral lesson. In no fewer than twenty-two instances is 'docte' (or 'doctement') used with reference to the poet's work.[5] The presence of terms like 'sçauoir', 'eloquence', 'motz ingenieux', 'magniloque guttere', 'stil elegant', 'magnificis verbis', and 'stille magnifique'[6] provides further evidence of the great importance of style and especially a learned style for the tragedies' public. It was even accorded on occasion exceptional ability to move. Lamy wrote of the actions and passions in Hardy that they were described in such a way 'par les traits hardis de [s]es vers, / Que l'on ne les tiendroit pour feintes' (II, 4). A Iosue Gondovin wrote for Pierre de Bousy's *Méléagre* (1582): 'Ie me metamorphose au bruit de ta chanson' (f. [4ʳ]), and Oger said of the verses in Chrétien des Croix' *Albouin*: 'en les oiant lire, on voit la chose méme' (sig. A4ᵛ). The last quotation makes particularly clear that recitation did not appear to the public in question a betrayal of the concept of theatre and that style and action, far from clashing in these plays, was seen to coexist quite naturally.

When the poets' friends turn to the content of the tragedies, they see in effect only one thing—what the play teaches. We shall all die, the French should keep the Catholic faith, honour follows virtue, punishment follows sin, Christians should repent. The comments are too numerous for all to be quoted but it is interesting to note their sententious quality and the common interest between playwrights and audience in questions of vice and virtue, Christian behaviour to the complete exclusion of any concern for those glimmerings of Classicism so dear to the critics. The liminary pieces show also that certain perspectives among the poets were not theirs alone. That longstanding distinction between profane and sacred subjects reappears in four poems published with Bardon de Brun's *Sainct Jacques*, one with Beaubrueil's *Regulus*, and one with Matthieu's *Esther*. The comparison of a tragedy to a mirror can be found in as late a work as A. Du Breton's Latin poem to Hardy, whose work is referred to as 'HVMANÆ SPECVLVM VITÆ' (I, 8).

Ought we to be surprised when confronted by the unanimity among these men and the longevity of views that they expressed to learn from an article by H. C. Lancaster that a 1640 prologue by Guérin de Bouscal described certain tragedies before *Le Cid* in the following terms: 'Qui veut bastir sur le vice / Esprouve tot ou tard quel est ce fondement' [Mairet's *Sophonisbe*]; 'l'amour / Desrobe le lustre & le jour / Aux belles actions d'vn Empereur de Rome' [Scudéry's *Mort de Caesar*] ('Leading French Tragedies', p. 376)? We might rather be surprised at certain judgments of modern critics such as Henri Chamard's contrast between the mystery play as an '*œuvre de foi*' and the tragedy as an '*œuvre d'art* [qui] ne vise plus à l'édification' (*La Tragédie*, p. 11), or Rigal's remark on Jodelle's *Didon*: 'tout cela était hors d'état de frapper l'esprit d'un spectateur' (*Alexandre Hardy*, p. 268). How telling to see the critics define and disparage as if their own views automatically coincided with those of the sixteenth century.

The striking similarity in concerns between the liminary poems and the poets' own declarations raises again the problem of the grammarians' definitions as a limited source of information on sixteenth-century views on tragedy. Our debt to Lanson for having established the primacy of Donatus and Diomedes over Aristotle in dramatic theory during this century must not be underestimated. It remains one of the key elements in any attempt to dissociate French Classicism from earlier tragedy, but the emphasis on style and moral lessons, coupled with the recurrence and persistence of such ideas among poets and public alike, points to the existence of greater factors at work in the century than the definition of Donatus and Diomedes.

Lanson's discussion of the relationship between Badius and Seneca provides a precise example of our dilemma. The critic was convinced that regarding the tragedies of antiquity 'la doctrine traditionnelle servit à les interpréter, plutôt qu'on n'y trouva de quoi changer la doctrine' ('L'Idée de la tragédie', p. 546), and he gives specific examples from Badius' 1514 edition of Seneca to show how the editor sees the ancient author through the eyes of Donatus and Diomedes. Lanson's point about Badius cannot be questioned but it leads to an effect, not a cause. In Badius and other commentaries on classical tragedy published before and after 1514 we find not only the influence of the grammarians but the same interest in style and moral truths exhibited by the dramatists of the sixteenth century and their friends. Badius' 1512 edition of Seneca (without commentary), praises the writer for his tragedies 'in which can be found that splendid abundance of eloquence: that proper use of words and weight of *sententiae*' (sig. a4^{r-v}). A 1491 edition of the same plays considers tragedy useful because of 'the elegant splendour of the poetry and agreeable richness of the rhetoric: the varied knowledge of things, namely that men recognize that fortune is fickle: and that because of its inconstancy it must not be trusted: and that virtue alone should be cultivated and one should prepare for the blessed life' (sig. a2ʳ). From these words in Bernardus Quncta's 1547 edition of Sophocles, one would hardly know that Sophocles had written plays. 'It is he who with both the weight of *sententiae* and that wondrous style of oratory and the most excellent union of things and arranging of fables, is so distinguished that he has no equal. And although there are those who esteem Euripides the wiser and call him the philosopher of the stage, nevertheless, as all learned men agree, [Sophocles] has attained first place in this great poem and for that reason the Sophoclean style shall be changed into adages' (sig. *2ᵛ).

It is true that Lanson's analysis recognizes that this moral purpose associated with tragedy is not specifically present in the grammarians and attributes the ethical dimension of tragedy to Horace's influence. But if such thoughts from the *De arte poetica* as 'Poets want to be useful or to delight or to say things which are at the same time pleasing and suited to life' (vv. 333-4) could inspire the period to seek moral truths in literature, Horace speaks in broad terms whereas we have witnessed a remarkable precision and uniformity in documents of the day. After returning so many times to this uniformity of views among commentators, dramatists, and their admirers we might well wonder what other sources of information and concepts on tragedy existed for the sixteenth-century dramatist besides Donatus, Diomedes, and Horace. I believe there are at least two—one, a medieval tradition represented in particular by Petrarch's *Trionfi*, by Boccaccio's *De casibus virorum illustrium*, *De claris mulieribus*, and by certain works of fiction, especially the 'histoires tragiques'; the other, curricula of the day and the role attributed to tragedy by rhetoric.

There can be no doubt that the *Trionfi* and both works by Boccaccio were available to literate Frenchman in the sixteenth century. A French translation of the *Trionfi* appeared in Paris in 1514 and was reprinted at least six times between 1519 and 1554. The *De claris mulieribus* had a Latin edition in Bern (1539) and appeared in French translation in Paris (1493 and 1538) and in Lyons (1551). The *De casibus* was translated into French by Laurent de Premierfait as *Des nobles malheureux*. His first version was completed in 1400, circulated widely in manuscript form and appeared in print in 1476 (Bruges) and 1483 (Lyons). The much expanded second version was printed in Paris no less than five times (1483, 1484, c. 1503, 1515, 1538). Claude Witart published yet another version of Boccaccio's work in Paris in 1578. Manuscripts of Premierfait's longer version were owned by the last dukes of Burgundy, Louis XI's Queen Charlotte of Savoy and sister Jeanne de France.

In typical medieval style, Boccaccio treated history as parables and private lives as examples. Helen and Clytemnestra emerge from the *De claris mulieribus* as proof of the evil effects of lust. Penelope and Dido teach us, on the other hand, to admire the powers of fidelity. In presenting the stories of Polyxena and Thisbe, Boccaccio explains their unhappy fate with one word 'fortune'. For Thisbe: 'Thus, out of envy, fortune at least allowed them to be joined in a gentle embrace, [but] she could not prevent their unfortunate blood from mixing' (f. ix^v); for Polyxena: 'I can easily believe that she [was] the work of generous nature, as her indifference to death shows; what a woman she would have become, if hostile fortune had not snatched [her] so quickly' (f. xxii^r). His prefatory pages to the *De casibus* specify that almost from the beginning of time fortune has chosen to exercise her power and although he cautions the proud to prepare for a fall, Boccaccio does not associate with those undone by fortune the moral censure accorded to Helen and Clytemnestra. This is not to say that fortune's work has nothing to teach us; quite the contrary. When adding more unfortunate souls to the *De casibus*, 'Aucuns par aduenture diroient que par les exemples dessusdictes iay assez monstre quelles sont les forces de fortune et quelle est la muablete des choses de ce monde et commẽt lesperance des mõdaines bienheuretez est deceuable et la gloire de ce monde est muable et vaine' (Premierfait, f. xxiiii^r), Boccaccio says enough in passing to demonstrate that long before Donatus and Diomedes were reprinted (1472 and 1476 respectively), the association was made between fortune's reversal and a moral lesson. But more important, it was made in a popular book and in a context that treated the stories not only of illustrious men and women, but of those very souls who would populate the humanist tragedies, Medea, Theseus, Phedra, Jocasta, Meleager, Hecuba, Lucretia, Dido, Oedipus, Cleopatra, and Agamemnon, some of whose stories Petrarch had also presented under the headings of diverse triumphs. The triumph of love includes Piramus and Thisbe, Brutus and Portia, David and Bathsheba, Amnon and Thamar, Judith and Holofernes; the triumph of chastity, Lucretia, Virginia; the triumph of death, Marc Anthony, Saul, Diocletian and Maximian.

The *De claris mulieribus*, too, reads like the roll call of tragic as well as famous women and no fewer than twenty of its subjects would find their stories retold in tragedies of the sixteenth and seventeenth century. It is not difficult to see how the mind which had learned to associate the stories of Hecuba and Helen with lessons on fortune and morals would transfer these lessons to the same stories when told in dramatic form; yet, the grammarians can be responsible for only a part of the transfer of ideas. By identifying tragedy with the same 'illustrious' people and their misfortunes, they aided the entry of these stories into tragedy but Boccaccio, not Donatus or Diomedes, specifically linked misfortune with the extolling of virtue and the punishment of vice in addition to the general lesson of life's vanity. Bosquet's poem to Montchrétien underscores the greater rapprochement with Boccaccio:

> Il a voulu monter sur la Tragique Scéne,
> Et chanter l'incertain de la grandeur humaine,
> Monstrer qu'il n'y a point en ce monde d'appuy,
> Enseigner le bonheur par le malheur d'autruy,
> Representer des grands les peines et les fautes,
> Et le malheur fatal des puissances plus hautes;
> Faire voir aux effets que le pouuoir humain
> N'empesche point les coups de la diuine main.

> > (*Tragédies*, sig. d7^r)

Moreover, Boccaccio intended his stories to have an emotional as well as a moral impact. The reflections on Thisbe or Polyxena quoted above illustrate this fact and again Boccaccio's presentation proves more in keeping with the tone of humanist writings. In this remark by Billard on the fate of his heroine Panthée and her husband, 'la fortune ennemie iuree des personnes de valeur ne les laissa iouir vn seul demi-an des delices' (f. 86^v) there is little of Diomedes but much to recall the situation of Polyxena also snapped away by 'hostile fortune'.

We are told that a German scholar of the sixteenth century, translator of the *De casibus*, so enjoyed his task that he wrote of the book: 'Ich habe ni etwas gelesen was mehr Vergnügen und Belehrung gewährt (Lydgate, p. xii). Jean de La Taille, dedicating his brother Jacques' tragedy *Alexandre*, points out that the great men 'meurent presque tous de mort violente. Voyez de quelle mort Cæsar, Pompee,

Brute, Caton, Daire, & tous les nobles malheureux que descrit Bocace, & tất d'autres de nostre temps, ont finé leurs iours' (f. 3ᵛ). As late as 1617,[7] we find Pierre Matthieu, author of a significant number of tragedies, publishing an *Histoire des prosperitez malheureuses d'vne femme cathenoise, grande seneschalle de Naples,* which Matthieu acknowledged as taken from the last tale of Boccaccio's *De casibus.* In Matthieu's words, the story shows 'vn tragique effect de l'inconstance de la fortune qui n'est moins ingenieuse en ses tromperies qu'estourdie en ses faueurs' (sig. A2ᵛ).

As important as these and other indications of the prolonged interest in Boccaccio's work may be, we do not need to rely on them alone to relate views on tragedy and trends in contemporary literature. Despite the great attention accorded to Rabelais, Montaigne, and the Pléiade in studies of the sixteenth century, they are not necessarily representative of the kind or of the volume of literature published in their day. Coexisting with the familiar titles are such relatively unknown works as Pierre Boaystuau's *Le Théâtre du monde* (1558, reprinted in 1572, 1580, and 1593), Jacques Tahureau's *Les Dialogues* (1565), Louis Le Roy's *De la vicissitude ou variété des choses* (1577), Antoine Du Verdier's *Diverses leçons* (1577), or the 1547 translation of Fregoso, entitled *Le Ris de Democrite et le pleur de Heraclite, philosophes sur les follies, & miseres de ce monde.* All preached about fortune, the force of love, the fall of tyrants, the constancy of some, the miserable end of others, and above all continued to remind Frenchmen that the way of the world proves that when man is 'au plus hault degré d'honneur, c'est alors qu'il perïst soudain' (*Le Théâtre,* p. 62). Boaystuau also singled out ambition, pride, and love as prime sources of human misery. He even speaks of love as 'ceste potion qui est l'entiere corruption & ruine de la plus part de la ieunesse de nostre siecle' (p. 167). Tahureau's text, too, often has nothing good to say of women and love. In the words of one of his interlocutors: 'nous voyons tous les iours que l'amour fait deuenir la personne de peu d'esprit, fole du tout: outre que c'est bien la plus grande sottise qui sçauroit entrer dedans le cerueau des hommes, de se rendre suiets aux femmes, creatures tant imparfaittes qu'elles ne sont engendrees de la nature seulement que pour vne necessité de la conseruation humaine' (p. 8). He has examples to substantiate his accusations, such as David and 'pernicieuse Clitemnestre' (pp. 11 and 15), both, it should be noted, subjects of humanist tragedies written expressly to make the same point.[8]

The transposition may have been irresistible. 'Combien de pertes de royaumes' were a consequence of love, observe *Les Dialogues;* 'combien de regrets & lamentables cris se sont épandus en vain par l'air, & tout pour cette rage d'amour', not to mention those who 'se sont (de leur propres mains) donné la mort' (p. 12).

Romanesque literature in the sixteenth century is another facet of the period that has been rather neglected. Yet the *Deffence* invited the young French poets to choose 'un de ces beaux vieulx romans Francoys, comme un *Lancelot,* un *Tristan,* ou autres' from which to fashion a new *Iliad* or *Aeneid* (II, v, 129). Muret annotated copies of Heliodorus' *Historiae aethiopicae liber primus* (Paris, 1551) and Theocritus' *Idyllia* XXXVI (Venice, 1558). (See Nolhac, pp. 216, 220.) Etienne Pasquier, in a letter to Ronsard, dated 1555, speaks well of the *Roman d'Amadis* (II, I, 11) and in another letter praises Urfé's *Astrée* (II, XVIII, 533-4). Rivaudeau's firm denunciation of *Amadis* and *Tristan* as 'liures indignes et pernitieux' (p. 52) is but another sign of widespread interest at the time in such works.

Popular, these works, too, could propagate certain familiar ideas on fortune and love. In Heliodorus' tale of the vicissitudes of Theagenes and Chariclea, few characters escape misfortune, as Gnemon's lament reveals: 'O miserable fortune de la vie humaine, pleine de toute incõstance, & suiette à toute mutation! quel flux & reflux de miseres tu as faict de monstrer tant en plusieurs autres hommes, qu'en moymesme souuentesfois' (f. 66ᵛ). And against the fierce loyalty of the main couple to each other and to their vow of chastity until marriage, Heliodorus juxtaposes such totally passionate creatures as Arsacé. Doomed to kill herself, she provides the author with an opportunity to expose fully the terrible consequences of unbridled love. Characteristic is this passage where the princess, who wishes to conceal her desire for Theagenes, has just been asked why she holds to keeping the couple in her house. 'Quand Arsacé ouyt ces parolles, elle ne se peut plus contenir, ainçoys fit ce que font ordinairement presque tous les amantz: car tant qu'ilz cuydent que leur affection soit incogneuë, ilz ont vergoine de la confesser: mais quand ilz sont vne fois descouuertz, ilz en deuiennent eshontez' (f. 88ᵛ).

According to Gustave Reynier, the development of the novel in France paralleled the country's internal situation. The Religious Wars, he felt, interrupted the growing importance of romanesque fiction (as distinct from the *roman d'aventures*). During Henry IV's reign romanesque literature flourished only to give way upon his assassination and the reappearance of trouble to a recrudescence of adventure tales with a continued interest in Greek novels and 'histoires tragiques'. However, it is not always clear to what degree one can distinguish absolutely between romanesque fiction and a *roman d'aventures*. Reynier's own bibliography of fiction between 1500 and 1610 casts certain doubts on the advisability of such a distinction.

Reynier includes *Les Amours de Cléandre et Domiphille* by Nicolas de Montreux under the heading of 'Roman chevaleresque et Roman d'aventures' although the wars, abductions, and so forth occupy the smallest place possible with respect to analysis of sentiment. For the first sixty pages the only 'event' is Domiphille's illness. When she recovers, Cléandre passes to his second concern, the love he has inspired in a princess who kindly harboured them after many misfortunes. This episode includes a war story because the princess, out of love for Cléandre, has refused the hand of a neighbouring ruler who proceeds to invade her land. Here is the total account of the turn in events:

le Roy fist de la sorte, qui voulut employer tout son pouuoir à tirer vengeãce du mespris de la Princesse, & à conquerir par force, ce qu'on luy denioit d'amitié. De sorte qu'il amasse vne forte & puissante armée, & sans aduertir la Princesse de son cruel dessein, se resout de luy faire cruellement la guerre. Ce mesme subject iadis arma les Romains contre les Sabins, qui leur auoient refusé leurs filles à femmes: & le Roy d'Epire les suiuit, qui fut plustost aux portes de Corinthe, qu'õ n'eust appris sa resolution à la guerre.

(f. 38ᵛ)

Cléandre reacts to the danger presented by war to his beloved sister Domiphille, who will be safely installed in a castle away from the city. His thoughts, her thoughts at separation and their goodbyes extend from folio 39ʳ to folio 51ᵛ—a perfect example of the proportions between analysis and adventure in the novel. The long passage reveals also to what degree all of Montreux' material derives from the particular amalgam of analysis and moralizing to be found in the literature we have been discussing. The war derives from the king's desire to take the princess and Montreux is so conscious of the archetypal quality of the emotions in play that he cannot resist comparing the situation with that of the Romans and the Sabines.

Author of both novels and tragedies, Montreux never resists the temptation to generalize, moralize, or declaim. The following passage, spoken by Domiphille, shows a familiar attitude toward the gods, change, and classical figures:

Et quoy? à toutes choses, fors à l'ire cruelle des Dieux contre moy se trouuera il quelque fin? Hé! qu'vn mesme sort ne conduit auec ma peruerse fortune, mon heureuse & calme, à fin au moins que parmy tant de malheur, i'eusse quelque sentiment du bien! Tout sera-il donc en ce monde subiect au changement, à la mort, à la fin, fors ma cruelle infortune? hé! quay ie faict? suis-ie comme Oreste matricide, côme Aiax meurtrier de la chasteté, comme Aspasia aduersaire des Dieux, & comme Helene infidele?

(f. 86ᵛ)

Virtue, constancy, and chastity receive undying praise in the novel. Domiphille's declaration of eternal love for her brother prompts this remark, 'O paroles enfantées d'vne belle ame? [*sic*] ô Constance fille d'vn cœur heroyque!' (f. 18ʳ) Virtue is not necessarily a private affair. The presence of the princess allows Montreux to make observations about rulers also and the princess' nurse reminds her that virtue is the richest gift she can give her people. Why all this sententious talk, these monologues, and rhetoric? Montreux gives us early in the book this explanation: 'Et veritablement la parole ayde beaucoup à gaigner la volonté des escoutans. Car elle est trompette de la perfection de l'ame, qui par elle se fait paroistre: & comme les fleurs par leur douce odeur se font cognoistre, de mesme par les paroles l'ame donne notice de son excellence' (f. 7ᵛ). The phrasing is doubly related to sixteenth-century drama. It offers yet another example of that faith in the power of words which brings us closer to understanding why speeches, not action, predominate in humanist tragedy. Secondly, Montreux shows here that interest in moralizing had considerable effect upon characterization. If this same tragedy seems to lack the psychological insight one finds a century later, these remarks show that when creating Cléandre and Domiphille, he had no desire to explore the complexity of the human personality but wished to lay bare the beauties of a virtuous being.

I would not want to imply that all fiction published in the sixteenth century resembles this work. The popular *Amadis de Gaule* or Heliodorus' *Histoire éthiopique* could on occasion approximate the genre which Reynier understands by the term *roman d'aventures*. At the same time, it is important to recognize that Montreux was not an innovator in his story of Cléandre and Domiphille but rather

B

was following the example of someone already quite popular with the period: Boccaccio, the Boccaccio of the *Fiammetta* and the *Filicopo*.

Miss Daele's study of Montreux' novels accentuates the influence of Heliodorus on the French novelist and, indeed, there are undeniable resemblances between their plot structures. She also calls attention to Montreux' own enumeration of his sources in the 1595 novel *Les Amours de Criniton et Lydie*, which the story of Cléandre and Domiphille continues. The list includes Achilles Statius, Heliodorus, and Boccaccio 'en ses AMOURS DE FELIX ET BLANCHEFLEUR' (Daele, p. 165). Blanchefleur's story (*Filocopo*) and the *Amorous Fiammetta* present the same structure used by Montreux—a love story told essentially through long speeches exchanged by the various characters. The speeches are interspersed with references to the events that keep the narrative moving and give rise to the situations which agitate the characters. There is also a similar perspective on the subject matter. Montreux lauded constancy and chastity. Boccaccio urged young ladies in love to read his *Filocopo* because they would then recognize 'combien plaist à Amour vne ieune personne seigneuriant sa pensée sans se dõner à plusieurs' (sig. A3ʳ). Adrian Sevin, Boccaccio's French translator, in recommending his translation to those pursuing felicity so that one's love might be brought '(sans concupiscence) à vertueuse & heureuse fin, telle qu'eurent Fleury & Blanchefleur' (sig. a3ᵛ), demonstrates that in yet another literary context Boccaccio continued to inspire the sixteenth-century writers.

Of all the diverse elements in the fiction of this period, the short story had probably the most decisive influence on humanist tragedy. Marguerite de Navarre's famous *Heptaméron* exemplifies a continued interest in using the short story to extract from human events pronouncements upon the respective effects of vice and virtue. The century produced a wealth of tales of this kind, often entitled interestingly enough 'histoires tragiques'. The largest collection to carry this designation is an anthology of stories by Bandello, translated into French in part by Pierre Boaystuau and completed by François de Belleforest. Boaystuau translated six stories and published them in 1559. The same year these six plus twelve stories translated by Belleforest were printed as volume I of the *Histoires tragiques extraites des œuvres italiennes de Bandel & mises en langue françoise*. Their success cannot be overestimated. I have found in major American and European libraries eleven separate printings of volumes I and II, nine of volume III, six of volume IV, ten of volume V, four of volume VI, and three of volume VII. They were published in Paris, Lyons, Rouen, Antwerp, and Turin.

In subject matter and examples, this long collection not only afforded the sixteenth century a continuation of the Boccaccio material, but may well be a direct source of the popularity at that time of the stories dealing with Sophonisba, Panthée, and Rosemund. Tales 43, 71, and 73 relate respectively their lives while the numerous introductions by Boaystuau and Belleforest allude to the lessons to be learned from David (5), Amnon (11), Porcia (23), Saul (37), Dido (66), Cesar and the Duke of Guise (76), Absalom (108)—all characters who reappear in humanist tragedies. One tale, the sixth, is definitely the source of Jean Behourt's tragicomedy *La Polyxène*.

The same introductions reveal that their relationship to the theatre is not restricted to subject matter. It is semantic—a story in the collection is often referred to as a 'tragedie', a 'comédie', and even a 'tragicomédie' (I, 690, III, 57, VII, 301)—and above all conceptual. Both translators are insistent about their own moral intent to the point of tedium. 'C'est sans doute que la varieté instable, & incertaine du cours de nostre vie est fort merueilleuse', writes Belleforest before story 47. He reminds us of the same instability when presenting number 64. Boaystuau's dedication sounds almost like a sermon. His book will be useful, he says, 'Car sous l'escorce d'vn petit monceau de paroles assez malagencees, les Rois, Princes, Pontifes, Empereurs, & Monarques, & generalement tous ceux qui font trafique en la boutique de ce mõde, peuuent contempler par bon ordre quel rolle ils ioüent en ce theatre humain' (I, 4).

At the same time, if we compare the range of topics translated from Bandello with the works of Boccaccio discussed above, we find some significant changes already noticeable in Boaystuau's *Théâtre du monde*. While chastity and love (whether lust or fidelity) figure in the *De claris mulieribus* and the *De casibus*, they are subjects among others and as I have pointed out, Boccaccio presented Fortune as a fact of life, not as an avenging force. The *Histoires tragiques*, like Montreux' novel, place a constant emphasis on chastity as a virtue and passion as a vice and all misfortune as a reflection of acceptable or unacceptable behaviour. When introducing story 7 Boaystuau defines his view of Fortune. What others have labelled Fortune, he writes, is in fact God's will. God's will implies judgment and it is precisely as such a judgment that most misfortunes are presented by the translators.

By calling love in his *Théâtre du monde* the undoing of his century's youth, Boaystuau announced both the precise moral his co-translator would seek to convey and the particular vehicle used by the genre to depict the familiar effects of fortune. Listen to Belleforest present story 114, 'l'amour est suyuy ordinairement de tous ces vices, & imperfections à sçauoir de soin, fascherie, douleur, & de trop d'elegance, & mignardise' (VI, 459) or to Meslier (?) in his *Histoire véritable des infortunees et tragiques amours d'Hypolite & d'Isabelle, néapolitains:*

De tous les accidens qui tirent les hommes en plus grande admiration & qui leur apportent le plus d'estonnement il ne s'en voit point de si estranges & de si prodigieux que ceux que l'amour nous produit, qui est vne passion, ou plustost vne fureur si violente, que deiettant toute raison de l'entendement de ceux qu'elle saisist, elle ne leur laisse aucune consideration des euenemens de ce qu'elle leur fait entreprendre. Et encore les exemples des guerres qu'elle a si souuent excitees des renuersemens des Royaumes, & des grands estats qui en sont procedez, des erreurs qu'elle a fait commettre aux plus sages, des malheurs ou elle a conduit les mieux aduisez. Et les ruines ou elle a precipité les plus grands nous soyĕt si ordinaires & voire en si grăd nombre qu'ils ne sont ignorez de personne.

(pp. 9-10)

The author's phrase 'deiettant toute raison de l'entendement' reveals their prejudice to have distinct philosophical grounds. Running throughout the introductions is the fundamental Stoic distinction between reason and passion, between a proud, sometimes fatal attachment to honour and the unprincipled abandon created by emotion. Belleforest summarizes his thoughts at the beginning of story 22, 'les effets [d'Amour] suyuis auec raison, laquelle doit regir toute action humaine, sont necessaires & honorables à nostre vie, si sont autrement disposez qu'en bonne part, & si aueuglément lon se lance és precipices d'vne folle fantasie, n'est rien tant pernicieux, qui aproche de la ruine, que telle folle passion aporte à la vie des hommes' (II, 202-3). Telling also is this remark by the anonymous author of *Les Tragiques Amours du braue Lydamas et de la belle Myrtille*. Myrtille's father was without ambition, he notes 'Qui estoit cause que mesprisant tous les vains hŏneurs de la Cour, il ne bougeoit de sa maison, se contentant des moyens qu'il possedoit, qui est ce que Seneque nome la vraye richesse' (f. 4^r).

Not unexpectedly in a century that revived the Querelle des

Femmes with vigour, a moral stance on love could easily become a judgment of womankind and the tales of passion, the incrimination of the female. The writers of these 'histoires tragiques' are in fact not always kind to women. Habanc's condemnation is total, 'Ainsi est il qu'apres que Dieu eust creé la femme à mesme instant il y eut quelque mauuais esprit qui luy vuida tout son ceruueau, & n'y laissa autre chose que du vent' (sig. [ã7ᵛ]). Bandello's translators prefer to use the Stoic yardstick of reason—extolling the women who protected their chastity at the cost of their lives and denouncing those others who become 'furieuses & entreprennent des choses qui les plus cruels tyrans auroyent horreur d'exercer' (I, 154). To discuss at length all the attitudes expressed in this long chain of moral tales would be out of place here, but the existence of the most frequent cannot and should not be ignored if we are to grasp the context of sixteenth-century tragedy.

Boccaccio's *De casibus* and *De claris mulieribus* and the 'histoires tragiques' shows us that the association of a great prince's fall with moral truths and broad didactic generalizations is an old concept and that it was widely disseminated in the vernacular in the form of popular reading quite different from the treatises of Donatus, Diomedes, and Horace, whose precepts on tragedy were, nonetheless, so thoroughly reinforced that for the playwrights and their friends to have discussed tragedy in any way other than the one they chose would have been exceptional indeed.

Why the liminary poems spoke so often of the dramatists' style obliges us to explore another facet of the period—the importance of rhetoric. The topic is large and filled with unexpected ramifications concerning tragedy, so many in fact that the subject deserves to be treated under a separate heading.

2 SIXTEENTH-CENTURY EDUCATION

We have been slow to recognize the pervasive influence of rhetoric in sixteenth-century France despite the fact that writers of the day did little to hide its importance. In introducing *Les Œuvres & Meslanges d'Estienne Jodelle* (1574), Charles de La Mothe begged the reader to note in addition to the poet's independence of the ancients, 'la propreté des mots bien obseruee, les phrases, & figures bien accommodees, l'elegance & maiesté du langage, les subtiles inuentions, les hautes conceptions, la parfaite suite & liaison des

Discours, & la braue structure & grauité des vers' (sig. ẽ1ᵛ-ẽ2ʳ).
Louis Le Roy presents his translation of Isocrates to Marguerite
de France with these words:

Il y a une perfection de bien parler & escrire, qui nous mõtre traitter les matieres
hautes grauement, les basses subtilement & les mediocres en style temperé: &
par mesme moyen, enseigner, delecter, & esmouuoir les auditeurs ou lecteurs,
leur persuadãt ce qu'on pretend. Puis accomoder les termes & sentences au
temps, au lieu, & aux personnes: obseruant la qualité de chacune matiere:
telement que le langage soit pur & correct, ayant nombre & douceur, & les
propos leur ordre & disposition. C'est sans doute la uraye espece d'eloquence,
qui ne peult estre muee par la diuersité des natures, des temps, & des nations.

(sig. A2ʳ)

Neither quotation mentions the word 'rhétorique' and yet both
derive their observations from its teachings.

To Cicero and Aristotle, rhetoric was primarily the art of persuasion. All rhetoricians believed in the power of rhetoric to accomplish great things and many humanists echoed this sentiment,
speaking now of rhetoric, now of poetry.[9] The repetition is not due to
chance. Poetry had long been recognized as a branch of rhetoric.
'Il est', wrote Fabri in 1534, 'deux gerres [sic] ou deux manieres de
parler: l'vng est prose, l'autre est rithme' (p. 27).[10] The humanists,
steeped in the ancient literature that established such a view, did not
question the relationship. Rules for oratory and rules for poetry
once appeared so synonymous (if one left aside the question of form
and rhyme), that from Aristotle to Quintilian classical rhetoricians
quoted indiscriminately from prose and poetry to exemplify these
rules. When sixteenth-century authors of works on rhetoric did
likewise with poets of their own day (Antoine Fouquelin constantly
cites the Pléiade and Pierre de Courcelles, Marot), they were following this tradition but also reaffirming their readiness to continue
to emphasize the rhetoric in poetry and poetry as the second rhetoric.

Quintilian did not agree with the definition of rhetoric put forward by his predecessors. After all, 'many other things have the
power of persuasion, such as money, influence, the authority and
rank of the speaker' (II, xv, 6). He insisted that rhetoric was rather
the 'science of speaking well' (II, xv, 34)—a more far-reaching definition than it sounds because Quintilian was convinced that to speak
well one had to be a good man and that good men would urge only
what was useful. These ideas, as well as Quintilian's emphasis in
his twelfth book on the necessity for the orator's education to

embrace all fields, were not absent from other rhetoricians but he insisted upon this more than Cicero or Aristotle and formulated for the Middle Ages, if we may believe E. R. Curtius, that particular interlocking network of concepts which made rhetoric, poetry, philosophy, and ethics all variations on a single intent. Since mastery of oratory in Quintilian cannot be distinguished from acquiring a knowledge of all things, striving to be upright, and learning to discourse on moral questions, his 'speaking well' is in some ways a play on words. 'Well' means both 'in a morally acceptable way' and 'in an artistically acceptable way.' The sixteenth century missed none of this. When Scaliger insisted that philosophical exposition, oratory, and the drama were all intended to persuade, when the humanists wedded moral values and element style in their praise of their contemporaries, they were living up to a practice as old as Quintilian's *Institutio oratoria*.

Quintilian twice reminds us that the orator teaches, moves, and delights (III, iv, 2; VIII, Pr., 7). His 'in fact true beauty and usefulness always go hand in hand' (VIII, iii, 11) is yet another means to make the same point. Preparation for an orator's career was to include work with *sententiae, chriae, ethologiae* (when the boy was too young for the schools of rhetoric), and later, *theses*. In that these *theses* dealt with such questions as 'which deserves the greatest praise, the lawyer or the soldier' or 'whether marriage is desirable' (II, iv, 24-5), their use to provide practice in thinking as well as writing is patent. The three other exercises receive little treatment from Quintilian and are more difficult to describe. He insists that the *ratio* is similar for all three; only the form changes. It seems possible to conclude that in the case of the *sententiae*, students were asked to write about an aphorism. In the *chriae* the themes were generally presented as a statement by someone whereas the *ethologia* required the student to imagine a famous individual's words on some prescribed subject.[11] Given that the themes to discuss most assuredly dealt with moral truths, the dual training of soul and speech was to begin very early.

The greatest portion of works on rhetoric was devoted to remarks on execution, that is, clarifying the various kinds of speeches, describing their subdivisions, and pointing out what styles and stylistic devices were appropriate. The effort to categorize fairly overwhelms the modern reader; yet Quintilian had his reasons. Through categorization and definition he hoped to make it possible to understand the nature of each potential aspect of oratory. He recognized that it is impossible to teach everything but, using an analogy between orator and painter, he observed that 'once [the painter] has acquired the general principles of imitation, he will be able to copy whatever is given him' (VII, x, 9).

Common to all rhetoricians is their division of oratory into *inventio, dispositio, elocutio, memoria, pronuntiatio* and of styles into an ornate, simple, and middle variety, insistence upon clarity as the prime virtue in oratory, and the conviction that amplification and ornamentation are absolutely necessary in order to achieve excellence. It is this last consideration that explains the inordinate detail afforded figures of thought and style by the rhetoricians. Oratory and a fullness (*copia*) of expression were synonymous to the ancients. In Cicero's words, 'the whole essence of oratory is to embellish in some fashion all, or, at any rate, most of the ideas' (*Orator*, xxxix, 136). Quintilian insists that the *narratio* should be adorned 'with the utmost grace and charm' (IV, ii, 116). His image—the streams of eloquence 'must not be conveyed through narrow pipes like the water of fountains, but flow as mighty rivers flow, filling whole valleys' (V, xiv, 31)—may not strike the modern reader as anything but bombast. Still Erasmus' *De duplici copia* exists to testify to the force of Quintilian's ideas in the sixteenth century. Erasmus even justifies his enterprise through reference to the Roman master: 'I am instructing youth, in whom extravagance of speech does not seem wrong to Quintilian, because with judgment, superfluities are easily restrained' (p. 14). Like his classical predecessor, Erasmus sees the dangers of both brevity and exuberance but the total effect of the *De duplici copia* and *Institutio* is one of exceptional interest in the multiple forms of stylistic embellishment.

No prolonged analysis is necessary to see that from his very first sentence Le Roy reveals to what extent he is familiar with the principles of Quintilian. The phrase 'bien parler & escrire' as well as the aims 'enseigner, delecter, & esmouuoir' are veritable translations of key definitions in the *Institutio*. The tripartite division of style, the mention of *sententiae* and correct language continue the association and touch on elements La Mothe expected us to notice in Jodelle's poetry. That both Le Roy and La Mothe single out *dispositio* ('ordre & disposition' in Le Roy, 'la parfaite suite & liaison des Discours' in La Mothe) not only underscores the use of rhetoric to furnish canons for literary judgments, but also provides another example of continued use of rhetorical writings to approach poetry.

Rhetoric's influence explains why Chapter II of Laudun's *Art poétique* (1597) bears the title 'De l'invention', III, 'De la disposition, & elocution' and why it is clear to him that 'le Poëte en son poëme, garde toutes les parties d'oraison, comme l'orateur, excepté que l'vn est plus contrainct de nombre que l'autre' (p. 7). Where tragedy is concerned, that influence is even more pervasive and more decisive than is generally recognized. We should no longer be surprised when Laudin insists that 'sentences, allegories, similitudes, & autres ornemēts de poësie' be frequent in tragedies (p. 284) or when Vauquelin de la Fresnaye chooses to say nothing about the dramatic qualities of Garnier and praises him as 'sçauant et copieux' (p. 95), but we should also have greater insight into the origin of Laudun's observation that in tragedy things must be 'bien disposées & ordonnées, afin de tenir tousiours les spectateurs beants' (p. 281). The remark repeats a commonplace of rhetorical theory; if it results from any serious thought by Laudun on the structure of tragedies, the remainder of his comments shows no signs of such a study.

I would observe the same regarding La Taille's sentence from *De l'art de la tragédie* mentioned above, 'Qu'il n'y ait rien d'oisif, d'inutile, ny rien qui soit mal à propos'. The sentiments are quite similar to cardinal precepts of the rhetoricians on style[12] and scarcely out of place in a treatise on tragedy if we consider that one of the century's prime sources of information on tragedy—Horace's *De arte poetica*—also deals extensively with style and general questions of rhetoric. I even suspect strongly that La Taille's description of the plot's desired effect on the listeners ('qu'elle change, transforme, manie, et tourne l'esprit des escoutans') may owe more to rhetoric than to Aristotle. At no time in the *Poetics* does Aristotle describe tragedy's effect in terms of a constant manipulation of emotion. Pity and fear are aroused through a discovery. Construction is a question of action that will excite these two emotions. La Taille's observation sounds much more like two lines (99-100) from Horace ('It is not enough that poems be beautiful; they should delight and lead the emotions of the listener where they will'), the same two lines which Chamard uses to gloss the statement by Du Bellay in the *Deffence* that 'celuy sera veritablement le poëte que je cherche en nostre Langue, qui me fera indigner, apayser, ejouyr, douloir, aymer, hayr, admirer, etonner, bref, qui tiendra la bride de mes affections, *me tournant ça & la à son plaisir*' (II, xi, 179, my italics). Quintilian said that 'it is in its power over the emotions that the life and soul of oratory is to be found' (VI, ii, 7) and maintained that Euripides was of greater use to a future orator than Sophocles since 'although admirable in every kind of emotional appeal, he is easily supreme in the power to excite pity' (X, i, 67-8). In addition to associating oratory and tragedy through emotional appeal, Quintilian offered remarks of interest to dramatists when discussing human character.

The rhetoricians were concerned about appropriateness with regard to all aspects of their performance. Thus, when Horace's *De arte poetica* spends several verses describing the ways of the young man and the quite different tastes of old men (vv. 161ff.), it is rephrasing long passages from Aristotle's work on rhetoric in which, in Book II, the orator/poet was apprised of the appropriate way to depict individuals. There was nothing sophisticated about such advice. 'It is evident', wrote Aristotle, 'that the character of those in the prime of life will be the mean between that of the other two [the very young and the very old], if the excess in each case is removed. . . . Their self-control is combined with courage and their courage with self-control, whereas in the young and old these qualities are found separately' (II, xiv, 1, 3). Effectiveness, not sophistication was the orator's aim. As Quintilian notes, 'the *narratio* will be credible, if in the first place we take care to say nothing contrary to nature, secondly if we assign reasons and motives for the facts on which the inquiry turns, . . . and if we make the characters of the actors in keeping with the facts we desire to be believed' (IV, ii, 52). How quaint and curious it sounds to hear nature referred to in a context where Quintilian considered Aristotle an expert. We would be missing the point, however, to assume that nature is here associated with human nature as the post-Freud world understands the phrase. The rhetoricians viewed character in terms of moral truths: 'it is the *property* of a good man to act rightly, of an angry man to be violent in speech or action' (Quintilian, V, x, 64), and to contradict these truths was to destroy the moral effect of rhetoric. Basic to rhetoric's perspective on character was the feeling that persuasion could not stem from the exceptional or the unfamiliar. The orator would not persuade his listeners of a man's worth by describing the crosscurrents of his behaviour. Oratory preached about qualities, guilt, innocence, vice, and virtue; to mix them as indeed Aristotle suggested when urging that the tragic hero be neither too evil nor too good was to complicate dangerously one's case. The liminary poems, Montreux' praise of the words of the virtuous, Scaliger's definition of the uniform purpose in literature and oratory show that the sixteenth century was more disposed toward rhetoric's simplification of character in order to persuade than toward the kind of aesthetic considerations that brought Aristotle to define the tragic hero as he did. The sixteenth century was interested in and content with the victory of virtue and the punishment of sin. None of this required sophisticated characterization. Quite the contrary. Having learned their rhetoric well, the humanists could only have felt uncomfortable with such characterization.

In some instances, the rhetoricians brought tragedy directly into the framework of their discussions by way of illustration. The beginning of Euripides' *Medea* provides Quintilian with a point on argumentation (V, x, 83). Sophocles and Euripides are to Aristotle one means of showing that a speechmaker must make his subject clear at the outset (III, xiv, 6). It was only natural, therefore, for Erasmus to point out that messengers in tragedies are especially good at *descriptio* (*De duplici copia*, p. 48) or for Muret to note that some consider Sophocles and Euripides the essence of eloquence (*Scripta selecta*, p. 70). However, in view of such repeated association of tragedy and style, we must be certain to explore *all* the influential works on style available to the sixteenth century.

In addition to Quintilian's *Institutio oratoria*, the main classical sources on rhetoric included Cicero's *De oratore*, *Orator*, and the *Rhetorica ad Herennium*, which was attributed to Cicero. Aristotle's volume on rhetoric, referred to in the Latin works, had several editions in the sixteenth century but does not appear to have been printed in Greek-Latin form before the fourth decade of the century except for earlier printings of Book III. Despite the relatively simple Latin of Cicero and Quintilian, students probably learned the rudiments of rhetoric through the handbooks of Hermogenes and Aphthonius. The difference between these popular school texts (Aphthonius was edited in 1624 by no less a scholar than Heinsius), and the classical works is both great and significant.

Hermogenes and Aphthonius present a rhetoric stripped of all but definitions and examples. Hermogenes in a 1540 Paris edition offered rhetoric as a description of the following topics: De fabula,

De narratione, De usu, De sententia, De refutatione, De loco communi, De laude, De comparatione, De allocutione, De descriptione, De positione, De legislatione. In 1521 Froben published an anthology of works on rhetoric. The Cantanaeus translation of Aphthonius contains: Definitio fabulae, Definio narrationis, Definitio chriae, Definitio sententiae, Definitio confutationis, Definitio confirmationis, Definitio communis loci, Definitio laudationis, Definitio vituperationis, Definitio comparationis, Definitio ethopoeiae, Definitio descriptionis, Definitio causae, and Definitio promulgationis legis. Other works in the volume are, significantly, three guides to the figures of style and one on rules pertaining to the principles of oratory.

Aphthonius always follows his definition with an example. The story of the ant and the cicada demonstrates *fabula*; a retelling of the love of Venus for Adonis and its consequences exemplifies *narratio*— a story destined to be used by none other than Du Bellay in his 'Metamorphose d'vne rose'. There is no discussion beyond what is required to present the particular subject, its various parts or various manifestations. In short, these writers offered exactly what the classical rhetoricians on occasion firmly declared rhetoric should *not* be: a list of rules. (See Quintilian, II, xiii, 1, and Cicero, *De Oratore*, III, xxx, 121.) Quintilian even more than Cicero peppered his writings with nuances about the precepts he proposed. Rules, they both insisted, were important but practice was even more essential. Quintilian criticized over-elegant and affected style, pointing out the dangers in excessive use of the very figures he so carefully described. Yet contemporary manifestoes such as the *Deffence* or works on rhetoric such as those written by Pierre Fabri, Antoine Fouquelin, and Pierre de Courcelles present none of these nuances. All are much closer in approach to Hermogenes or Aphthonius and suggest that what we consider the wisdom of the ancients interested the sixteenth century less than their precepts, a fact not unimportant with respect to the link between tragedy and rhetoric.

To say that a speech is different from a tragedy or a poem would hardly create an argument today. We might be willing to admit that all three genres have some common elements such as structure but the differences far overshadow the resemblances. Rhetoric made the contrary more obvious to the sixteenth century. Its purpose was to codify a method of composing that applied to all serious forms of expression and the humanists responded in kind. They discussed precepts and not the act of creation, models and rules, not exceptions and nuances. In addition, the particular fashion in which Hermogenes and Aphthonius handled the subject of rhetoric could only accentuate the distance between the stylistic elements in a work and the work as a whole. Consider, for example, Peletier's curious inclusion of Niobe among suitable tragic subjects. Aphthonius, defining the kinds of *ethopoeiae*, has recourse to this possibility, 'quae nam uerba dicere posset Hecuba cadente Troia' (what words Hecuba might speak at the fall of Troy), but chooses for his inevitable illustration, 'QVAE VERBA DICERE POSSET Niobe iacentibus liberis' (what words Niobe might speak before her dead children) (Froben, p. 218). Hecuba was already enshrined in tragedy; Peletier's certainty that the subject of Aphthonius' moving *ethopoeia* would also be perfect for tragedy leaves no room for speculation on the relative importance of style and genre for Peletier.

The atomization of the work of art shows up especially in the century's intense interest in elevated diction and *sententiae*. When Erasmus defined tragedy's style, he borrowed Horace's phrase 'ampullas & sesquipedalia uerba' (swelling and polysyllabic words) although it is not at all clear in the *De arte poetica* that Horace intended these words as a recommendation. (See vv. 93-9.) We have seen how often the humanists were told that aphorisms were both beautiful and useful and well into the 1580's we find continued publication of a work like Octavianus Mirandula's *Illustrium poetarum flores*, which is nothing but an amalgam of sayings arranged alphabetically by subject (e.g. Fortuna, Clementia). The force of such thinking with respect to the dichotomy between style and genre can be seen in Scaliger's remark concerning the relationship of *sententiae* to tragedy: '[*Sententiae*] are like columns or basic pillars so to say of that structure' (III, 96). This is the remark of a man who has studied rhetoric, not tragedy. It is also reflected in Pierre Grosnet's treatment of Seneca's tragedies, published in 1534: *Les Tragedies de Seneque desquelles sont extraictz plusieurs ẽseignemens avthoritez & singulieres sentences tant en latin cõme en francoys tresutilles & prouffitables a vng chascun.*

Oversimplification is not the only way in which Aphthonius differs from Quintilian or Cicero. *Fabula* to Quintilian did not designate Aesop, whose works he called *fabellae*. *Fabula* was rather a narrative form, found especially in tragedies and poems, that is 'not merely not true but has little resemblance to truth' (II, iv, 2).

For the author of the *Rhetorica ad Herennium* the term meant similarly a work whose events are 'neither true nor probable' (I, viii, 13) and he, too, equated *fabula* with tragedy. Cicero's early *De inventione* makes no such association but merely states: '*Fabula* is the term applied to a narrative in which the events are not true and have no verisimilitude' (I, xix, 27). Here is how Aphthonius speaks of *fabula:*

> The *fabula* originated with poets but even orators use it when they wish to give advice. However, a *fabula* is an untrue story that imitates the truth and has various names. It has been called now Sybaritic, now Cyprian, the names having been changed to account for the variety of originators. Nevertheless, it has been maintained that it is preferable to use the term Aesopian because Aesop has written the best of all *fabulae*. Some *fabulae* are 'reasonable', some 'moral', others 'mixed'. In the 'reasonable' variety we describe a man doing something; the 'moral' ones imitate the acts of the irrational; the 'mixed' have traits of both the 'reasonable' and the 'moral'.
>
> (Froben, p. 191)

Aphthonius has telescoped words and predecessors so that Aesop is now a prime example of that basic (both Aphthonius and Hermogenes begin their works with *fabula*) narrative form, separated even from *narratio*, where Aphthonius never uses the word *fabula*. Most important is the loss of association between *fabula* and the invraisemblable. A *fabula* may not be true but to Aphthonius it imitates truth. Thus, when a 1555 edition of Aphthonius glossed the general definition of *fabula* with 'Fabula versatur maximè in tragoediis' (*Fabula* is found very often in tragedies) (p. 5), we may legitimately wonder whether the intention was to repeat Quintilian's words on *fabula*, accenting the supernatural side of tragedy or to follow Aphthonius and associate tragedy with a story that contains a moral. Aphthonius' own example of *fabula*—the ant and the cicada—leaves little doubt that to him the genre was a moralizing vehicle and this scholium on *fabula*'s *sermo falsus* in the 1555 Aphthonius makes clear how complete the confusion between fable and *fabula* had become: 'Although the subjects are incredible and appear to have none of the force of truth, they do, nevertheless, have a message in comparison with which the truth may be made manifest and possess a true meaning beneath the fictive narration' (p. 5).

The confusion appears quite early. Both Donatus and Diomedes consider tragedy and comedy as varieties of the single genus called *fabula*. Scaliger parrots their view (I, 2). Such uniformity, important in itself, leads to the even more crucial agreement that in *fabula* lay truth, but moral truth, and not necessarily a realistic rendering of human life. While Aphthonius, Donatus, and Diomedes all possess some awareness of drama as imitation, they offer nothing to suggest that such imitation bears any relationship to Aristotelian *mimesis*. By that term the *Poetics* understood a representation rooted in the basic human pleasure that comes from recognition or admiration of an artist's skill. Imitation to the gramarians meant providing the action with a moral drawn from human experience. Expressed another way, what Aristotle presents as a portrait emerges from Aphthonius as an allegory. That tragedy uses kings and generals, not an ant or a cicada, can be considered immaterial. Kings and generals are merely tragedy's agents for instructing the audience and I suspect that Aphthonius' distinction between the 'rational' and 'moral' varieties of *fabula* is based simply on whether rational man or other creatures not endowed with reason are involved. Even if Donatus insists that these men must behave like kings or generals, we have not necessarily moved any closer to Aristotle because without the concept of pleasure in recognition the rule remains what it is: a principle of rhetoric mouthed like so many others.

The confusion between fable and *fabula* lasted long enough for La Mesnardière to feel obliged to redistinguish between them in the seventeenth century.[13] I do not think that the implications of this confusion can be emphasized too strongly. Its acceptance attests to the strength of that medieval tendency to moralize through art, a tendency that continued into the seventeenth century. Its propagation made even more difficult the possibility of wrenching tragedy from the dictates of rhetoric and the compulsion to allegorize.

Throughout the Latin scholia accompanying the 1555 text of Aphthonius, we find that the didactic cast given to the many examples stimulates the commentator to explain in kind and to display the extent of his own understanding that stories have morals. The moral essay (*chria*) mentioned by Quintilian, for instance, prompts Aphthonius' commentator to include other sample essays, including one on 'Omnia uincit amor' (Love conquers all). Here we learn that in his verses Euripides 'judges Love to be supreme over all the Gods' (p. 70) and witness this use of *copia* in the sample essay to prove Euripides' point: 'What caused the house of King Philip of Macedonia to be overthrown? And too the immoral marriages of Cleopatra. Iole daughter of Eurytus, was the reason Hercules' family was destroyed. The house of Theseus was reduced to nothing because of Phaedra' (p. 73). Euripides is mentioned again regarding love to substantiate the statement that 'Love is the worst of all things that try the human mind' (p. 109). I will not belabour the evident. The sentiments, the subjects are those of the 'histoires tragiques'. Indeed, Belleforest cites Euripides and Sophocles before stories 7, 51, 56, and 111 in the same spirit, showing how truly widespread the association had become between classical tragedy and *sententiae*.

One could add, however, that just as Aphthonius represents a reduction in scope and understanding from Quintilian, so the scholia vent pious precepts where Boccaccio had caught a glimpse of human passion. Compare the compassion in these observations by Boccaccio on the Thisbe tragedy, 'Injurious fate erred and perhaps so did the unfortunate parents. . . . Passion is a desire of immoderate force, and in adolescents a veritable curse and urgency' (f. ix^v) with the simple sentiment of Aphthonius' commentator, who finds that the story 'teaches that those who disobey their parents and join themselves by love bonds, will have a very unhappy end' (p. 31). His analysis of Virgil's Dido deserves to be quoted in full:

When he decided to put in his Aeneas a portrait for men of human things and to teach through it what each must do or not do, it was not enough to show from time to time true emotions in fictional characters, as some poets are in the habit of doing, but in fact he added several real things. Among those which must be judged as most genuine [is] that which tells (to keep youth from insane love), of Dido, Queen of the Carthaginians, who killed herself because of her inability to endure her love.

(p. 136)

Here is a side of the sixteenth century that does not coincide well with such ideas as a discovery of ancient letters or a preparation for French Classicism but I hope that the preceding pages have made abundantly clear how extensive is the mentality we are dealing with and how its many manifestations are linked to tragedy. When a 1562 translation of Euripides noted beside certain speeches 'Tyrannidis vituperatio et laus Democratiae' (A censuring of tyranny and praise of Democracy), 'Pulchra disputatio de causis miseriarum humanarum' (A lovely argument about the causes of human miseries) (McDonald, p. 112), when in the closing years of his life Ronsard called tragedy and comedy 'du tout didascaliques et enseignantes' (II, 1017), each brought to bear one of the two contemporary perspectives on tragedy: its rhetorical style and its moral lesson—

the perspectives which return again and again in the liminary poems to tragedy.

If rhetoric had much to say about tragedy, tragedy gained considerably in importance by the role it was assigned in the teaching of rhetoric. While medieval texts such as those by Boccaccio discussed above helped to determine thinking about potential tragic subjects and the lessons of history, generations of young Frenchmen were being introduced to tragedy from the earliest years of their education. If Boccaccio's works taught moral behaviour through misfortune of the great, tragedy, constructed of the same material, could do the same, only better since tragedy possessed over prose the advantage of helping children learn eloquence.

In his 1561 treatise *Liber de liberali, et pia institutione iuuentutis*, Nicolaus Agricola exhibits the mentality which drew tragedy naturally into the purview of education: 'Fabius says that poems furnish an abundance of figures and a variety of things both to instruct and to please the soul. Tragedies offer several examples of the character and misfortunes of tyrants. Comedies are a most attractive mirror of private lives' (sig. [*7^r]).

The collected edition of Melanchthon's letters contains a document so complete and so explicit regarding this instructional value of tragedy that I feel obliged to quote the entire opening portion:

Often when thinking of the ways and customs of men, I marvel at the decision of the Greeks who first showed tragedies to the people not so much that they consider it a source of enjoyment but more importantly that by means of a contemplation of atrocious examples and misfortunes tragedies might turn our rude and fierce passions toward moderation and curbed desires, since in these misfortunes of kings and states they showed the weakness of human nature, the inconstancy of fortune, the irenic outcome of truly good deeds and inversely the very very sad wages of crime. In all this it was particularly wise to choose subjects not about everyday happenings, but exceptional and terrible ones at whose evocation all the audience would shudder. Indeed, people are not moved at seeing trivial and middling misfortunes, but a terrifying kind must be thrust before their eyes to penetrate their feelings and be fixed [there] for a long time and move them through pity to think about the causes of human catastrophes and to make each one associate himself with these sights. Nor was it a petty faculty or art to express somehow the magnitude of events through the eloquence of the dialogue and the variety of acts.

I myself often feel a shudder passing through my whole body when merely reading, not seeing acted the tragedies of Sophocles or Euripides. And there is no one so made of iron who can read of the struggle of the Theban brothers without some emotional upset, or of the fate of the mother Jocasta, who about to delay the battle, when she arrived too late, drew forth the sword from the wound of one of her sons, and with this very sword which was soaked with the blood of her son, this most unfortunate mother transfixed herself. Then, she thrust herself between her sons, throwing out her arms, as if she were intending to die in the embrace of them both. Who can imagine anything more lugubrious? These things were thus acted, were seen, were read, were heard both by the wise and the people, not as entertainment but as a code for governing one's life. These events impressed upon men the causes of human misfortunes, which they observed in these examples being evoked and accumulated from depraved desires. And just as Pindar said, Ixion, bound to his wheel shouts in Hell these words which Virgil repeated: 'You have been warned, learn Justice and not to spurn the Gods'.

Thus the most important part of all tragedies is the subject. They want to fix in the minds of all the thought that there is an eternal mind which always punishes terrible crime with illustratious examples and generally sets a more tranquil course for the moderate and the just. And although sometimes fortuitous misfortunes befall even them, (for there are many hidden reasons) nevertheless that moral which is obvious will not for that reason be vitiated, viz. it is always clear that the Furies and dire calamities are the consequences of atrocious crimes. This thought indeed bends many to moderation which ought the more to move those of us who know that it was often propounded by the clear voice of the Church and God.

Consequently, there is no doubt that the reading of tragedies is most useful for adolescents, as much for impressing upon their minds the many obligations of life and the restraint of their immoderate desires as for [teaching] eloquence. For the splendour of the words is indeed great and the action superbly suited to exciting every emotion of the soul as it falls upon our eyes. And these are the two brightest stars of oratory. And although many reasons can be related, which invited the eager to read tragedies, nevertheless, certainly this one ought to persuade the more sound minds, namely that all those at every age who have become acquainted with this literature the more they reread the same tragedies the more they admire the morals of the works, the succession and nature of the events and make themselves become aware of the miseries, the remedies and the governing of human life. For this reason, they are all the more desired the more they are examined. And just as the art in an excellent painting cannot be estimated with a rapid look, so in these works so very wisely composed, all aspects cannot be grasped immediately. This is why it was often the custom in the theatre to repeat the same stories. . . .

I have spoken too long regarding the intentions with which tragedies are devised, and how they are useful for governing behaviour and eloquence and why the examples of behaviour and eloquence are more prominent in tragedies than in comedies.

(pp. 567-69)

From beginning to end Melanchthon's discussion accentuates the moral truths to be learned from tragedy. Most are quite familiar and the coexistence of the theme of inconstancy of fortune and lessons on vice and virtue should be noted. Melanchthon also has a sense of tragedy's cathartic value, perhaps derived from Hermannus Alemannus,[14] but this dimension, so hotly debated in Italy, becomes quickly submerged in other matters, such as the utility of tragedy for adolescents. Similarly, while Melanchthon sounds like Aristotle when he calls the subject 'the most important part of all tragedies', he rapidly destroys any possible comparison by showing, as Aphthonius had done before him, that the importance of the subject lies in its moral and Melanchthon's pleasure in tragedy emerges more as a rational phenomenon—the gradual understanding of the play's message—than as an aesthetic appreciation of the poet's overall accomplishment.

The use of tragedy to teach eloquence and morals proved an enduring practice, whether the teacher was Nicodemus Frischlinus, trying to inscribe Virgil's memorable verse upon the minds of his students, or Grégoire de Hologne, convinced like Théodore de Bèze, that religious subjects were worth more than any earthy love verse. But, as might be expected, Jesuit colleges did the most to maintain an atmosphere in which tragedy and rhetoric could flourish. That Frischlinus and Grégoire were advocating the study of Latin tragedies might surprise us less today if we could appreciate to what degree the Jesuits insisted upon teaching Latin as a living language. In 1587 at Grenoble an earlier rule was reactivated making Latin the only language to be used in the school. The attitude was not reserved for the sixteenth century. Henri Lantoine reports that 'en 1612, M. Camus, principal du collége de Tréguier, avait annoncé qu'il enseignerait la philosophie en français. . . . L'Université défendit au novateur d'appliquer son programme et d'enseigner en français sous peine d'exclusion' (p. 138). As late as 1623 the Jesuits authorized an edition of Aphthonius for their colleges to be used along with the classical sources for the teaching of rhetoric. We know how large a place this training enjoyed in their system thanks to the publication in 1586 and successive years of the *Ratio studiorum* (a detailed exposition of the Jesuit curriculum) that also includes an interesting remark on tragedy: 'Que le sujet des tragédies et des comédies, lesquelles doivent être en latin et très rares, . . . soit sacré et pieux, qu'il n'y ait entre les actes aucun intermède qui ne soit en latin et décent, qu'aucun personnage ou costume de femme n'y soit introduit' (Schimberg, pp. 370-1). The many titles listed by Gofflot in his study of the Jesuit theatre reveal that plays were not always restricted to Biblical material or church history. An *Hyppolyte* and a *Jules*

César were performed at the écoles de Saint-Maixent in 1576 and 1580 respectively. Still, the subjects are hardly out of line with general humanist practice.

One gauge of the Jesuit influence, I suspect, is the remarkable interest shown George Buchanan's two Latin tragedies *Jephthes* and *Baptistes*. We are all familiar with Montaigne's revelation that he took leading roles in Buchanan's plays when in college (I, 27). Frischlinus in 1584 pays the Scot the compliment of mentioning him in the same breath with Seneca: 'Although we have not imitated', he says in a preface to his tragedy *Venus*, 'that grandiloquence which Seneca [did] in his tragedies or our Buchanan in his Jephthes, we nevertheless gave ourselves the task of retaining Virgil's phrasing' (sig. A2^v). Florent Chrestien translated *Jephthes* in 1587; Busset translated it again in 1590 and Pierre Brisson published and translated *Baptistes* at Rouen in 1613, *Jephthes*, in 1614. The influence spread even to high places. That indefatigable diarist Jean Héroard tells of a performance of *Jephté* at the French court on 7 November 1612 given by 'des petits garçons' (Lough, pp. 35-6). Also, is it purely coincidental that the town of Pont-à-Mousson, where two French tragedies were published (Jean Robelin's *Thébaïde*, 1584 and Nicolas Romain's *Maurice*, 1601) was also the site of a Jesuit college that in 1595 had to turn the populace away from a performance because of the large number of 'personnes de qualité?'[15]

There can be no better proof of the effectiveness and the prevalence of this training in rhetoric than the number of playwriting lawyers at this time, especially between 1595 and 1620. Robert Garnier, Pierre Matthieu, Jean de Beaubrueil, Jean Prévost, all were trained in the law and therefore were required by their profession as well as their professors to be familiar with rhetoric. La Croix du Maine, in fact, duly noted that in addition to his talents with verse Garnier 'a encores ce rare et excellent don d'orateur, qui est une chose fort peu commune' (Myssing, p. 19). Payen reproduces this 1564 statement by a French lawyer, which, if typical, proves that the Solons as well as the Ronsards of the day spoke Greek when speaking French: 'cet œil du Parlement qui a sa rondeur également proportionné, œil plus droit que celui de Polyphème, lequel aucuns ont estimé, sur Philostrate, être œil de la France, qui regarde cette Galathée ou cette Vérité, de laquelle ce grand Polyphème, qui est ce grand corps de la Justice, est amoureux' (p. 66).

Others, such as Roillet, Grévin, Le Coq, d'Amboise, represent the professions of medicine, theology, and teaching and among those who took time to write polite verse printed with their tragedies, the percentage of lawyers, doctors, professors, and clergymen, those who had undergone a similar education, is also extremely high.[16] Thus, when H. C. Lancaster attempts to show that the tragi-comedy appealed to various classes because 'its authors included Barran, a preacher; Behourt, Heyns, and Jean-Georges, schoolmasters; Du Chesne, a physician; Bonet and La Fons, lawyers; Le Jars, the King's Secretary of the Chamber; Papillon, a retired captain; Garnier, Sainte-Marthe, and Mlle des Roches, who occupied themselves largely with literary pursuits' (*French Tragi-Comedy*, p. 77), he has surely missed the point that behind this variety lies a uniformity of education and attitude toward serious drama to which contemporary evidence continually returns us.

NOTES TO CHAPTER I

[1] From the *Catalogue of Lucubrations* (1523), quoted in *The Epistles of Erasmus*, ed. Francis Morgan Nichols (3 vols. London: Longmans, Green, 1901-18), I, 393.

[2] Erasmus, *Opus Epistolarum*, ed. Percy S. Allen (12 vols. Oxford: Clarendon Press, 1906-58), I, 418.

[3] See Bernard Weinberg's 'Scaliger versus Aristotle on Poetics', *Modern Philology*, 39 (1942), 337-60.

[4] Etienne Jodelle, *Les Œuvres et Meslanges poétiques*, ed. Marty-Laveaux (2 vols. Paris: A. Lemerre, 1868-70), II, 178.

[5] See before Bardon de Brun's *Sainct Jacques*, the poems by I. Granaud, (sig. [π8r]) and M. Petiot (sig. [π8v]); before Chantelouve's *Pharaon*, the poem by François de Balauoine (sig. ã4v); before Chrétien des Croix' *Albouin*, poems by P. B. Argent. (sig. A5r), Oger (sig. A4v), and O. Du Mont-Sacré (N. de Montreux), (sig. A3r); before Belyard's *Le Guysien*, the sonnet by M. E. P. P., (sig. [A7r]); before Philone's *Tragédie*, the unsigned sonnet and the Quatrain by Franc. Rolland, (p. 7); before the 1585 edition of Garnier's tragedies, poems by Belleau (sig. [ã7v]), and Binet (sig. [ã8v]); before his *Cornélie*, the ode by Belleau (f. 38r); before his *Hippolyte*, the sonnet by N. D. B. (f. 111v); before Hardy's collected works, poems by Théophile (I, 11), Saint Iaques (I, 13), and before his *Daire*, a poem by Guillebert (IV, 6); before Laudun's *Horace*, poems by Guillaume de Roques (f. 32r), M. Rigal, and Loys Delaudun de Gatigues (f. 32v); before Matthieu's *Clytemnestre*, the poem by Benigne Poissenot (sig. **5r); before Prévost's *Edipe*, the poem by F. Gaultier (sig. ã5v); before Thierry's *David persécuté*, the ode by Franc. Bigeot (sig. A6v).

[6] See, for example, Bernier de la Brousse's poem to Prévost (sig. [ã6r]), an anonymous Latin poem to Matthieu's *Vasti* (sig. [*8r]); Iean Vuillemin and B.

Poissenot's remarks before Matthieu's *Clytemnestre* (sig. **4ᵛ and **5ʳ), François de Balauoine's poem before Chantelouve's *Pharaon* (sig. ã4ᵛ), and A. Dubreton's Latin poem before Hardy's collected works (I, 8).

⁷ The copy I have consulted is dated 1619 but Cioranescu lists an earlier edition for 1617.

⁸ See p. 123.

⁹ Compare Quintilian's 'Never in my opinion would the founders of cities have induced their unsettled multitudes to form communities had they not moved them by the magic of their eloquence; never without the highest gifts of oratory would the great legislators have constrained mankind to submit themselves to the yoke of law' (II, xvi, 9) and Fabri's 'c'est [l'eloquence] qui descript les loix, les droictz et les iugemens, et est le plus grant tresor qui puisse estre a la chose publique que d'auoir de bons zelateurs d'icelle' (pp. 6-7) with Peletier's 'La Poësi¢ à congregè les homm¢s, qui eto¢t sauuag¢s, brutaus e epäues. . . . La Poësi¢ à etè caus¢ des edificacions des Vil¢s e constitucions des Lo¢s' (p. 8).

¹⁰ See Castor's chapter 2, 'Poetry as the Art of Second Rhetoric' for a full and excellent discussion of this phenomenon.

¹¹ Quintilian's editor H. E. Butler says this about *ethologia*: 'The meaning of *ethologia* is doubtful, but probably means a simple character-sketch of some famous man' (I, 156). I have been led to describe the term a bit more narrowly by the fact that Aphthonius gives as a definition of the related term *ethopoeia* 'quae nam uerba Hercules imperante Eurystheo dicere potuisset' (what words Hercules might have spoken after Eurystheus' orders) (p. 217).

¹² Compare Quintilian's 'there must be propriety in our words, their order must be straightforward, the conclusion of the period must not be long postponed, there must be nothing lacking and nothing superfluous' (VII, ii, 22), which is translated almost word for word in Fabri's treatise, p. 23.

¹³ See p. 194.

¹⁴ See William F. Boggess, 'Hermannus Alemannus and Catharsis in the Mediaeval Latin *Poetics*', *The Classical World*, 62 (1959), 212-14 and Weinberg's *A History of Literary Criticism in the Italian Renaissance*, I, 352-8.

¹⁵ See Gofflot, p. 153. On the college and Nicolas Romain's involvement with the university at Pont-à-Mousson, see Eugène Martin, *L'Université de Pont-à-Mousson* (Paris and Nancy: Berger-Levrault, 1891).

¹⁶ A sample list of men identified in the text: Benigne Poissenot, 'docteur aux loix', in Matthieu's *Esther*—1585, sig. **2ᵛ; I. Oger, 'Aduocat Argent.', in Chrétien des Croix' *Albouin*, sig. A4ᵛ; Mon. Estienne, 'substitut de M. le Procureur General de Barois', in Romain's *Maurice*, sig. A6ʳ; Monsieur Mauljean, 'Licencié és Loix, Aduocat au Pont', in Romain's *Maurice*, sig. A6ʳ; G. Durand, 'maistre és Arts', in Romain's *Maurice*, sig. A7ʳ; I. H. de Saint-Iaques, 'Aduocat en Parlement', in Hardy's collected works, I, 13; Iean Vuillemin, 'Docteur en Medecine', in Matthieu's *Clytemnestre*, sig. **4ᵛ; N. Bergerius, 'Aduocatus', in Soret's *La Céciliade*, sig. π6ᵛ.

Here is a partial list of others that I have been able to identify myself: Pierre Hévin (Prévost) was 'docteur en droit'. See the article on his son in the *Biographie Universelle ancienne et moderne*, ed. Michaud (45 vols. Nouvelle Edition Paris, n.d.), 19, 400. Claude Binet (Garnier—1585) was 'avocat au Parlement'. See the

Dictionnaire de biographie française, ed. M. Prevost and R. d'Amat (Paris, 1933-—), VI, 494. Bernier de la Brousse (Prévost) was 'avocat'. See the *Biographie universelle*, 5, 635. Jacques Dalechamps (Bousy) was a doctor. See the *Nouvelle Biographie générale*, ed. Hoeffer (46 vols. Paris, 1862-70), 12, 804. Jacques Levasseur (Poullet) was an 'érudit et littérateur' according to the *Nouvelle Biographie générale*, 31, 21.

II OLD AND NEW DRAMA

Although the relevance of Quintilian and Boccaccio to our topic is, I hope, absolutely clear, it is also true that we are not primarily concerned with rhetoric or short stories but with the humanists who wrote plays and that these men were subject to the additional influence of medieval and classical drama. Speculation on the relationship between the humanist theatre and these pre-existing traditions has produced a number of judgments that extend the realm of those prejudicial attitudes discussed in the Introduction. When, for example, Maurice Valency states, regarding humanist tragedy and antiquity, 'Judging by their prefaces, the Renaissance dramatists considered that their tragedies were elegantly classical; but it is obvious that, with the exception of Trissino, they were more strongly influenced by the Senecan horror plays and the medieval story forms than by anything derived from a study of the Greek' (p. 22), there is more than a suggestion that Greek tragedy is rather different from Seneca and that the humanists were somehow confused about their own inspiration. On humanist and medieval theatre, Lebègue has this to say: 'Comme ses successeurs, Jodelle rompt complètement avec le théâtre médiéval; il ne lui emprunte rien. . . .' The rupture is described in terms of the appearance of a new form ('cinq actes, séparés par les strophes d'un chœur, très peu d'action, beaucoup de lamentations, des sentences . . .' (*La Tragédie française*, p. 33). Valency returns us to the eighteenth-century view that tragedy had to await French Classicism for its true flowering; Lebègue, to the related concept of a sixteenth-century Renaissance which breaks with the past and inaugurates French Classicism.

We have already seen enough to know that it is not possible to distinguish neatly between medieval attitudes toward tragedy and the views held by such great classical figures as Quintilian. Also, if the humanists were as strongly influenced by rhetoric as contemporary documents suggest, it is hard to believe that the sixteenth century would have placed form over expression when reading Greek and Latin playwrights. Form is only part of theatre. The formal differences between Jodelle and a mystery play are admittedly great but so is the uniformity of views on tragedy among the writers available to the sixteenth century. The well-established fact that medieval theatre did not die in 1548 but survived into the seventeenth century also suggests that formal changes may be a poor gauge of the sixteenth century's relations with the past and that we must be willing to study tragedy as a concept as well as a form.

I   THE MEDIEVAL THEATRE

It is a critical commonplace to speak of a decline in medieval drama at the end of the fifteenth century and the beginning of the sixteenth. The action of the Parlement of Paris, which in 1548 forbade the Confrères de la Passion to play 'mystères sacrés' gave a formal date to this decline. It has been explained by some in religious terms. Comic, even scabrous episodes had alternated with stories from the Bible while the spectators used the occasion not to deepen their religious fervour but to amuse themselves by shouting obscenities, fighting, and so forth. Practical and literary reasons have also been advanced. According to Lebègue, plays had reached gigantic proportions requiring many days and much money to perform. Already in the fifteenth century a pedantic style heavy in scholastic reasoning and bizarre etymologies had developed and a study of the various reworkings of Les Actes des Apôtres shows that these tendencies were by no means dead in the early sixteenth century.[1] For all this evidence of decadence, however, the medieval theatre was to exercise an influence even beyond the end of the sixteenth century and this talk of decline will not tell us why, perhaps because it does not explain wherein lay the drama of a Christian theatre.

It has been said that because Christianity offers a promise of redemption and an after life, its world view is not tragic. However, hope may be immediately realized or endlessly awaited. Also the portrait of the saved does not exclude the horror of the castigation of the damned. Such nuances are particularly noticeable in two of the earliest plays of the French medieval theatre, the *Sponsus* and the *Jeu d'Adam*. The former drama, written near the end of the eleventh or the beginning of the twelfth century, relates the story of the wise and foolish virgins; the *Jeu d'Adam* (c. 1146-74) presents in trilogy form the fall, the first murder, and a march of prophets to announce the Messiah. In addition to a Biblical source, the dramas have in common a presentation of two vital aspects of man's spiritual life. By recounting man's fall and first crime, the *Jeu d'Adam* turns toward the past to illustrate the drama which weighs upon man from his birth. The story of the wise and foolish virgins, a prefiguration of the last judgment, looks rather to the future and to the moment of decision that awaits every man at the end of his life. They both depict a struggle between the forces of good and evil. Moreover, the force of each play depends directly upon the immediate failure of good to conquer its opposite, that is, upon the portrait of a tragedy.

The *Sponsus* dates from the period in medieval drama when plays were still produced exclusively within the churches and incorporated into the liturgy. The verses were sung; the use of Latin, extensive. There is great fidelity to the scriptural source and the entire text concentrates on underlining the weight of the parable lesson 'vigilate'. The play makes no concession in its development to entertaining the spectators. The sense of ritual dominates as all innovation or addition is subordinated to the allegory's message.

At the same time, the verses in Old French suggest the awareness of a lay public, one for whom the Latin had to be translated to insure the communication of the lesson. I say 'translated' because the French does not add to the Latin verses. The Latin always precedes the Old French which repeats the Latin like a gloss. Nevertheless, the French varies the tone of the Latin verses in certain places to produce a distinction that is all-important for the history of medieval drama.

This theatre was not always to remain within the church walls or continue to be chanted in harmony with its liturgical origins and context. It moved outside the building toward a public that knew little Latin and would demand to be entertained as well as educated. To answer these needs, the drama required more and more a tone of action in contrast with the tableaux of the nativity scene or the resurrection. Its characters underwent a process of humanization whereby the dramatist developed individual and human traits within the

universal, archetypal aspect of the religious figures. If added movement would help maintain interest, a more human dimension could
establish a link between actor and spectator that was useful for
effective propagandizing. Within the text of the *Sponsus* appear
examples of each of these developments, examples that prove to be
essential elements of the play's dramatic technique.

Regarding movement and action, it is significant that the oil
merchants do not speak in the Latin text, just as they are silent in the
Bible. The Latin text remains throughout the more faithful to the
Biblical account of the parable. Even the preamble of Ecclesia, who
is not specifically mentioned in the Bible, can be justified by the
unnamed voice that cries, 'Ecce sponsus venit' (Matthew 25:6).
Ecclesia's announcement ('Here is the bridegroom who is Christ /
keep watch, virgins' vv. 1-2), the interpretation of the coming of
Christ ('For he comes to free / the origins of nations' vv. 5-6) and
of his death are didactic and dramatically very neutral. An action is
not being set in motion so much as explained. Christ's speech in
Latin, too, paraphrases the Bible. 'A men dico, vos ignosco' (vs. 99)
repeats 'Amen dico vobis, nescio vos' (Matthew 25:12) and preserves the didactic tone: 'Those who waste proceed away from /
the threshold of this palace' (vv. 101-2). The verses are also as neutral
as those of Ecclesia. The drama is not specified and the spectator
himself must translate these words within the context of the parable
to feel the human tragedy of those who did not 'keep watch' and
'wasted'. The remaining portion of the Latin verses partakes of the
same dramatic neutrality. The foolish virgins beg the wise for aid,
are refused and told to seek the merchants. The next Latin stanza
shows the foolish virgins lamenting their fate, as in the Bible.

The French verses, on the other hand, depict a conversation
between the merchants and the foolish virgins. Here the gloss
translates the suggestion of the wise virgins into action since the
addition of dialogue assures a verbal confrontation. Of equal
importance is the fact that the confrontation with the merchants
also enhances the drama inherent in the action: hope. The warning
to keep watch has been sounded and the foolish virgins sense the
tragedy that awaits them, but before the drama is played out, the
author introduces a gloss that places the foolish virgins before their
final hope of salvation. With this exchange the tableau comes to
life and becomes theatre; the parable turns into tragedy.

Just as the French verses add the crushing encounter between the foolish virgins and the merchants to a static tableau, so the remaining French verses, in glossing the Latin text, transform the characters' neutral, didactic language into an individual and emotional exchange. When the first group of French stanzas begins to translate Ecclesia's introduction, the difference in tone and language is immediately apparent. The allegorical 'vigilate' is rendered 'Gaire noi dormet!' The description of Christ, saviour of the world, is at the same time maintained and recast with two verses whose accent on brutality and suffering has no equivalent in the Latin. Finally, 'Gaire noi dormet' becomes a refrain that announces its counterpart spoken by the foolish virgins, 'Dolentas, chaitivas, trop i avem dormit!' There is no longer any ambiguity to the vocabulary. The foolish virgins were told not to sleep and did. I think that we can also say that the French gloss of 'vigilate' definitely creates a second plane of action within the play. A specific drama has been lived by individuals who confess their mistakes and lament their fortune. The two planes continue to the final scene. Christ refuses to recognize them and sends them away from the palace threshold but then, in French, he makes clear that the foolish virgins are to be damned, repeating the adjective 'chaitivas' of the refrain. It may be true that there are wise virgins present to substantiate the theory that Christian drama is not essentially tragic but given that all within the play focuses upon the fate of the foolish, not the wise virgins, and the impossibility for the former to reverse their fate, I find it extremely difficult to deny the play the title of tragedy or to ignore its tragic structure of warning, hope, and catastrophe.

By mid-twelfth century and the *Jeu d'Adam*, the drama had moved to the church front. The development of action and human characterization had reached new heights and with it dramatic techniques also made advances. Irony, psychology, exploitation of themes and planes now deepened that tragic structure.

The *Jeu* begins with a lesson, in Latin, that is followed by a choral chant also in Latin. Once the dialogue is opened, however, the characters speak only in French. Figura (God) addresses Adam and Eve. His words announce the play's first and most important theme: obedience. Adam responds that he will obey his creator. In giving Eve to Adam, Figura tells them to love one another but warns Adam, 'Ele soit a ton comandement, / E vos amdeus a mon talent' (p. 7). The hierarchy of allegiance is clear and it will prove essential to the elaboration of the drama. Because both man and woman are to obey Figura, yet Eve's position on earth is subservient to Adam's, their marriage forms a mirror of their relationship to Figura and a second plane, the human plane, which will be developed until the dramatist can transfer the action to that plane and effect the kind of humanization of the allegory we have witnessed in the French verses of the *Sponsus*.

Figura's remarks to Eve repeat the theme of obedience and introduce the second important motif of the play: glory. Eve is told to love and obey her creator and her husband 'Car ço est droiz de mariage' (p. 8). If this is done, 'Se tu le fais bon adjutoire / Jo te metrai od lui en gloire' (p. 8). Glory is the fruit of obedience. The lesson is repeated for Adam by Figura whose words

> Ja n'avras faim, por besoing ne bevras,
> Ja n'avras froit, ja chalt ne sentiras.
> Tu iers en joie, ja ne te lasseras,
> E en deduit ja dolor ne savras

> (p. 8)

evoke the lyrical quality of an existence in glory. By linking glory and obedience, the author is of course justifying the future loss of paradise through Eve's disobedience. But through such a lyrical description of Eden, the sense of 'gloire' has been made concrete and the public must contemplate its loss in fully understandable terms.

Figura follows the portrait of Eden with an allusion to free will:

> En vostre cors vos met e bien e mal;
> Ki ad tel don n'est pas liez a pal.
> Tot en balance or pendiez par egal;
> Creez conseil que soit vers moi leal

> (p. 9)

and counsels them to abandon evil and follow good. Figura recognizes the dual nature of his creation, a duality exploited in the two planes of the action.

Figura's final act and the end of the exposition concerns the tree of knowledge. He warns Adam, 'Se tu en manjues, sempres sentiras mort; / M'amor perdras, mal changeras ta sort' (p. 11). Adam understands. He swears fidelity to Figura and twice in his speech he scoffs at the possibility of losing so much for so little, 'Por une pome se jo gerpis t'amor, / Ja en ma vie comperrai ma folor' (p. 11). The couple have been warned. Man has vaunted his sense of values. Eden for an apple! The stage is set for his fall.

With the appearance of the devil, the second plane of the drama becomes dominant. The devil begins by asking Adam how goes his life. When Adam answers, 'Ne sen rien qui m'enuit' (p. 12), the devil retorts, 'Puet estre mielz' (p. 12) and attempts to interest Adam in the means to remedy this situation. Adam agrees to do all save disobey his creator. The forbidden fruit is offered but Adam refuses it. When the devil tries to instill in Adam a desire to rival his creator, who after all made man to be his gardener, Adam recognizes Satan and sends him away.

This scene has no equivalent in the Bible. Its invention by the dramatist affords a singular insight into his effort to make the encounters with the devil realistic and human. The devil poses no questions of a theological nature. Their confrontation is not a debate. Rather, the devil speaks directly to Adam the man and attempts to uncover in his human make-up the possibility of injured pride at being God's inferior.

The devil's meeting with Eve follows the same pattern. He quickly adapts his tone to the situation, addressing Eve with all the flattery of a courtly lover: 'Tu es fieblette e tendre chose, / E es plus fresche que n'est rose' (p. 18). But flattery is only to dispose Eve's mind to darker thoughts about her marriage: 'Mal cople en fist li Criator: / Tu es trop tendre e il est trop dur' (p. 18). The temptation with the apple follows, replete with the vision of a greater glory for Eve as a 'dame del mond' (p. 19). She is visibly attracted, but the devil will not be content until he has involved Adam in Eve's disobedience. She is directed to taste of the fruit and to give it to Adam despite what he may say. Eve accepts.

Of the actual eating of the apple and Adam's sin, the Bible says only that Eve ate and gave the apple to Adam, who also ate. The *Jeu d'Adam* gives a fuller account. Again the accent falls on a careful sounding of the psychological situation. Eve wants Adam to eat the apple. Fresh from the serpent's counsel, she suggests to Adam that he really does not know what the fruit is or how good it is. Adam is momentarily tempted, then refuses. Eve retorts, 'Del demorer fais tu que las' (p. 22), which I take to mean, 'En hésitant tu agis comme un lâche'. Adam accepts to eat. Eve has succeeded, but through an insult that cleverly signals Eve's disobedience to Figura without leaving the context of the couple's private existence. The dramatist has been able to remain on the second plane of his story and still propel the drama to its tragic close. Although the *Jeu* possesses its equivalent of the wise virgins in Adam's announcement of Jesus' coming or Eve's 'Mais neporquant en Dieu est ma sperance' (p. 33), hope is not the main emotion created by the play. In her final speech, Eve recognizes that 'De nostre mal long en est la mecine' (p. 32). Hope is long in the future and the audience is left with a portrait whose essential traits are the weakness of man and the irreparable loss of the earthly paradise. The entire second part of the trilogy, by depicting the first human crime, demonstrates even more brutally how far mankind has come from Eden. And all 'Por une pome'. Could the prophets' march completely efface this impression?

With the vogue in later centuries of the miracle play, the conventional technique of medieval drama began an evolution that continued into the sixteenth century. The dramatists' development of the human as well as the allegorical plane in the story grew increasingly difficult to discern. Irony and psychology, those cardinal elements of the tragedy of the foolish virgins and humanity's first couple, all but leave the stage.

The miracle play was not by its nature suited to any tragic scheme. The miracle performed by the Virgin or saint restored happy circumstances immediately. There could be no dwelling upon the unfortunate present with a distant hope foreseen as in the *Jeu d'Adam*. In addition, the miraculous act was performed by an agent other than the protagonist so that interest in his psychology proved minimal. In the *Miracle de Théophile* (13th century), where Théophile makes a pact with the devil and brings about a miracle through repentance, Rutebeuf did make some effort to probe the action which leads to the pact and recantation. But in the *Miracle de la Marquise de la Gaudin* (14th century), the author puts preparing the miracle well above developing his characters. Of these two famous miracle plays, it is significant that the later work has the less psychological orientation. Several other differences between the plays indicate how very representative they are of the evolution outlined above.

Albert Pauphilet has said in his edition of the *Miracle de Théophile*, in view of its 'scènes juxtaposées plutôt qu'enchaînées', that this is 'plus qu'un drame, un beau *vitrail poétique*' (p. 136). The point is well taken, but the growing independence of individual scenes is only an effect whose cause lies in a new concept of the drama's narrative. The technique of the *Jeu d'Adam* with its interlocking themes, its 'Por une pome', cannot be separated from a sense of the narrative as a story of increasing intensity where characters evolve to bring about a reversal of their fortunes. Like the *Sponsus'* Latin verses, the *Miracle de Théophile* offers a series of tableaux which are related, but instead of a complete evolution, the author depicts only those crucial scenes that are necessary for an understanding of the story's moral. Soon after Théophile has made his pact with the devil, Rutebeuf inserts a scene between Théophile and his friends: 'Ici va Theophiles a ses compaignons tencier, premièrement a un qui avoit non Pierres' (p. 148). The scene has no dramatic value and does not advance the action. It simply shows the change that has come over Théophile now that he is in the hands of the devil. In the following scene seven years have elapsed and Théophile has repented.

The *Miracle de la Marquise de la Gaudin* seems much less disjointed. There are no scenes so unnecessary as Théophile's quarrelling with his friends nor does time elapse so abruptly. The play has a number of idiosyncrasies of its own, however. Notable is the disproportion in focus. Here is a résumé of the action. The marquis must take a trip and leaves his wife in his uncle's care until such time as he will return. The uncle unsuccessfully tries to seduce his niece and arranges for her to be discovered in bed with his dwarf whereupon she is falsely accused of adultery. The husband returns, learns what has happened and condemns her to die. A passing knight who had known the marquise is told of her fate, challenges the uncle, overcomes him and forces him to reveal the truth. The plot permits a number of dramatic moments: the unsuccessful seduction, the husband's return, the husband's decision, the knight's appearance. Only the first and last moments are exploited in the play and even then to no greater degree than much of the peripheral material. The exposition, for example, runs for some 181 verses during which the couple attend mass and listen to a sermon (not included in the text). The attempted seduction, however, is accomplished in sixty-five verses, less than half the time necessary to place the marquise in the hands of the uncle. We never learn what the woman's sentiments are following the harrowing event. The action passes directly to the uncle who arranges his plot and then to the marquise's preparation for bed. The husband never expresses his sentiments. Only the marquise and the knight are permitted to vent their feelings when alone and in both cases their monologues are prayers to the Virgin.

These prayers constitute the longest speeches in the play and contrast with the rapid pace of events. There is one sequence where the contrast is particularly noticeable. The marquis has left; the uncle has promised to protect his charge. She takes leave of her servant to ask the Virgin to protect her husband and give her strength in his absence. The devil appears proclaiming, 'Je li feray meschief avoir / Se j'oncques puis' (vv. 216-17). But the marquise takes up her prayer to the Virgin and the devil sees that all is useless. He turns instead toward the uncle. Immediately we have the seduction scene. Such suddenness recalls the rapid passage of the seven years in Rutebeuf's *Miracle de Théophile*. Yet there the poet had devoted several prior scenes to the main character and to his state of mind. Of the first five sequences, two are devoted to Théophile alone and in only one is Théophile absent. The scene following the time lapse contains a long lament in twelve quatrains written in alexandrins. The lament is complemented by Théophile's prayer to the Virgin in nine twelve-verse stanzas. These passages can be attributed to Rutebeuf's essential profession of poet, not dramatist, but I see no reason to deny the fact that in spending so much time with the inner feelings of Théophile Rutebeuf is also closer to the theatre which had preceded him than to the theatre to come.

The only person to evolve in the marquise's story is the uncle and the change is so rapid that we never see it. We see only the result. It exists, furthermore, not as the centre of the drama but as the mechanism to produce the drama. We are not invited to witness the tragedy of evil triumphing over good in a person but the victory of good (the Virgin) over evil (the uncle). From this shift in emphasis from a personal tragedy to a supernatural victory follow the many changes we have just noted between the miracle plays and the earlier dramas.

In the *Sponsus* the wise virgins answer their sisters' plea for oil with these words:

Nos precari, precamur, amplius,
desinite, sorores, ocius:
vobis enim, nil erit melius
dare preces pro hoc ulterius.

(vv. 56-9)

(Cease, we beg, to implore us further, sisters, for nothing will profit you to ask us any longer for it.)
The tone is harsh and final as will be the words of Christ at the end.

C

The play is not concerned primarily with such condemnation, however. It focuses on the plight of the fallen, their warning, their hope, their final realization of failure. In the story of the marquise, we see the world through the eyes of the wise virgins exclusively. Divided between the good and the bad, the prepared and the unprepared, it seeks to identify properly the two species and to offer their fate as an example to all. Théophile's anger at losing his post— the seed of discontent that grows into his sinful pact—is one of the last vestiges of the second plane on which such examples had previously acted out their destiny in human terms. By ignoring this dimension, the story of the marquise automatically dispenses with any necessity to offer a verisimilar narration. Its particular pace, its disproportionate interest in prayers and the hearing of mass become quite natural if we accept that the narration seeks only to define the respective moral positions and prepare the drama's lesson. The Virgin, God, the Church are constantly on the lips of the marquise. We discover that the prolonging of the exposition by a church scene is directly related to the author's desire to accentuate her piety. The marquise will not let her husband undertake his voyage without asking God's protection:

> Mais je vous pri pour Dieu qu'avant,
> Sire, que faciez ceste emprise,
> Au mains que nous deux a l'eglise
> Aillons vous a Dieu conmander
> Et li sa grace demander.

(vv. 24-8)

As unchanging and incorruptible as the wise virgins, the marquise may have possessed a faith that produced miracles but her perfection also returned dramaturgy to the simplicity of parables.

The *Mistére du Viel Testament*, written in the fifteenth century, played in Paris in 1542, dramatizes literally all the major episodes of the Old Testament, including the story of Adam and Eve and the drama of Saul and David, destined to become one of the great subjects of late sixteenth-century tragedy.

From its inception the Adam and Eve story shows a different organization from the *Jeu d'Adam*. God creates Adam, leads him to Eden and then creates Eve. In the *Jeu*, it will be remembered, Figura confronts both Adam and Eve before placing the couple in their earthly paradise. The *Mistére* follows the Biblical account; the *Jeu* is willing to rearrange for reasons of its own internal drama.

The presence of all three characters in the opening scene of the *Jeu* permits the dramatist to introduce naturally the theme of obedience. Figura charges his creatures and each swears to be 'feel'. Like the vassal's oath of fealty, a certain rite is performed and even greater gravity is given to the eventual transgression. In the *Mistére*, Adam rises after his creation 'et puis ce doit mettre humblement a genoulx, les mains joinctes, disant ce qui s'ensuit':

O divine illustracion,
Pére puissant, plein de bonté,
De ma noble creacion
Vous rends graces en humilité;
Hault recteur de divinité,
Mon Dieu, mon pére et plasmateur,
Mercy vous rends par charité
Comme a mon maistre et createur.
O souverain gubernateur,
Principe du ciel et acteur
De toute chose primeraine,
Mon sieur, mon prince et recteur,
De tout bien auxiliateur,
Mercy vous rends d'entente pleine.
Bonté souveraine
Puissance haultaine,
Noble sapience,
En ce bas demaine,
Par amour certaine,
Vous faitz reverence.

(I, 30)

When God ushers Adam into Eden, Adam 'a genoulx' exclaims:

O mon createur et mon maistre,
Mon Dieu, mon pasteur honnorable,
Soubz vous je doy bien joyeux estre
D'avoir ce lieu tant delectable.

(I, 31)

Eve will do and say no less after her creation. The scene, the tone, the relationship between characters could not be more different from the *Jeu d'Adam*. We witness a scene of adoration where God is recognized immediately as Creator and power supreme. Adam does not speak to God so much as praises him, repeating certain phrases until his words acquire the tone of a litany. God's new creations are not charged. The idea of obedience appears spontaneously in the speeches of Adam and Eve and the moment loses all the dramatic potential of the *Jeu*'s covenant.

When the first man and woman are placed in Eden, God warns them against the fruit of knowledge and the couple swear allegiance in keeping with the Biblical sequence, but the theme of glory and its explicit involvement with the necessity for obedience are absent, as can be seen from this exchange at the end of the scene:

Dieu   Vous deux en ce lieu precieux,
          Estes creez par providence,
          Pour remplir en noble excellence
          Lassus le haut siége des cieulx.
Adam Vray Dieu, puissant et glorieux,
          A vous ferons obeissance.
          . . .
Eve   Nous sommes soubz vostre regence
          Pour obeyr de cueur joyeux.
Dieu   Vous deux en ce lieu precieux,
          Estes creez par providence,
          Pour remplir en noble excellence
          Lassus le hault siége des cieulx.

(I, 37)

I have quoted several verses to show that the lyrical quality of Adam's praises to God is not exceptional in the *Mistére*. These lines, with the marquise's prayers to the Virgin or Théophile's lament, demonstrate to what extent the characters are less and less appreciated for their human as well as pedagogical significance, for in the absence of any human plane within the action, how could the characters appear except as perfectly predictable figures in a prescribed tale or voices that intone religious commonplaces?

The scene of the fall, too, makes this point. The devil appears, delivers a monologue, and turns immediately to Eve. (Adam will not be given any more of a role than is commensurate with the Bible account and the devil adopts none of the gallant tones of the *Jeu d'Adam*.) From Eve's reply, 'Je croy que de franc cueur loyal / Me conseillez bien sagement' (I, 47), we learn that little is required to entice her to eat. When she sees Adam, she admits her act and repeats the devil's promise that the fruit will make them great. Here is Adam's response:

Pour esprouver se j'aurai mieulx,
J'en mengeray, quoi qu'il advienne.
Le fruit est plaisant et joyeux,
Il ne peut que bien ne m'en vienne.

(I, 49)

There is no insult, no cajoling, no flattery. The author neglects all psychological possibilities inherent in the couple's situation and offers fidelity to the Bible in lieu of the imaginative adaptation of the *Jeu d'Adam*—at least until we arrive at the judgment of man's first transgression.

Justice is swift in the *Jeu* in keeping with the warning of the introduction and its clear definition of man's obligations. When punishing Adam and Eve, the *Mistère du Viel Testament* invents extensively for the first time and adds a scene of some 265 verses. Justice, Mercy, and God discuss the transgression committed by Adam and Eve. Justice demands damnation; Mercy, some less excessive punishment. They argue until God pronounces sentence. The obvious imitation here of a courtroom scene points to what Lebègue calls 'l'appareil de la scolastique' (*La Tragédie religieuse*, p. 16) in describing the decadence of medieval drama. Still, I think that the scene's precise function comes to light in these words spoken by God to Justice:

> Dictes; je vous escouteray
> Avant que de donner sentence,
> Et juste jugement feray
> Que on verra par experience.

> (I, 56)

Through the debate of Justice and Mercy the audience is to learn of the gravity of man's crime and of God's love for his fallen creation, in short, each of the essential points of theology related to the Biblical event.

The lyricism of the exposition, the absence of characterization, the pedagogical orientation of the allegory, all point to the same conclusion: the evolution in technique from the *Jeu d'Adam* to the *Mistère*, if gradual, has also been decisive. At each stage we have moved further from the *Jeu's* powerful combination of moral tale and human drama. In the *Mistère* Adam turns to Eve after God's sentence saying:

> Voir, l'ung l'autre sommes honteux.
> Ainsi, o povre humanité,
> Monceau de terre lymonneux,
> Ragarde ta fragilité.

> (I, 69)

Does 'humanité' refer only to Adam and Eve or is it directed to the

audience as well? It is impossible to tell. The two have fused completely in the author's mind.

Despite the decline of dramatic content in medieval theatre, the
tradition continued. Its products were played in the sixteenth
century and imitated by new dramatists. Prominent among these
new plays are the works of Marguerite de Navarre, who composed
four 'comédies spirituelles' (*Comédie de la nativité, Comédie de
l'adoration, Comédie des trois rois, Comédie des innocents et du désert*)
and seven other plays that have been published together by V.-L.
Saulnier as her 'théatre profane'. The distinction between 'spirituelle'
and 'profane' here pertains exclusively to the subject. 'Spirituelle'
is used to mean derived from the Bible; 'profane' to designate stories
created by Marguerite. For, in tone, technique, and conception of
subject there is little to distinguish between the two groups of plays.

The Biblical plays, written probably around 1536, form a connected story but each is constructed to exist alone as a separate work.
The subject of Jesus' birth is one of considerable interest to the
medieval theatre and Jourda refers in his critical edition of the
Comédie de la nativité to an impressive number of medieval works on
this theme which Marguerite could have known and imitated. Subject
is not the only link between Marguerite's comédie and her medieval
predecessors, however.

At the beginning of the *Comédie*, Joseph is worried about a trip
to Bethlehem, given Marie's state. Marie answers:

> Danger n'aura ie le nous certifie;
> Car le Puissant qui en moy fructifie,
> Tient en sa main et la mere et le fruit.
>
> (vv. 31-3)

The decision is made.

> Joseph Or puisque tel est vostre saint desir,
>   Allons nous en vous et moy à loisir;
>   Obeïssons à DIEV en toute chose.
> Marie   Certes amy, mieux ne pouons choisir
>   Que d'obeïr; car lá gist mon plaisir;
>   Qui obeït à DIEV, il se repouse.
>
> (vv. 41-6)

As they advance on Bethlehem, Marie speaks of this little village:

> O Bethleem, maison de pain nommee,
> Quelle sera de toy la renommee,
> Quand tu seras le coffre du pain vif?

Courez icy, vous la gent affamee,
Courez icy, vous Ame bien aymee,
Et receuez ce pain d'vn cœur naïf.

(vv. 61-6)

There can be no mistaking the tone, We are again confronted with
that very particular religious lyricism of the *Mistére du Viel Testament*. There is no attempt at a natural conversation but rather the
opposite—to give a systematic glossing of every aspect of the
historical event in order to bring out its religious connotation. The
couple go to Bethlehem because one must obey God in all things.
Marie is not afraid because God will protect them. Bethlehem is
already seen as the 'coffre du pain vif' and as Christ's birthplace,
the symbolic site to which man must turn for spiritual nourishment.

When they arrive in Bethlehem, Joseph is obliged to visit three
innkeepers, all of whom refuse them a room, but each for a different
reason. The first hates the poor and seeks only rich guests; the
second welcomes only 'Princes et Roys' (vs. 105). For the third,
Marie and Joseph are much too saintly. 'Sy sages gens ne voulons
receuoir' (vs. 135). Such confrontations are in no way justified by
the Biblical text or by the texts of Marguerite's predecessors.
Joseph's response to each refusal explains Marguerite's intent.
After the first meeting, he says,

O Charité, qui rendz l'ame parfaite
Difficile est que lon te trouve au cœur
De l'homme riche, si DIEV n'y est vainqueur!

(vv. 92-4)

After the second, he berates pride; after the third, 'volupté'. The
entire scene is conceived in allegorical terms and exploited for its
pedagogical content only.

Similarly, when Joseph returns to the stable, Marguerite speaks
of his 'deuoir' in such a way as to confuse it with every man's duty to
God's son. Joseph the husband, the discomfort of the rudimentary
lodging, Marie's state, none of these realistic elements are pertinent.
It is characteristic that, when Joseph is close enough to the stable to
see the mother and infant, he describes first the light, dazzling and
unique. Like the wise virgins, who by their state of preparedness have
begun to enter a different world from that of the foolish virgins long
before the final scene, Marguerite's characters walk a line between
the immediate context and a timeless continuum. Reality fades

because the essence of the nativity must be seen as then, now, and forever true.

Reality and drama are terms that have meaning for Marguerite but they do not designate what we have encountered in a play like the *Jeu d'Adam*. Reality is no longer the complexities of marriage or the weaknesses of human psychology in which religious problems can be mirrored. Life is seen as a moral existence where there are moral choices to be made (going to Bethlehem), vices and virtues to be met (the three innkeepers), duties to perform (Joseph's return). These are the 'events' in the *Comédie de la nativité* and in each instance they are expanded to bring out their full moral value. The 'drama' of the *Comédie* is similarly moral. 'Heureux ie suis', says Joseph on entering the stable, 'Dont voir le puis / O heureuse et digne veue!' The repetition of 'happy' is hardly a slip of the pen. The imparting of such happiness is the drama of the nativity and its effect, also rendered by the symbolism of light, touches all the characters, except Satan.

Satan appears in the final segment of the play as part of a *bergerie* in which the devil confronts a group of shepherds and shepherdesses who have just visited the stable. If, according to Jourda (p. 72), Marguerite's extensive use of Satan in the *bergerie* is original, her treatment of the scene has a rather familiar resonance. Satan exhorts the group to leave God and to follow him. The characters affirm one after the other their undying faith in God and Satan responds with a barrage of questions: 'Estes vous Dieux' (vs. 1087), 'Cuydez vous pas auoir son saint Esprit' (vs. 1091), 'Pensez vous bien entendre l'Escriture?' (vs. 1101) But the group has learned its catechism well and knows how to answer each question. The devil pursues another tactic. He challenges them to explain their poverty if their father is what they claim. 'Si en toy fust le Filz de Dieu trescher, / Te lairroit il ainsi souuent pecher?' (vv. 1129-30) But Elpsion replies: 'Plus nous souffrons, nostre ioye redouble, / De voz plaisirs ne donnons pas vn double' (vv. 1127-8). Here is Dorothee's reply:

Nous confessons que nous faisons peché,
Et ne pouuons rien sinon peché faire;
Mais Dieu en nous pour son œuure parfaire
Ioint dedans nous sa tresiuste iustice,
A qui sert bien de fueille nostre vice.

(vv. 1137-42)

Without being properly an allegory, the *bergerie* serves the same purpose as the judgment scene in Paradise. It is a debate in which the pertinent theological questions are reviewed and explained. Following the general pattern of the opening episode of the *Mistére du Viel Testament*, Marguerite performs her pedagogical tasks first through a lyric style, moving later to a more intellectual presentation. She never forgets, however, her 'drama' of joy. When the shepherds leave the stable, they sing:

> Pasteurs, menons trestous ioye,
> Et chantons bien hautement;
> Car en quelque part que soye,
> Viure veux ioyeusement.

(vv. 964-7)

The same techniques reappear throughout the remaining 'comédies spirituelles' and her 'théâtre profane'. The particular thematic and pedagogical orientation with its tinges of Neo-platonism and Evangelism remind us, of course, of Marguerite's own profession of faith, but the technique again and again points back to the medieval tradition Marguerite knew and so repeatedly practised. This is not to say that no distinctive technical innovations appear in Marguerite's plays. Jourda maintained that 'Elle annonce peut-être involontairement la tragédie classique profane ou sacrée'.[2] His conclusion is based in the main on an examination of Marguerite's handling of the traditional medieval material. In arranging the nativity scene, for example, Marguerite suppressed much more than she borrowed. Marie's traditional sage-femme, the ox and ass, preambles, allusion to the annunciation, all this disappears. Her *bergerie* is a single episode, carefully structured through the debate with Satan, whereas her predecessors had used the pastoral material intermittently for a comic effect. Such limiting of the action produced, Jourda points out, a reduction in the number of 'lieux' ('la scène n'a plus les dimensions énormes qu'elle avait dans les *Passions* du XVe siècle, . . . Premier effort vers l'unité de lieu' (I, 455). Finally, Jourda calls attention to Marguerite's division into four very separate plays of a subject which in the preceding century would have formed one continuous work.

These remarks show that the fascination with form has been applied to theatre even before *Cléopâtre captive*. Frankly, I am not convinced that the simplicity of Marguerite's play is more easily explained by some instinctive movement toward Classicism than by her overwhelming preoccupation with the symbolism of her material. The greater unity of place derives from Marguerite's marked lack of interest in the more picturesque episodes associated with the nativity. She focuses on those elements whose meaning is most central to her own beliefs. The simplicity of the play is a direct reflection of the singlemindedness of Marguerite's religion.

At the same time, by Jourda's own admission, in every other respect these plays do not depart from the technique we have come to associate with late medieval drama: 'La forme dramatique n'est plus pour la Reine qu'un moyen commode de donner forme vivante à ses théories religieuses. A ce point ses comédies ne sont même plus du théâtre, mais de la poésie lyrique mise en dialogue' (I, 462). Such uniformity assures us not only of the tradition to which Marguerite belongs but of the degree to which this theatre's conventions were accepted without question. Lyricism, didacticism, allegory, the use of a *décor simultané* which permitted the particular multiplicity of events and swiftness in transitions figure prominently in these conventions. All suggest that the stage could not have been equated in the minds of the playwrights or the public with the representation of a real event. All, moreover, worked together to create the desired effect. *Décor simultané* and didacticism most certainly contributed to each other's success. The increasing tendency toward debate, lament, explication, and abstract characters required that no clash exist between the spectacle and the staging, that the staging make precise certain 'lieux' without attempting to be in its entirety one of these 'lieux'. In furnishing such, the *décor simultané* permitted the playwrights to concentrate on their moral or the symbolism of places and characters while encouraging them to continue in this direction since each 'lieu' was more of a convenience than a slice of reality to be respected. It will be interesting to note, therefore, not only which classical dramatists the sixteenth century came to know and how well, but also what effect a sympathetic reading of the ancients could have upon a society so accustomed to these conventions.

2 THE CLASSICAL HERITAGE

When Jodelle produced the first humanist tragedy in French to be acted in France, his feat was without precedent in his career. How he prepared for this task, why he among the new young poets should have adopted it, remains a mystery. There is no mystery, however, as to the official source of Pléiade interest in the drama. Restitution of classical tragedy and comedy was openly asked for in the *Deffence*: 'Quand aux comedies & tragedies, si les roys & les republiques les vouloient restituer en leur ancienne dignité, qu'ont usurpée les farces & moralitez, ie seroy' bien d'opinion que si tu t'y employasses, & si tu le veux faire pour l'ornement de ta Langue, tu scais ou tu en doibs trouver les archetypes' (pp. 125-6). The unfavourable comparison with medieval genres is standard practice in the *Deffence* and when Du Bellay speaks of the 'ancienne dignité' of the classical theatre, it is tempting to suppose that he is talking in aesthetic terms and to conclude that these young insurgents at the mid-point in the sixteenth century had so penetrated into classical letters, thanks in great measure to their teacher Dorat, that all the deficiencies of the pre-existing medieval genres were forever laid bare. In truth, we are hardly in a position to make such a statement, especially with respect to tragedy. The contemporary material quoted in Chapter I would disprove any conclusion we might want to make about the Pléiade's preference for classical tragedies because of their structure, their characterization, or their dramatic qualities. I suspect, therefore, that Du Bellay meant by 'dignité' above all dignity of expression—the *copia* of rhetoric for which so many humanists were praised by their friends and ancient playwrights cited by the rhetoricians. This is only an hypothesis, of course, but there is more evidence to support it than to support the possibility of an interest in dramatic structure, for once stylistic preferences drew the humanists to Euripides and Seneca, the formal changes followed naturally.

My choice of Euripides and Seneca is not fortuitous. The humanists sometimes mentioned Aeschylus and Sophocles but most likely read nothing of the former and little of the latter. Sophocles' *Electra* was translated into French by Lazare de Baïf and published in 1537. (A translation of Sophocles' *Antigone* by Calvy de La Fontaine was never printed and Jean-Antoine de Baïf's rendering of the same play was not published until 1573.) Although Sophocles was edited in France as early as 1528, the ability of large numbers of French humanists to read Greek well may be seriously doubted. Only Euripides—and only a few of his plays—were translated with any frequency.

Several early attempts to translate his plays into Latin or French went unpublished: Tissard's *Medea, Hippolytus,* and *Alcestis;* Amyot's *La Troade* and *Iphigénie;* and one anonymous effort, *Les Suppliantes.* The loss is less considerable than it might appear. Some of these plays could still be read in Latin or French thanks to the publication of Erasmus' *Hecuba* and *Iphigenia in Aulis* (1506), Buchanan's *Medea* (1544) and *Alcestis* (1556), Hervet's *Antigone* (1541), Bochetel's *Hécube* (1544), and Sébillet's *Iphigénie à Aulis* (1549). The repetition of titles has some importance. It provides evidence of a further limit on the range of Greek works available to those who did not know that classical language. Moreover, it is not an insignificant fact that France's greatest hellenists at the time as well as all the above translators save Buchanan never wrote tragedies. The same repetition points up the deficiencies of even the translators. Bochetel and Sébillet produced their work *after* Erasmus. Studies by Sturel and Delcourt have shown that Bochetel used Erasmus more than Euripides and that Sébillet's *Iphigénie* is, in fact, a translation of Erasmus with occasional glimpses at the original.

Given the range of translations available, it was probably inevitable that Euripides' greatest successes among sixteenth-century playwrights should be *Hecuba* and *Iphigenia in Aulis.* Amital in Garnier's *Les Juives* plays a role clearly patterned on that of Hecuba (though seen through Seneca's play on the same subject, according to Lebègue). Théodore de Bèze and George Buchanan, pioneers both in the development of humanist drama, imitated Agamemnon's situation in *Iphigenia* for their *Abraham sacrifiant* and *Jephthes* respectively.

Euripides' *Hecuba* begins with a prologue recited by the shade of Polydoros, who tells of his own death and the approaching death of his sister Polyxena. Euripides has no interest in surprising his audience or in unfolding his drama slowly. The dreadful death accomplished and the one to come are made to weigh on us at the outset as they do on Hecuba. She has dreamed and relates her dream to the chorus. After Polydoros' prologue the meaning of the dream as prophesying the children's death is unavoidable but Hecuba is made to hope: 'Dieux souterrains, sauvez ce fils, qui, seul appui de notre race, réside en la neigeuse Thrace, sous la foi d'un hôte paternal. Il va se passer quelque chose d'affreux' (II, 136). Only two characters have spoken and already Hecuba appears a pathetic figure, dreading the future, begging the gods to prevent what has been preordained.

The succeeding scenes offer no respite from this initial technique. Whatever the circumstances, Hecuba will beg or pray or both, but her misfortune is sealed. When Ulysses comes for Polyxena, Hecuba reminds him that she once saved his life. He is moved but just as swiftly Ulysses declares that the sacrifice must be. Before being led away to die, Polyxena intones a good-bye to Polydores whom she believes still lives in Thrace. Hecuba wonders if he too has not died but Polyxena answers with the strong affirmation that Polydores is alive. There is no positive statement which can be made for Hecuba that destiny has not undone.

The second part of Euripides' play concerns Hecuba's vengeance against the man who killed her son Polydoros. After Talthybios has narrated Polyxena's death, Hecuba sends a servant for water to wash the dead girl's body. The servant obeys and finds Polydoros, whose corpse she brings back to Hecuba. Such is Euripides' transition. The new sequence mixes Hecuba's fierce pride and strength with horror and gore. Polymestor's children are murdered offstage and he is blinded by the old queen, again offstage, but the bodies and the blinded Polymestor are later revealed to the audience. The raging Polymestor speaks first to Hecuba to announce the circumstances that will lead to her death and to that of her last living child Cassandra. Then he turns to Agamemnon to forecast his doom at the hands of his own wife. The horror thus spills over into the future beyond the limits of the play. When it finally closes, the theme of continued suffering persists; the chorus prepares for 'le dur apprentissage de la servitude' (II, 175).

The chorus is composed of Trojan women waiting to set sail with the victorious Greeks whom they will serve as slaves. When Ulysses has taken Polyxena, they sing of their new homes across the sea and ask which city shall be theirs. When Talthybios finishes telling of Polyxena's death and Hecuba has done her mourning, the chorus sings of its destiny, of Paris and Helen, who brought misfortune upon the people of Troy. Aristotle disapproved of such detachment from the principal action and said so: 'The Chorus should be considered as one of the persons in the drama; it should be an integral part of the whole and have a share in the action—following the practice of Sophocles, not Euripides' (pp. 314-5). However, Euripides knew what he was about and the meaning of his *Hecuba* resides as much in these laments of the chorus as in the story of the Trojan queen.

We are initially struck by Hecuba only. She seems perfect for Euripides' play of pathos and lament not only because her misfortunes were endless but because they contrasted so sharply with the life she had known previously. She was the queen of a great and wealthy city; her children were numerous, beautiful, proud. When *Hecuba* opens, this queen has become a slave. Her family is decimated, destroyed with her city and her glory. The theme of the fallen queen runs throughout the tragedy. Upon first seeing Hecuba, Talthybios compares her miserable state with her former glory. When the body of Polydoros is brought to his mother, a servant enumerates again all that Hecuba has lost. The queen herself makes use of the contrast between what she once possessed and what she has become in hopes of moving Ulysses. Such repetition is no accident; it defines Hecuba's tragedy. It defines as well what might be termed Euripides' tragic vision. This vision passes over inner struggles and 'tragic faults' to find its *raison d'être* in the spectacle of an individual forsaken by fortune after a prosperous existence. Here and there we find allusions to Helen and to Paris but in the last analysis Euripides is less interested in exploring the why of Hecuba's tragedy than in depicting the bitterness of its accomplishment.

If the attraction of Hecuba for a society that had ample urging to associate tragedy with the misfortune of the great is too obvious to require comment, the technique used to communicate her situation should not be passed over quickly. I have noted that Aristotle hardly approved of Euripides' use of the chorus; he must have approved still less of Euripides' plot line for *Hecuba*. This is no single action, complete in itself, with a beginning, middle, and end but two distinct events related yet not united. Beneath this distinction we have two different concepts of how to move the audience. Aristotle accentuates the force of interacting elements moving toward a single climax. Euripides has produced in *Hecuba* a work that relies rather on accumulation—the two deaths, the repetition of laments on Hecuba's fate. A single climax would not have accomplished Euripides' aim and he avoided such a technique. It is interesting to read in the *Poetics* how Aristotle recognized the power of Euripides' plays without admiring their structure: 'Euripides himself, although he sometimes handles his subjects badly, is still the most tragic of poets' (p. 306).

By recognizing that Euripides sought to move in this play through accumulation and repetition, we have also given his treatment of the chorus and the double plot a definite purpose. It was important in Aristotle's eyes for the chorus to be an essential part of the action because the effects of tragedy as he conceived of them lay in the plot. In a play like *Hecuba*, where the effect derives rather from the quality of the spectacle, there had to be a means to bring out this quality. By singing of slavery and war, misery past, present, and future, the chorus extends the queen's own unhappiness until it becomes all-pervasive.

The chorus is not Euripides' only means of heightening Hecuba's misfortune. The play possesses much melodrama and rhetorical display. Talthybios' narration omits no detail of Polyxena's death. The exchange between Hecuba and Ulysses brings the queen to her knees as a suppliant begging for a life in return for having once saved Ulysses. Hecuba tells of her dream with abundant apostrophes, questions, and imperatives. Was a student to doubt Erasmus' definition of tragic style ['To speak in the manner of tragedies is to use more highsounding words. For tragedies have a sublime character and love swelling and polysyllabic words' (*Adagiorum*, p. 466)] after hearing Polymestor decry his fate thus: 'Atroce, atroce traitement! Hélas! Affreuse torture! De quel côté me tourner? Où me diriger? Vais-je m'envoler dans la céleste palais aérien où Sirius et Orion de leurs yeux de flamme font jaillir des rayons brûlants' (II, 168)? When Lanson says of Hecuba, 'Quel exemple de la fragilité des choses humaines! quel cas admirable et effrayant d'infortune royale!' ('L'Idée de la tragédie', p. 550), he has exposed only part of the play's attraction. *Hecuba* was exemplary in subject and execution. That we are talking about a rather un-Aristotelian concept of execution could hardly have mattered to the humanists but it is yet another important clue to explaining the particular nature of humanist tragedy.

Between *Hecuba* and *Iphigenia in Aulis* the differences are few, the resemblances legion. The plot is more unified in that all fixes on Iphigenia's death but it is not free from some befuddlement. Agamemnon for some time explains the necessity of Iphigenia's sacrifice in terms of his own fear of the army who will not permit her to escape. Later he sees the sacrifice in a more grandoise light. 'C'est la Grèce pour laquelle il faut . . . se sacrifier', he says to his daughter, 'Car il faut . . . que notre patrie soit libre' (I, 84). Confusion enters into the motivation of others characters as well. Iphigenia at first does not want to die; then she eagerly agrees to the sacrifice. Aristotle could not accept that. Euripides not only could; he had already done the same thing before, and in *Hecuba*, where Polyxena recoils before her death only to see it eventually as a welcome salvation.

Although with *Iphigenia in Aulis* we move from a melodrama of the many misfortunes of the Trojan women to the single horror of a father's sacrifice of his own daughter, Euripides still maintains the accumulation of pathetic moments by adding a multiplicity of characters who play or help the others to play a role similar to that of Hecuba. Her suffering and her abortive pleas are now those of Agamemnon, Menelaos, Clytemnestra, Iphigenia, and Achilles. Even the pathos and the lament are created by similar techniques. As Hecuba seeks in vain to preserve Polyxena from the inevitable fate announced in the prologue, so the main characters of *Iphigenia* concern themselves for most of the play with the prevention of the inescapable. When the play opens, Agamemnon has reneged on his promise to sacrifice Iphigenia and written a letter telling his wife and child not to come to Aulis. No sooner does the faithful servant depart to transmit the letter than he is intercepted by Menelaos who discovers its contents and proceeds to berate Agamemnon for his treachery. Argument ensues between the brothers. Only when Agamemnon adopts a tone of lament on hearing that Clytemnestra and Iphigenia have reached the Greek camp does Menelaos relent and agree to help save his niece. But Agamemnon recognizes that Menelaos' aid is alas too late. Ulysses knows of Artemis' order that Iphigenia be killed and now that Iphigenia has arrived in camp, the army will never let her leave.

The play has no prologue, but the very first exchange of words in the play, spoken by Agamemnon and an old servant, serves in a more subtle fashion to accentuate the inevitable misery that awaits Agamemnon. The king arouses the old man before dawn and rushes him out of his tent. The servant does not understand Agamemnon's rashness and advises that they return to their beds. But Agamemnon prefers to reflect on the tranquillity of the anonymous and the obscure and to emphasize the precarious nature of the great's existence: 'Tantôt les dieux irrités de quelque manquement à leur culte brisent une carrière humaine, tantôt les hommes, sous leur caprice ondoyant et hargneux, vous font saigner' (I, 44). The first contingency probably alludes to the legend in which Agamemnon killed a deer sacred to Artemis. It was for this reason that the goddess demanded the sacrifice of Iphigenia. Regarding the second, we have to look more deeply into the plot.

A bitter barb directed at Agamemnon by his brother concerns the former's ambition and in particular his burning desire to become Commander-in-chief of the Greek forces. That honour is now his and he is powerless to save his own daughter. He commands the Greek army but must carry out the army's wish that Iphigenia die. Gods, men, and lastly destiny track Agamemnon, for as the old man reminds him: 'Pour un bonheur sans nuage, Agamemnon, ne t'engendra point Atrée' (I, 44). A king powerless, a commander who must obey, a son of the cursed house of Atreus, Agamemnon provided with Hecuba one of the finest spectacles of Euripidean tragedy.

It, too, indulges in melodrama. A mother's plea for the life of her child returns as a tragic situation with the debate, now between brothers. Menelaos' change of heart after the quarrel reminds us that rhetoric has been preserved along with melodrama as a basic Euripidean ingredient for tragedy. Agamemnon's lament at the news of his wife's arrival contains the familiar questions: 'Que dire, infortuné? Par où commencerai-je' (I, 55). When he is finished, the chorus exclaims, 'Autant qu'une femme, et une étrangère, peut compatir à une princière détresse, je verse, moi aussi, des larmes de pitié' (I, 56) and Menelaos follows suit. The author's intent in this scene strikes all the more when one considers its complete lack of influence upon the play's action. Again rhetoric and melodrama work their effects at the expense of a strict linking of events. Moreover, *Iphigenia* shows that this tendency to work in terms of individual scenes could also produce occasional moments of moralizing such as the sententious nature of the remarks exchanged by Agamemnon and the old man. *Sententiae, narratio*, melodrama, misfortune of the great, these aspects of tragedy stud the plays by Euripides best known to the French humanists who were not to find, however, either psychological drama or plots of carefully integrated elements.

Some may feel that I have been unfair to Euripides in accentuating those aspects of his plays that most recall the humanists' own conception of tragedy. If I have, several distinguished Greek scholars seem to have made a similar error. Warner Jaeger points out the debate aspect: 'Throughout his plays we can trace a novel competition between tragedy and the rhetorical contest of opposing litigants which so delighted the Athenians, for now verbal duels between contrasting characters on the stage became one of the principal excitements of drama' (cited in McDonald, p. 25). Henri Berguin describes the structure of *Hecuba* as one in which 'il n'y a pas d'apogée; c'est une succession de cris de douleur ou de haine' (I, 14). Harsh states flatly that 'exploitation of the sentimental and of the melodramatic is a marked characteristic of Euripides' later plays' (p. 159), and both he and Decharme remark on the playwright's repeated use of children to heighten the sentimental. Decharme spends several pages in his study of Euripides showing how in contrast to the other great Greek dramatists he was wont to 'assombrir ses dénouements sans nécessité' (pp. 268-9). Webster observes that 'scenes of voluntary self-sacrifice are obviously good theatre and may have been invented by Euripides' (p. 279).

Readers familiar with Euripides will, I hope, forgive this enumeration of views but it cannot be stressed too forcefully how Euripides, *the* Greek influence on French humanists does not conform to popular conceptions of classical drama. This is not 'stille Grösse und edle Einfalt'. The diverse parts are not cemented together to form an ineluctable concatenation of events. The chorus often furnishes mere mood music; individual scenes are milked for pathos, not psychology or dramatic action. There is a unity of effect more than of action as debates, description, and monologues reveal the playwright's pronounced interest in displays of emotion.

For the very reason that these rhetorical displays must have fascinated the humanists, I doubt that they were struck by another quality of Euripides' work: his rationalistic, sceptical treatment of the gods. At least I can find no evidence to suggest that they saw his *Alcestis* as a criticism of the legend or *Iphigenia in Aulis* as a contrast 'between modern human muddle and epic heroism' (Webster, p. 264). Indeed why should they; we are still at a moment when tragedy is a moral lesson and a style, not a subtle commentary.

It is one of the many ironies of literary history that Euripides has remained a reputable dramatist whereas Seneca, the other major classical influence on French humanists, has had abuse heaped upon his plays from all sides. No fewer than four Senecan dramas (and among them the Senecan dramas most imitated in France), *Medea*, the *Troades*, *Phaedra*, and *Hercules furens*, are direct imitations of plays by Euripides. Moreover, several of Seneca's trademarks—the prologue, dreams, violence, messengers—can be traced directly to Euripides. A dream appears in *Hecuba* exactly as Seneca will exploit the device; Talthybios' speech and that of the messenger at the close of *Iphigenia in Aulis* are no different in kind or function from Seneca's use of *narratio*. The blinding of Polymestor in *Hecuba* and the display of his murdered children can hardly be interpreted as a sign that Euripides shunned violence. Even worse scenes awaited those who could read his other plays in Greek. If extensive use or abuse of rhetoric, too, distinguishes Seneca, then again the Latin poet can not be said to have betrayed his model.

Despite such strong resemblances between Euripides and Seneca, Rivaudeau saw primarily a difference: 'En [la tragédie] depuis les premiers Grœcs nul homme, à mon auis, a fidelement versé ni s'est composé au vray et naïf artifice que Seneque seul, qui encores ne se est du tout formalizé ni à l'art ni à la façon des anciens' (p. 44). This observation, we must regret, was not elaborated upon. It nevertheless must give us pause and obliges us to ask if differences of some magnitude as well as significant similarities exist between Euripides and Seneca.

The quality of Seneca's plays and his hold over sixteenth-century dramatists have produced much discussion. In its more open-minded form the discussion recognizes that violence is probably a poor means to explain the period's attraction to Seneca. As H. W. Wells points out, the medieval theatre could often outdo Seneca in creating violent scenes. Many call our attention rather to the pessi-mistic mood of Seneca's dramas, his moral philosophy, and use of political themes to explain his popularity.[3] I personally feel that it would be a great mistake to place any of these aspects of Senecan drama ahead of the lure of the rhetorical display, of which Seneca is an avowed master but since these other traits offer valuable clues to some of the differences to which Rivaudeau might have been alluding, they cannot be passed over lightly.

Both playwrights produced a *Medea* and Buchanan's Latin version of Euripides' drama made it possible for humanists who knew no Greek to contemplate the respective treatments of this powerful theme. Most prominent in Seneca's adaptation are the aggrandizement of Medea's role and the heroine's isolation. In the Greek play the nurse, the pedagogue, the chorus, and Egeus all help Medea or express sympathy for her plight. Seneca omitted Egeus and the pedagogue. The chorus condemns Medea. Jason, who appears in Euripides as a heartless *arriviste*, and thus creates more sympathy for Medea, becomes in Seneca a defenceless foreigner who fears for his children and sees marriage to Creusa as his only opportunity to secure their future. Euripides' Medea is an unfortunate woman whose unhappiness is contemplated with pity and whose actions are viewed with horror primarily because of the fearsome logic that eventually makes crime her only recourse. That logic gives the Greek play a distinct legal quality. Medea first defends herself before the chorus and then debates with Jason, who is told by the chorus that his speech is well done but that he has not acted 'selon la justice' (IV, 133). The aggrandizement of Medea's role in Seneca is directly related to his omission of this legalistic material.

Euripides studied a proud woman's reaction to her situation; Seneca studies rather the passion that brings about Medea's crimes. The Greek play opens with the nurse both fearing Medea and recognizing the piteous state in which her mistress finds herself. The pedagogue enters and announces Creon's decision to exile Medea. Only then do we hear Medea's voice (but from within the palace). Seneca opens directly with Medea, already set on vengeance, invoking the Furies, and providing Seneca with the first of the many long passages such as verses 397-424 or 740-844 in which he exhibits his command of rhetoric. Euripides concentrates on a human portrait whereas Seneca tends toward examination of an abstraction. Here are two excerpts from Medea's meeting with Creon as conceived by Euripides:

C. C'est à toi, œil sombre, qui t'irrites contre ton mari, Médée, que je parle. Quitte ce pays pour l'exil, emmène avec toi tes deux enfants, et sans tarder! C'est moi-même qui ferai exécuter cet ordre et je ne retournerai pas au palais avant de t'avoir jetée hors des frontières de ce pays.

M. Hélas! je suis anéantie! Malheureuse! je suis perdue! Car voici que mes ennemis mettent toutes voiles dehors et il n'est plus pour moi de port où m'abriter sûrement de la malédiction. Je te poserai pourtant une question, Créon, malgré mon malheur: pour quel motif me chasses-tu du pays, Créon?

C. J'ai peur de toi,—à quoi bon m'en cacher?—j'ai peur que tu ne fasses à ma fille quelque mal sans remède. Beaucoup de raisons à la fois contribuent à ma crainte: tu es habile, savante en maints maléfices, et tu souffres d'avoir perdu le lit conjugal. J'entends dire—on me le rapporte—que tu menaces de te venger sur son beau-père, sur l'époux et sur l'épousée. Aussi, avant d'avoir eu à souffrir, je prendrai mes précautions. Mieux vaut pour moi aujourd'hui ta haine, femme, que la faiblesse à ton égard, et plus tard, les longs gémissements.

(p. 126)

...

M. Tu me chasseras? Tu n'auras aucun égard à mes prières?
C. C'est que tu ne m'es pas plus chère que ma maison.
M. O ma patrie! Combien en ce jour je me souviens de toi!
C. Après mes enfants, pour moi aussi c'est le bien de beaucoup le plus cher.
M. Hélas! hélas! pour les mortels, quel mal terrible que les amours!
C. Cela dépend, je crois, des circonstances.
M. Zeus, qu'il ne t'échappe pas, l'auteur de mes maux!
C. Va-t'en, insensée, et délivre-moi de mes ennuis.
M. Les ennuis sont pour moi, et je n'en manque pas.
C. Bientôt la main de mes serviteurs va t'expulser de force.
M. Ah! non, pas cela.—Je t'en supplie, Créon.

(pp. 127-8)

Creon could not be more frank. The sententious quality of Medea's remark on love elicits no similar response from Creon but rather a sarcastic retort. Now here are excerpts from the same scene in Seneca's *Medea*. (I quote the Latin because the French does not convey that lapidary quality of certain lines.)

M. Quod crimen aut quae culpa multatur fuga?
C. Quae causa pellat, innocens mulier rogat.
M. Si iudicas, cognosce, si regnas, iube.
C. Aequum atque iniquum regis imperium feras.
M. Iniqua numquam regna perpetuo manent.
C. I, querere Colchis.
M.   Redeo: qui aduexit, ferat.
C. Vox constituto sera decreto uenit.
M. Qui statuit aliquid parte inaudita altera,
   aequum licet statuerit, haud aequus fuit.
C. Auditus a te Pelia supplicium tulit?
   Sed fare; causae detur egregiae locus!
M. Difficile quam sit animum ab ira flectere
   iam concitatum quamque regale hoc putet
   sceptris superbas quisquis admouit manus
   qua coepit ira, regia didici mea.

(pp. 143-4)[4]

The point of departure has not changed. Medea is defiant and Creon set on ridding himself of her but the development of the givens is quite different. Creon, the man of honesty, is effaced by the king and judge to whom Medea responds with *sententiae* on justice and politics. Similarly, in explaining earlier her future actions to the nurse, Medea resorts to *sententiae*:

M. Leuis est dolor qui capere consilium potest
   et clepere sese: magna non latitant mala.
   Libet ire contra.

N.   Siste furialem impetum,
alumna: uix te tacita defendit quies.
N.   Fortuna fortes metuit, ignauos premit.
N.   Tunc est probanda, si locum uirtus habet.

(p. 141)[5]

The scene should be compared with that between Medea and the chorus in Euripides. Medea's defence is put under the rubric of the misfortune of women and the necessity to be faithful to a single being. Her final word: 'Une femme d'ordinaire est pleine de crainte, lâche au combat et à la vue du fer; mais quand on attente aux droits de sa couche, il n'y a pas d'âme plus altérée de sang' (IV, 125-6). Thus, even when Medea employs a more general context, justified by the formal presentation she is making for her defence, Euripides relates the argument to Medea's situation in a fashion that Seneca feels no need to imitate.

Comparisons between the two *Hercules furens* or *Trojan Women* would reveal that the differences noted above pervade the other dramas Seneca took from Euripides. The presentation of Hercules is completely recast along the lines used to catapult Medea into prominence. Whereas Euripides' play opens with the frightened exiles Amphitryon and Megara discussing their fate, Seneca chose to depict the enraged Juno, who, in cursing the prowess of Hercules and evoking the Eumenides to crush him, establishes not only the plot but also an immediate portrait of Hercules the mighty demigod. When Amphitryon and Megara do appear, Seneca thinks nothing of adding to the worried exchange we might expect of two defence-less persons threatened with death a long enumeration of the labours of Hercules—a task Euripides left for the chorus. The arrival of Hercules in the Greek play could not be more simple. He merely appears before his father and wife. Seneca precedes the actual arrival with a shaking of the temple and a great roar. 'Un bruit infernal a retenti du fond de l'abîme', says Amphitryon. 'J'ai été entendu. C'est, oui, c'est le bruit que font les pas d'Hercule!' (p. 23)

Such histrionics, used in *Medea* to depict the force of avenging passion, become the appropriate background in *Hercules furens* for the study of the hero who is called upon to bear an even greater burden—his own guilt. Again Seneca has changed quite radically the orientation of his Greek model. Euripides' play emphasizes friendship, underscoring first the desertion of Hercules' family by his friends during his absence and the magnanimous gestures of

Theseus, who gives Hercules a home and brings the hero out of his despair. Theseus has no such function in the Latin work. Amphitryon alone argues with his son: 'C'est maintenant qu'il te faut être Hercule: supporte l'immense poids de ce malheur' (p. 50). With this 'Nunc Hercule opus est' we see how symbolic the early labours have become, how symbolic Hercules himself is about to become.

In the *Trojan Women*, Seneca preferred to present his symbols with the play's very first lines, spoken by Hecuba: 'Que quiconque se fie à sa royauté et, maître tout puissant d'une cour grandiose, loin de craindre l'incontance des dieux, livre à la prospérité une âme crédule, me contemple et te contemple, ô Troie: jamais la fortune n'a montré par de plus éclatants exemples combien sont fragiles les bases sur lesquelles se dressent les superbes' (pp. 58-9). From the outset we must lose sight of the pathos Euripides exploited in Hecuba's private love for Troy to contemplate the handiwork of fortune. The lesson is so central to Seneca's handling of the material that he adds to the Euripidean plot a scene between Pyrrhus and Agamemnon in which Agamemnon expounds the significance of the Greek victory. The following gives an example of the tone of Seneca's passage: 'On ne saurait garder longtemps un pouvoir fondé sur la violence tandis que la modération le rend durable, et plus la Fortune élève et exalte la puissance des hommes, plus ceux qui sont dans la prospérité doivent se modérer eux-mêmes, et craindre des accidents opposés, en se défiant de la faveur excessive des dieux. La grandeur peut être anéantie en un instant: voilà ce que j'ai appris par ma victoire même' (p. 68). This is not to say that Euripides never generalizes or points out morals. His chorus does; his characters do. But the sententious remarks crown personal statements and are not, as happens so often in Seneca, the very substance of conversation.[6] Thus, for a public accustomed to long discourses and moralizing, the differences between Euripides and Seneca must have seemed more a question of degree than of kind. I shall even go so far as to say that with respect to dramaturgy or tragedy's function in general, the differences between these classical dramatists and medieval techniques probably appeared far less great than we might imagine. Hecuba's loss of country and position could be compared with the change of fortune in the lives of Saul or Eve as depicted so lyrically in the *Mistére du Viel Testament*. The arrival of Egeus just in time to help Medea is no more improbable than many encounters in medieval drama. The detached chorus in works by both Seneca and Euripides, used to comment repeatedly upon the action, must have struck the humanists as a singularly convenient means of improving upon the medieval desire to instruct through drama.

Lanson assures us that 'on risquerait de ne rien comprendre à l'imitation que la Renaissance fit du théâtre grec, si on oubliait que celui-ci vint non pas apporter une connaissance neuve, mais s'insérer dans une connaissance antérieure' ('L'Idée de la tragédie', p. 548). The precise context of his remarks attributes to Donatus in particular the responsibility for this 'connaissance antérieure'. The grammarians definitely have their place; yet what we have just observed suggests also that on the one hand it was and is still possible to read carefully the Greek theatre available to the humanists and be struck by the same phenomena the humanists appreciated, and on the other hand, that the success of the grammarians may not be calculated without reference to the evolution of medieval drama. In order to counteract the influence of Donatus or Diomedes and to discuss Greek theatre as Jaeger or Kitto have done far greater scholarship than the humanists possessed would have to accrue. In the absence of that scholarship, the period exhibited the most natural of reactions. It responded to what it recognized from general reading and indigenous traditions to be the traits of tragedy.

Possessors of more extensive investigation concerning both the classical world and the medieval era, we find innumerable reasons to oppose these worlds and miss the strong lines of continuity. Readers of Boccaccio's *De casibus* found similar truths being stated in the classics. The chorus leader in Euripides' *Medea* closes the play with the observation that '[Maintes choses] que nous attendions ne se réalisent pas; celles que nous n'attendions pas, un dieu leur fraye la voie' (IV, 159). Seneca's *Medea*, like Euripides' *Hecuba*, makes clear that fortune is fickle and inconstant (vv. 219, 287). When Seneca's Hecuba describes Troy—'Voyez: ces murs hauts et magnifiques gisent confusément ammoncelés' (p. 59)—her intentions parallel the thoughts of both Boccaccio and Du Bellay's *Antiquitez*. The stylistic device Seneca uses to introduce the Trojan queen, 'Quicumque . . . fidet . . . me uideat' (p. 58), re-occurs through Petrarch (*Rime*, CCXLVIII) to Ronsard (*Amours*, 1552, I). Berthe Marti's conviction that Seneca's plays represent a dramatic exposition of his Stoic philosophy may not be accepted by all scholars but her arguments give us ample evidence of the didactic nature of his plays. By warning us that 'Most medieval ideas about literature are themselves classical in ultimate origin' (p. 13), Miss Doran helps to explain further why it was not difficult for Badius and other humanists to identify the intent of the ancients through reading the grammarians. When a humanist praised a writer of tragedy for carefully assigning the appropriate end to vice and virtue, it is unlikely that he would have been able to define his inspiration as being either the 'medieval ethic' or Cicero's pronouncement that 'By one and the same power of eloquence the deceitful among mankind are brought to destruction, and the righteous to deliverance' (*De oratore*, II, ix, 35).

Within this continuity the two examples of change that we have discussed both lead to the dominance of Seneca among possible models for tragedy. It is not insignificant that the traits which distinguish Seneca from Euripides—overt sententiousness, characters presented as symbols—bear a striking resemblance to developments in late medieval drama. It is crucial that Seneca offered far more than Euripides a model for the technique that highlighted and facilitated the *mise en œuvre* of those multiple dictates on tragedy to which the humanists were increasingly subjected.

Rhetoric brought tragedy into the realm of literature designed to move its audience and Seneca's prologues or first scenes abandoned the purely expository nature of their counterparts in Euripides, plunging the reader immediately into an atmosphere of intense emotion. 'Arme-toi de colère et prépare-toi à anéantir avec une fureur poussée au paroxysme', cries Medea toward the end of her opening speech (p. 137). Furthermore, Seneca knows how to maintain a mood of dread. In Euripides' *Hecuba* Talthybios arrives after the sacrifice of Polyxena to play the role of messenger. Seneca, telescoping his model's *Hecuba* and *Trojan Women* for his own *Trojan Women*, makes Talthybios inform the reader of Achilles' appearance to the Greeks demanding Polyxena's life. Did he fear that the particulars of the legend had been forgotten? It is more likely that he saw an occasion to sustain the play's general atmosphere. Talthybios is upset, 'Mon âme est effrayée, un frisson d'horreur agite mon corps' (p. 65) and he describes in detail the sight of Achilles' ghost.

Rhetoric also insisted upon the beauties in *copia*. Of the three stock characters in Seneca studied by Mendell—the messenger, the tyrant, and the nurse—the first represents an immediate source of *narratio* and *descriptio* and the other two, a means for moralizing, often through further rhetorical exercises and stichomythia. In particular the tyrant provokes comment on clemency and exempla of the fate of rulers; the nurse, words of caution and social conformity.

Thus, in Seneca the sixteenth century found not only the appropriate conceptions and conventions but most important, the dignity of a high style. This above all made him a model for French humanist tragedy. I seriously doubt that further translations from the Greek would have changed such a choice. They would not have matched the rhetorical display of Seneca; they would not have conveyed so immediately the 'message' of tragedy as it was then understood or portrayed a world where right, wrong, vice and virtue, morality and politics were so directly discussed.

The number of liminary poems placing a French humanist above Seneca and the Greeks is rather startling. Were the authors of this praise prompted solely by friendship and bombast to make such claims? The same liminary poems in which they flatter the playwrights have demonstrated also that vice and virtue, morality and politics, not dramatic technique, held their attention. The plays in question often outdistanced even Seneca in reiterating the appropriate *sententiae*. I suspect that these very excesses (by modern standards) explain in great measure a judgment that derives not from hyperbole but from the logic according to which what outdid Seneca surpassed Seneca.

That logic has deep roots in the humanist mentality. If humanism fostered tragedy through translation of Greek works and commentaries on Seneca, if it brought change in form to the theatre and insisted upon the 'dignity' of its style, it did little to discredit forcefully the moralizing, the lament, the use of exempla as they appear in late medieval drama and literature. In the models of the *Deffence*, in Peletier's feeling that Quintilian was too long, in Rivaudeau's assurance that he could be summary about tragedy since Horace and Aristotle provided the essential discussion, we encounter the humanists' preference for precept and model over discussion and nuance, a preference that so simplified matters as to encourage dramatists to outdo Seneca, not study him or Euripides. The approach suggested, moreover, that with the proper models, a certain command of *copia*, a knowledge of the most useful themes, anyone could write a tragedy and as the Frères Parfaict once noted, in the decades before Corneille nearly everyone did.

NOTES TO CHAPTER II

[1] For a more complete discussion, see Loukovitch, pp. 1-25 and Lebègue, *La Tragédie religieuse*, pp. 3-29.

[2] Pierre Jourda, *Marguerite d'Angoulême* (2 vols. Paris: H. Champion, 1930), I, 482.

[3] This is the view of the H. W. Wells, McDonald, Herrick, and Charlton.

[4]

M. Quel est le crime, quelle est la faute pour laquelle je suis condamnée à l'exil?

C. La cause de ton expulsion m'est demandée par cette femme innocente!

M. Si tu es mon juge, instruis mon affaire; si tu n'es qu'un tyran, donne des ordres [arbitraires].

C. Qu'il soit juste ou inique, tu dois te soumettre à un ordre royal.

M. Jamais une royauté inique ne dure longtemps.

C. Va te plaindre à Colchos.

M. Soit, j'y retourne: mais que celui qui m'en a amenée m'y ramène.

C. Ta réclamation vient trop tard puisque ma sentence est prononcée.

M. Quiconque statue sur quelque chose sans avoir ouï l'une des parties manque, même si l'arrêt rendu est équitable, à son devoir d'équité.

C. Est-ce après l'avoir ouï que tu as livré Pélias au suplice? Mais parle: donnons à une si belle cause le moyen [d'être plaidée].

M. Combien il est difficile de détourner de la colère une âme déjà surexcitée par elle, et combien on considère comme royal, lorsqu'on porte superbement le sceptre, de persister dans la voie qu'on a prise, [ce sont là des vérités que] j'ai apprises dans la cour de mon propre palais.

(pp. 143-4)

[5]

M. Légère est la rancune qui peut faire des calculs et se mettre en embuscade; les grands maux ne peuvent se cacher. J'ai décidé de marcher à l'attaque.

N. Arrête cet élan insensé, ô toi que j'ai nourrie: c'est tout juste si le silence et le calme peuvent te défendre.

M. La fortune redoute les gens de cœur: elle accable les lâches.

N. Le courage n'est louable que lorsqu'il trouve l'occasion de se déployer.

(p. 141)

[6] See, for example, *Hecuba*, vs. 228, 378, 592ff; *Iphigenia in Aulis*, vs. 408, vv. 688-90.

III HUMANIST DRAMATURGY

I DIDACTIC PATTERNS

The uniformity of views on tragedy expressed by the theoreticians and the liminary poems may appear less surprising now that we understand how great were the forces that created it. The accessibility of Seneca and Euripides, coupled with the evolution in medieval drama toward parable plays and away from a development of the characters' individuality reinforced what rhetoric, Donatus, or Diomedes had said about tragedy and insured that their concept of tragedy as a moral tale with an emotionally charged style would not disappear when formal changes brought tragedy closer to the classical models.

If, however, we wish to grasp the spirit that executed humanist tragedies, it is not enough to appreciate the staying power of contemporary views; we must recognize that those views were received with enthusiasm. What Miss Doran has written of some English dramatists is applicable to all the French humanists who wrote tragedies: 'They are apt to let the story, perhaps a good one in narrative form, take care of itself, and put their principal attention on writing speeches. Such an emphasis is what their training in rhetoric would have prepared them for' (pp. 61-2). To say that the humanists neglected characterization or unity of action is fair but to judge their work on this basis alone is not fair since they neglected characterization and structure in order to accomplish other aims of greater import to them. If we no longer respond positively to rhetorical display and blatant moralizing, the situation may say more about us than about the sixteenth century. At the very least, we should abandon any temptation to see humanist tragedy as some imperfect understanding of classical techniques. The humanists had a purpose and techniques that can be well defined. The remarkable similarity with which themes are handled in tragedies between Jodelle and Hardy assure all who read them that the humanists were not in constant search of an approach to tragedy. Their own was not Aristotelian in nature but armed with knowledge of other writers such as Horace, Seneca, and Euripides, they had every reason to believe that they were producing tragedies of the finest quality.

Judging this tragedy on its own terms also includes recognizing its popularity and relationship to other genres of the day. The humanists pursued tragedy in numbers to which no history of French literature does justice. Forsyth's bibliography lists 222 titles of French tragedies before 1640. Although he includes translations in his count, the total of original works remains very high. At the same time, tragedy was but one genre among several to which the century turned for lessons on passions and man's fate and I do not think it excessive to add that ultimately we will not understand the spirit of French humanist tragedy if we study it wholly within the context of a genre's development, neglecting its ties with a broader literary trend that also evolves. The humanists worked with literary models such as Seneca, theories such as those contained in the rhetorical tradition, and moral truths. Of these three elements, the humanists gave priority to the moral lessons, culled from the 'histoires tragiques', Boccaccio, Boaystuau's *Théâtre du monde*, and so forth. They employed the rhetorical principles to give these lessons an acceptable style, and only lastly turned to their dramatic models for inspiration.

Mrs. Jondorf's chapter on Seneca provides some refreshing insights into this hierarchy. Her aim is to warn against overemphasizing the Senecan quality of humanist tragedy and to suggest how different is, for example, the treatment of political themes in the two theatres. 'Sixteenth-century writers,' she concludes, 'even while using "Senecan" elements in their plays, can produce quite un-Senecan results' (p. 25). When Melanchthon called subject (fabula) 'the most important part of all tragedies', he made the point explicit. To the humanists plot equalled lesson. The appropriateness of a subject emerged from its potential to instruct and every playwright attempted to insure that the lesson became clear, using in particular the means outlined by the rhetoricians. Maurice Valency has, I think, confused means and end in claiming that 'the French thought [tragedy] should make one cry' (p. 28). The multitude of lamenting characters in their tragedies exists to teach us the effects of fortune; the weeping soul was a tragic type among others, just as the reversal of fortune proved to be only one tragic theme among many. All were destined to be food for thought, not tears, and nothing demonstrates this fact better than the plot lines devised by the humanists.

The theories on tragedy available to the humanists said little about plot. It was perhaps possible to derive from the general subject advanced—reversal of fortune in the lives of the great— some glimmer of structure but the evidence provided by the plays themselves suggests rather that didacticism, especially a didacticism which could be implemented by rhetorical exercises, directed the thinking of the period. Scaliger's sample plot, for example, based on Ovid's story of Ceyx and Alcyone, actually skirts the possibility of depicting a reversal, yet carefully exploits all chances for rhetorical exhibition:

Let the first act be a lament, the chorus then condemning sea voyages; the second act, a priest with votive offerings conversing with Halcyone and her nurses, altars, fire, pious sentiments, the chorus then approving of the vows; the third act, a messenger with news of the rising of a storm, the chorus then bringing forth examples of shipwrecks, and much apostrophising to Neptune; the fourth act tumultuous, the report found true, shipwrecks described by sailors and merchants, the chorus then bewailing the event as if all were lost; the fifth act, Halcyone looking anxiously at the sea, sighting far off a corpse, followed by the metamorphosis of both, just when she was about to take her life.

(III, 97)

Without violating the twenty-four hour rule of which he was aware Scaliger could have included a tender scene between the husband and wife on the eve of Ceyx's departure. As told by Ovid, the story contains such a scene with Ceyx's promise to return in two months. Scaliger's plot shows that reversal of fortune did not at all mean to him the inclusion of a movement from a happy to an unhappy state. It was sufficient for the main character to refer (in Hecuba fashion) to a happier past and this presumably would form part of her opening lament. That speech, the 'pious sentiments' of act two, the messenger of act three, the description in act four, not to mention the views of the chorus, all accentuate that concern for plot was much subordinated to interest in rhetorical display.

Although a few humanists did create plots in which a full revolution of Fortune's wheel appears, they remain a very small minority. The others who attempted to convey some sense of a reversal of fortune constructed their plays more along the lines of Scaliger's example. They did so because the unfolding of such a plot provided many more occasions for the kind of moralizing in which the humanist felt inclined to indulge. When the tragedy opened with misfortune already a fact, the writer had virtually all the remaining acts to exploit the lessons of such misfortune. Such a foreshortening of the action is diametrically opposed to the procedure of Classical tragedy and has evoked the usual censure.[1] Yet it is wholly compatible with sixteenth-century expectations.

The call to teach through the reversal of fortune brought with it an understanding that the lesson would be communicated in an appropriate style. The stasis resulting from the foreshortening provided the time to develop that style without interfering with the plot line. The standard procedures—lament, stichomythia, *narratio* —depended for their effect on some previous action and could be used only if the time (sometimes considerable) required for their exploitation could be made available. Both requirements were met by the foreshortening process. Moreover, what the dramatists lost in number of events, they more than compensated for in number of moral lessons. Not only do few humanist tragedies concern themselves with depicting the full turn of Fortune's wheel, even fewer (if any) restrict their message to the vagaries of Destiny. There is perhaps no aspect of humanist tragedy which so accentuates its didactic intent than the eagerness of playwrights to include in their works a variety of moral questions of interest to the period.

Some writers took pains to spell out their intentions. Most prominent is Pierre Matthieu, who included with the title of his tragedies lists of the subjects treated. Thus *Clytemnestre* portrays 'De la vengeance des iniures perdurables à la posterité des offencez, & des malheureuses fins de la volupté'; *Aman*, 'De la perfidie & trahison. Des pernicieux effects de l'ambition & enuie. De la grace & bien-vueillance des Roys dangereuse à ceux qui en abusent, de leur liberalité & recompense mesuree au merite non à l'affection. De la protection de Dieu sur son peuple qu'il garentit des coniurations & oppressions des meschans.' Heyns included in the Prologue to *Le Miroir des Vefues* an enumeration of the vices and virtues contained in the play's 'enseignement'. A sample of vices: 'L'iniquité des Roys: L'outrecuidance, la vantise & cruauté des Vice-Roys, Colonnels & Capitaines: le blaspheme des incredules: la deffiance envers Dieu'; and of virtues: 'L'utilité de la tentation: la necessité en laquelle tombent ceux-là qui en delices oublient le Seigneur' (p. 8).

Even more revealing of the humanists' mentality are the glosses inserted by Soret in the margins of *La Céciliade*. A priest, Soret also held the title 'Maistre de Grammaire des enfans de Choeur' in a Parisian church. It is not surprising, then, to find that his glosses resemble somewhat those placed by humanists beside verses of ancient tragedy.[2] Cécile's father speaks first, admitting that his daughter derives only her body from him; all else comes from God. The speech is called 'Deuoir d'vn bon pere touchant l'instructiõ de ses enfans' (p. 2). He feels that the time has come for his daughter to marry. His wife agrees to follow his advice. 'Honneste response d'vne femme enuers son mary' (p. 8), observes Soret. Matthieu and Heyns can break down their plots into convenient lessons; Soret was able to do the same for virtually every major speech. Together they suggest openly not only in what manner they composed their plays, but also how the many other playwrights of their day proceeded.

Although death by assassination, execution, or suicide closes most of these tragedies and satisfies the familiar definition of tragedy by occasioning remarks on the inconstancy of fortune and the fragility of earthly power, the humanists conceived of plot as a malleable vehicle, a mere continuity into which any quantity of material could be inserted. It is remarkable that any unified plots can be found among their tragedies at all. Their approach ignored the possibility of conflict among individual wills or psyches to thrive rather on ideas and the number of concepts that could be put into play.

Beaubrueil's *Regulus* charts the career of a Roman consul from victory to defeat and death—a perfect reversal pattern. Yet in truth the play dwells even more on the questions of reputation and service to country. Attilie and Manlie originally undertake battle against Carthage because 'celuy gaigne vn los magnifique / Sur les aultres humains, qui de la republique / Les affaires epouse' (p. 2). They know that others will try to obscure their honour and their country could prove ungrateful as has happened already many times in Greek and Roman history. (Examples are cited.) Still,

L'honneur des gens de bien ne depend du parler
De ses lourdz iugemĕtz qui rien n'y voyent cler,
Mais de la voix de ceux qui d'vne ame syncere,
Franche de passion pesent bien vn affaire.

(p. 7)

Their victory provokes a discussion of clemency which Attilie refuses to grant. Then he is in turn defeated in battle. Amid the lamenting over fortune's reversal the theme of clemency returns. Attilie is admonished: 'Il ne failloit pas tant estre enflé de ton gain, / Ains deuois te monstrer aux hõmes plus humain' (p. 43). The remainder of the play depicts Attilie's voyage to Rome under promise to return to Carthage, where he has been guaranteed a house, not a prison, if he arranges an exchange of hostages. Before the Senate Attilie argues against exchanging vigorous young warriors for an old man. He returns to Carthage and death but not before we hear him utter, 'i'ayme mieux souffrir ceste mort inouye / Que de viure à plaisir trahissant ma patrie' (p. 69). Example of fortune's inconstancy, Attilie dies an example of much more, just as his actions have permitted Beaubrueil to exploit more than one theme.

Pageau's *Bysathie* offers a similar range of preoccupations within an even more cavalier treatment of the reversal of fortune pattern. Bysathie's involvement in the plot does not begin until Act III, where the princess decides to overthrow her own father because he has condemned to death a handsome Roman soldier whom she loves. In Act IV the regicide is accomplished and Bysathie gives the sceptre to Crasse, her beloved. In Act V she kills herself, for Crasse has returned to Rome. Her death does not close the play, however. Crasse, desirous of seeing Bysathie again, learns of her death from a messenger who insists that he should 'remercier les Dieux / Qui [l']ont retirez du manoir Stygieux' (p. 83).

The sentiment is quite appropriate. Taken as a whole, *Bysathie* relates Crasse's life, in which Bysathie's machinations and death are but an episode. The first two acts belong to Crasse alone, to his courage, his love of country, and to his hope of a Roman victory over impossible odds. Most significant is Crasse's speech upon his return to Rome at the beginning of Act V. He makes no mention of Bysathie but praises *his* success ('I'ay dompté la rigueur, i'ay dompté la furie, / De ce peuple mutin' p. 54), and Rome's might ('Ainsi puissent touiours, se courber soubs nos loix, / Les Bretons esloignez, & les hommes Gregeois' p. 57). Although Ronsard's *Franciade* and

D

the ever-popular *Aeneid* made stories of foreign heroes and abandoned princesses lose none of their tragic tone, Pageau, like
Beaubrueil, found equally appropriate for tragedy the example of
valour and patriotism.

Although it is not difficult to see from these examples that to
define what *was* appropriate for tragedy could constitute a risky
undertaking, some critics have not considered all early plays entitled
'tragédie' worthy of the name. Elliott Forsyth, for example, does not
include Bretog's *Tragédie françoise* in his bibliography since it
belongs to a group of 'certaines pièces du XVIᵉ siècle qui, tout en
portant l'appelation "tragédie", ne sont en réalité que des mystères
ou des moralités' (p. 426). Yet we have seen that in the earliest stage
of humanist tragedy, Théodore de Bèze and Des Masures could
offer only awkward, inadequate descriptions of the works they entitled 'tragédie'. With the passage of time, the definitions did not
become more adequate and the plays did not become more uniform.
Matthieu's *Vasthi* has a reversal with no death. Behourt's *Esau* has
neither a clear-cut reversal nor a death. Virey's *La Machabée*
depicts numerous deaths but the reversal is total before the play
opens. The list of oddities is long and spans all periods in the genre's
history. Its length is a warning. Those, like Jean de La Taille, who
offered canons for distinguishing among subjects, must have been
rather few. The majority worked along the lines of Pageau or
Beaubrueil, expanding outward from misfortune to cover myriad
didactic possibilities and feeling content when some elevation in
style and much moralizing could be included.

To demonstrate how fluid techniques were, let us return a moment
to Bretog's *Tragédie françoise* and to Le Coq's *Cain*, also excluded
by Forsyth from his bibliography. The allegorical characters in
Bretog have one function: to explain a character's motivation. Venus
and Chasteté each try to win over the protagonist, a servant who
covets the wife of his master. Jalousie incites the husband to accuse
his wife. In Le Coq's play the allegorical figures symbolize the moral
consequences of Cain's act. Abel's blood cries vengeance. An angel
announces that Cain will hereafter be cursed. Peché appears, described as 'horrible d'appearance' (sig. C2ᵛ), and followed by La
Mort, who says, 'Ie suis fille, / De ton peché' (sig. C3ʳ). She informs
Cain that she will not advance the end of his days as he had asked.
He must await his natural death.

The humanists' abandonment of such characters and procedures was never total. Satan, Angels, and Furies were admitted on stage for decades after Le Coq and Bretog. If it may be objected that they are not allegorical figures in the mode of Chasteté or Peché, I must agree but point out at the same time that their function in the humanists' plays nevertheless closely parallels the use to which Chasteté was put by Bretog. They, too, incite, encourage, inspire in order to explain human conduct. Moreover, if allegorical figures disappear, scenes such as Chasteté and Venus debating with the protagonist will continue to abound. The humanists merely reassign the arguments, giving in general Chasteté's views to a nurse or a confident and letting the thoughts of Venus appear in the speeches of the lovesick interlocutor. When Peché and La Mort disappear, again little is lost because essential to innumerable tragedies is the concluding observation that sin has brought about misfortune and death will be the transgressor's wages. In other words, embracing a more classical style did not mean abandoning the mentality of medieval drama. It was simply transposed and for the excellent reason that the Venus / Chasteté debate or the appearance of Peché with her daughter La Mort constituted patterns of didactic exposition which the humanists felt as necessary in developing their plot as did their medieval predecessors. Although generations of scholars have emphasized a rupture between humanist and medieval technique, there is every reason to believe that the humanists were more concerned with 'classicizing' medieval didacticism than with fleeing it. From whatever perspective we attempt to approach the humanists' work, this realization awaits us.

Some years ago I argued that the structure of Garnier's tragicomedy *Bradamante* offered less of a departure from contemporary practice than had been suggested and that the first-act appearance of Charlemagne, like the prophet's speech at the beginning of *Les Juives*, had definite importance for the play's thematic unity.[3] It is now possible not only to present more evidence to illustrate the traditional quality of such a technique but also to show how this technique is linked to didacticism's influence on humanist tragedy.

Every story which fulfilled the simplest requirement for tragedy by relating misfortune in the life of an illustrious person did not provide the thematic richness that we have just noted as so attractive to the humanists. Other stories were recognized through the long tradition of citing *exempla* as possessing important moral lessons but did not fall conveniently within the reversal of fortune category, however broadly defined. Jodelle's *Didon se sacrifiant* typifies the first problem; adaptations of the Amnon and Thamar story, the second.

The conversation among Achate, Ascaigne, and Palinure which opens *Didon se sacrifiant* has no counterpart in the *Aeneid*. Virgil's Ascanius is a mere child, not the impetuous adolescent whom Jodelle portrays. Virgil does mention in verse 400 the Trojans' 'fugae studio' (eagerness for flight) in reference to their preparations to set sail but he includes no dialogue. Jodelle not only creates one but also makes at least one Trojan, Achate, not eager to flee. This hesitation forms the basis for Jodelle's opening scene.

Achate sees in the command to depart Dido's potential death and the gods' unceasing indifference to human suffering. He is made to accept the decision through such arguments as Ascaigne's 'l'amour & la haine / Des Dieux vont bigarrant la fresle vie humaine' (f. 253ᵛ) and Palinure's

Jamais aux bas mortels les Immortels ne rendent
Vne asseurance entiere: & tousiours ceux qui tendent
A la gloire plus haute, ont leurs ames estreintes
Aux soucis, aux trauaux, aux songes, & aux craintes.

(f. 254ᵛ)

Through them Jodelle also bridges the gap between Virgil's concentration on Dido and the desire to wrap a tragic suicide in far-reaching commentary on man's fortune.

The story of Amnon and Thamar provided the sixteenth century with a perfect example of the terrible effects of passion; yet it, too, existed at a distance from some obvious link with human destiny in general. Both Chrétien des Croix and Thierry wrote tragedies based on Amnon's desire for Thamar and both opened their plays with the tribulations of David, not Amnon. In Chrétien's work, David speaks to God, recognizes God's omnipotence, and adds, 'Mais qui sçait mieux que moy l'effet de ta puissance?' (p. 2). The scene ends with a request that the chorus sing God's praises and attempt through sacrifice to move God to be favourable to them. Thierry opens with the prophet Nathan, who contrasts God's patience with Israel's obstinate bent toward sin. David's adultery is but one more example and a sin not yet totally expiated. Even more misfortune will befall his house. David appears at the beginning of the second act, begging God not to punish man unjustly even though we are all tainted by original sin and he, David, has been guilty of pride since becoming king.

Again the dramatists withhold immediate entry into their plot (Thierry's Amnon will not appear until scene 2 of Act II) and again the interposition of a peripheral personality proves necessary to establish the general message. Chrétien and Thierry select David's tribulations in order to draw the act of incest and death of Amnon out of the category of isolated events and into the stream of misfortunes of David, of the Jews, and ultimately, of all sinners. We witness the Christian equivalent of Ascaigne's observation that our lives are subject now to the love, now to the hate of the gods to which the dimension of sin has appropriately been added. All tragic characters pray that the gods will be propitious but all recognize also that misfortune dogs the steps of every mortal. So intent are Chrétien and Thierry on their message that David closes both plays. Thierry's David is a more classical figure, lamenting in Hecuba fashion the series of misfortunes befallen him; Chrétien's character is profoundly Christian: 'Console toy Dauid, c'est pour vn bien que Dieu / A tiré ton Enfant de ce terrestre lieu' (p. 106). Still, each serves to make us take one step back from the sight of a particular sin and its particular punishment to grasp the greater pattern involved.

Another play to possess an interesting first act is Garnier's *Antigone*. Only Antigone and Edipe speak. Edipe will not appear again. They discuss primarily Edipe's wish to die. Antigone urges her father to overcome his sadness and swears that she will not abandon him. Edipe maintains his right to decide what is best for him. They debate his crime which Edipe calls 'une forfaicture, un prodige, une horreur' (vs. 131), but which appears to Antigone as 'une fortune, un hasard, une erreur' (vs. 132). Her father acted in ignorance. 'Personne n'est mechant qu'avecques volonté' (vs. 136). Only some two hundred lines later do we hear of that struggle between Polynices and Eteocles which occupies the major portion of the action. Antigone begs Edipe to live in order to put an end to this struggle but the link with the acts to follow proves quite contrived. Edipe agrees to go on living, but only because of Antigone's sighs and she, not he, departs at the close of the scene to calm the struggle at Thebes.

It is evident that the act bears only a most tenuous relationship to the story of Polynices and Eteocles; however, unlike the plays just discussed, such separation does not derive from any attempt to shower the plot with wider meaning. Another structural principle is at work.

Garnier entitled his play *Antigone ou la piété*. To bring out this quality, the dramatist bypassed both a unified plot and the story-within-a-framework procedure of *Didon se sacrifiant*. He selected a series of confrontations (Antigone and Edipe—Act I; Antigone and Iocaste—Act III; Antigone and Creon—Act IV), in which Antigone's stand would proclaim her concern for others, her strength, and determination. Garnier's peculiar handling of the Theban civil war in Act I remains quite justified in such a scheme. That Antigone urges her father to live in order to establish peace in Thebes shows her characteristic concern; that she, not Edipe, leaves for the city accentuates even more the same message. Given the popularity of debate and stichomythia with connoisseurs of rhetoric, it is not difficult to imagine why Garnier could have found action by confrontation an attractive pattern. Important for us is the fact that Garnier was not alone in relating structure and confrontation or feeling that a particular theme or idea could be best highlighted by juxtaposing it with its opposite.

The anonymous *Sophronie* is an avowed adaptation from Tasso. However, in the Italian verses which inspired the play, Tasso never once mentions an Orcan, who has a significant role in *La Sophronie*. (An Orcano appears in Tasso's Canto X to argue against resisting the Christians, ostensibly because of their strength, but in fact because a young bride has turned him away from war. If he is the model for Orcan, then the degree of adaptation is all the greater.) Orcan's function in *La Sophronie* consists, first, of opposing the king's projected treatment of the Christians through a discussion of the virtues of clemency, secondly, of preaching reason against the king's rage, and finally, of challenging the king's sense of his own importance with an affirmation of the omnipotence of God—ample demonstration that to the author of this French tragedy making dialogue out of Tasso's narration meant in part composing debates. He is not an exception.

Startling but true is the gradual realization which comes to anyone who reads these tragedies in large numbers that the genre quickly amassed stock debates to be repeated over and over until the reader can anticipate long segments of dialogue. Some topics for stichomythia appear purely situational pieces; others bear on the wider themes raised by the action. Of the first variety, we find discussion on the pros and cons of suicide, insistence that dreams and portents are meaningless, not divine warnings, as the other speaker claims, and assurance by servants, wives, or friends when the protagonist despairs that all is not lost. More consequential are the innumerable debates on the moral and tactical advantages of clemency versus severity as a political policy and urgings for steadfastness in the face of misfortune directed at those same despairing protagonists. Whatever the example, we find the humanists displaying their knowledge of rhetoric's principles and providing each speaker with a carefully constructed series of arguments. They are so well matched, in fact, that, as Griffiths has pointed out, it is extremely difficult to detect which position the author favours. I am not certain that he always intended us to make a choice. Part of the stylistic display had to be a convincing argument for each speaker. Cicero records (without criticism) that Aristotle trained young men to argue both sides of a case (*Orator*, xiv, 46). Moreover, there are certain indications that debates, as set stylistic pieces, were only superficially integrated into the dialogue. In Le Breton's *Adonis*, Venus and her lover clash early over Adonis' love of the hunt. This discussion ends abruptly with Adonis announcing, 'Baste, c'est trop parlé' (p. 12). Such sharp cuts in the dialogue are not infrequent. They underscore the isolation of the set piece and betray, I feel, that nonchalance on the part of the playwright with regard to overall structure which rhetoric often fostered.[4]

What the humanists enjoyed creating at the level of stichomythia, they were not adverse to implementing at the level of scenes or acts as well. When Philone pitted Joab's advice to Adonias against that of another friend, or when Montreux gave to Cléopâtre's two handmaidens opposing perspectives on their mistress' future course of action, we observe only the most obvious step which the dramatists could take to amplify the pattern. Others include repeating a debate and changing slightly the context in order to bring fresh arguments to bear. Faure has Gordian *père* confronted in Act I with one set of reasons why he should rebel against the emperor only to present the once convinced character as recanting so that in Act II he may confront his son, who then engages him in a second argument for revolt. This time Gordian *père* is won over for good.

In some works we are confronted by a simple division of attention between the two sides of an issue that cuts the play in half. A famous example can be found in Montchrétien's *La Reine d'Écosse*, divided rather equally between the exposition of Elizabeth's cares (Acts I and II) and Marie's sentiments (Acts III, IV, and V). Frances Yates has attributed this perspective to Montchrétien's fidelity to his source, Pierre Matthieu, who also presents a balanced story of the execution. The last to deny the power which source material exerted over the humanists, I, nonetheless, feel obliged to point out that Montchrétien was hardly alone in effecting such a division. For example, Garnier before him had devoted Acts II and III of *Cornélie* to anti-César sentiment. Yet the appearance of César in Act IV confirms none of this sentiment. He is even made to say that he did not want war and to show compassion: 'Victoire aucune où i'apperçoy gesir / Le corp d'vn citoyen, ne me donne plaisir' (f. 62ᵛ).

Occasionally, a play maintains a veritable interplay of opposing concepts throughout its development. Behourt's *Esau ou le chasseur* is just such a work. The author gives very little attention to the actual events of the Biblical tale. Jacob's visit to his father and Esau's discovery of his brother's deception appear wholly within the last act. For the preceding acts, Behourt develops a philosophical clash out of Esau's penchant for the hunt in contrast to Jacob's preference for the fields. Esau believes that all is determined by the stars, including his love of the hunt. When Jacob appears (Act IV), it is to condemn astrology; yet Esau is not present until the close of the act, and there they discuss Esau's birthbright. This encounter begins the retelling of the Biblical story. Thus, the juxtaposition of Esau's and Jacob's views remains purely gratuitous since neither of the scenes presents the other brother to stimulate (or justify) a philosophical *prise de position*. But, of course, Behourt was not working with a genre subject to the sort of logic provoked by the Querelle du *Cid*. I doubt that any of his contemporaries missed the calculated clash of ideas. They enjoyed the early acts as such and may well have complimented Behourt for having effected so fine an opposition.

Chrétien des Croix plays throughout *Amnon et Thamar* with the opposition between wisdom and self will. David, repentant, says in the first scene of Act I that he at last has begun to taste the supreme quality of wisdom, 'ayant assopi l'ardeur de ma ieunesse' (p. 3). Immediately thereafter we see Amnon in the throes of passion. Act II begins with Thamar's praise of those who have attained wisdom and passes to Absalon, who declaims: 'O que l'homme est heureux, qui n'a iamais esté / Esclaue d'autre ioug que de sa volonté!' (p. 28). As happens in *Esau*, Thamar and Absalon in effect speak to a situation of which they are yet ignorant. Clearly delineated, the clash remains until Act IV purely thematic.

Naturally, just as it was not easy to create well-balanced sticho-mythia and give an obvious edge to one of the speakers, so humanists who were willing to exploit freely the many facets of those questions raised in their plots sometimes made identification of any predominant message impossible. Lebègue admits in his critical notes to Garnier's *La Troade* that 'on ne voit pas nettement l'enseigne-ment moral et religieux qu'il avait coutume de tirer des événements dramatiques' (p. 248). The problem is attributed to a hesitation on Garnier's part between his personal feelings and material he found in Seneca and Euripides. Perhaps. But we should not forget that Garnier was quite free to engage in exposing both without necessarily labelling one his final opinion. If didactic literature in the sixteenth century had always meant the opposite, we would not be disagreeing today over so many passages in Rabelais or Montaigne. The humanists heaped scorn on argumentation without substance or conviction but rhetoric's influence, their moral and professional training would not let them forget the value of a well-exposed prob-lem, carefully debated.

That the subjects for humanist tragedy were derived in the main from ancient historians, Plutarch's *Lives*, classical dramatists, or earlier sixteenth-century plays, will surprise no one. To examine in what way this material struck the humanist and how he adapted it to the tragic genre nevertheless affords more insight into the particular mentality we have been studying. I hope I have already said enough regarding plot to explain why a dramatic plot line was generally not of interest to the humanists. Their reaction to the various inner dramas they encountered in their sources is another matter.

Among the commonplaces offered regularly to describe the Re-naissance, 'the discovery of man by man' stands high on the list. We are expected to observe this discovery in the wave of auto-biographies, nude paintings, and sensuous love verse of the period. If this is an accurate description of the Renaissance, French humanist tragedy cannot be used as a piece of substantial evidence. Whether confronted with some of the finest writing of antiquity or mere sketches of human passion, the humanists regularly passed over, transformed, or played down these emotions in favour of the traditional didactic patterns. In France, the fulfilment of man's discovery of man belongs to seventeenth-century tragedy and not to its humanist predecessor.

Readily available to the sixteenth century was, for example, the superb handling of characters in the *Aeneid* and, next to Sophonisba, Dido gave her name to more humanist tragedies than any other heroine. At the same time, Virgil's general influence is less than one might expect, and except for the Dido tragedies, such as Jodelle's *Didon se sacrifiant*, I know only of Prévost's *Turne* as representing an entire play derived from the *Aeneid*. The date of *Didon se sacrifiant* is uncertain; Balmas places it around 1560. According to Cioranescu, Prévost's work was first published in 1612. Despite the time span, Jodelle and Prévost treat Virgil in a similar fashion.

Numerous students of classical letters, including R. G. Austin and Michael Putnam, have demonstrated the care with which Virgil drew his characters. In the Turnus episode, Aeneas continues to display the singleness of purpose which in part justifies the familiar epithet 'pius', repeated in line 311 of the final book. It is true that Aeneas receives constant assurance—from the river god Tiberinus (VIII, 36) and from his mother (VIII, 531, 608)—but it is also true that the words of encouragement he speaks to his men at the opening of Book XI allow for no regrets, no hesitation. He is dedicated to the cause.

As Virgil shows us more and more of Turnus' character, certain contrasts seem in the making. Beside the 'pius' and 'pater Aeneas' (XII, 697), Virgil places the fiery Turnus, described variously by 'arduus' (IX, 53), 'audaci' (IX, 126), 'violentia' (XI, 376), 'furens' (XI, 486). Yet, as Putnam has pointed out, the closing lines of the *Aeneid* reveal in its hero no less fury. Aeneas is compared to a hunter's dog pursuing a frightened stag, jaws gaping (XII, 746), is said to speak 'saevo . . . pectore' (XII, 888)—the kind of adjective Virgil has heretofore lavished upon Turnus. So, too, at the moment of final victory over Turnus, any notion of nobility and generosity fades as Aeneas espies Pallas' belt and slays his enemy 'furiis accensus et ira / terribilis' (burning with fury and terrible in his anger) (XII, 946-7).

Prévost respects little in Virgil's scheme or complexity despite an intimate knowledge of the poet's text. Aeneas' first appearance shows him discouraged; his final scene portrays him as magnani-

mous. The fierce Turnus speaks some of the play's most lyric lines
and the play as a whole, instead of moving as the *Aeneid* does from
the general plane of the gods' designs to the clash of two individuals,
weaves its plot around the everpresent theme of fate.

In each case contemporary practices brought Prévost to transform
what he found in Virgil. Although Turnus opens the third act with
a denunciation of the effeminate Aeneas, contrasting the robust
country ways of the Italians with the Sybaritic Trojans, Prévost
does not hesitate to insert within this faithful portrait of Virgil's
Turnus an outpouring of amorous sentiment:

> O quel eslancement poussoit tantost la belle
> En mon ame amoureuse! ô que son œil vainqueur
> Me remplissoit de ioye, & d'angoisse le cœur!

(f. 43^v)

The fierce country boy has turned Petrarchist lover. Nowhere in
Virgil's final book was Prévost treated to such gallantry. We learn
only that once when Turnus looks on Lavinia, 'love throws him
into confusion' (XII, 70). The willingness to embroider extensively
upon Virgil and to be rather inconsistent (within a single speech)
derives not only from the ease with which readers of *Amadis* and
l'Astrée accepted gallantry in warriors but also from a more general
tendency to consider style above characterization. In a literary
world dominated by rhetoric the opportunity to wax eloquent was
rarely missed. Poetic conventions of the day had already refined the
vocabulary of a lover's declaration of fidelity; Virgil had included
an elegant comparison of Lavinia's face, streaked with tears, to
ivory stained with crimson dye or roses set among lilies (XII, 67-9).
In Prévost's play Turnus makes the comparisons as part of his outpouring of emotion. Humanist tragedies are replete with such
rhetorical flourishes.[5] It helped to insure the praise for a 'docte' or
'grave' style that all sought and many won. It also produced unexpected *longueurs* in moments of relatively great stress or, as in the
case of Turnus, puzzling shifts in tone or characterization. They will
remain unexpected or puzzling only if we do not recognize that
style, elegant, flowing, and especially moral was so often an end in
itself to the humanists.

It justified in particular the expression of sentiments appropriate
to a single scene but otherwise out of character with previous or
subsequent declarations. Laudun's Diocletian exhibits for four acts

the heart of the blackest tyrant. When the final act opens, we find 'L'Empereur Habille en Iardinier' (f. 27ʳ). Laudun has taken no pains to prepare this about-face, which, however, permits the author to write a long piece on the joys of the simple life—a traditional theme—and in itself of sufficient interest to obscure the lack of logic in Diocletian's conduct. Use of this technique is particularly noticeable in the numerous debate scenes on hope and despair, death and life, where the concern for a well-balanced debate fairly removes the scene from the plot's prior development. How else to explain the fact that although Behourt opens the last act of *Hypsicratée* with his heroine's resolution to die now that Mithridates' fortune has changed (to which her nurse responds with the characteristic call for hope and courage), he later places the same words of encouragement in Hypsicratée's mouth when she must listen to Mithridates' lament.

Griffiths and Doran, referring to such passages as Quintilian VI, ii, 8-24, stress the importance for the humanists of portraying an *emotion* in a speech, not a character's ever-unfolding personality. They point out also that since in the accepted view of men like Quintilian the violent emotions were usually of a momentary nature, the humanists saw no reason to prepare the audience for a character's many outbursts. I would not reject this observation, but see as even more fundamental in determining the characters' attitudes the humanists' tendency to work from set situations and set moral truths, not an integrated plan of presentation. The practice of printing quotation marks at the beginning of the sententious verses so that they might be more prominent in the text accentuates further this tendency.

To introduce Aeneas' uneasiness, Prévost chose this question, asked of Jupiter: 'Helas! quand finiront les iniustes fureurs / De ta femme implacable?' (f. 44ᵛ). Adapted from the Psalms, it echoes a standard complaint in humanist tragedy used by oppressed Christians and pagans alike.[6] Its immediate value to Prévost is to permit an enumeration of those long trials to which Aeneas refers. But eventually its moral value emerges. Prévost is leading to a typical confrontation between discouragement and hope. Achate counters Aeneas' complaints with the usual 'Enee il faut chasser cet inutil soucy, / Et penser à bastir vne autre Troye icy' (f. 46ᵛ). To Aeneas' pessimistic 'Bastir vn Ilium desert, inhabité' (referring to the number of Trojans killed by Turnus), Achate opposes the principle

that 'On ne pouuoit assoir que sur vn fondement / Fascheux &
mal-aiseé, ce braue bastiment' (f. 46ᵛ).

Similarly, if by the fifth act Aeneas has regained his tone of assurance and Prévost shows no interest in the personalities beneath
the Turnus-Aeneas struggle, it is because from his work must come
the realization that destiny controls all. Latinus cannot grant his
wife's plea to marry Turnus to Lavinia because: 'nostre destinee /
Ne nous ordonne point autre gendre qu'Enée' (f. 37ᵛ). Aeneas tells
the same Achate in Act V

> Ce n'est pas ma valeur, Achate, mais les Dieux
> Qui ont soucy de nous, & nous gardent des cieux,
> Recompensants chacun ainsi qu'il le merite,
> Qui redressent par moy nostre ville destruite.

(f. 56ʳ)

The play's final scene is left to Turnus' father, his lament, and his
predictable query, 'quels accidents soudains / Roullent diuersement
les affaires mondains?' (f. 62ᵛ)

As an earlier analysis has shown, this question was just as important to Jodelle when he composed his *Didon se sacrifiant*. We can now
note that it was certainly more important to him than examining
Virgil's portrait of Aeneas in the fourth book of the *Aeneid*. The
description is singularly indirect. In the entire book Aeneas speaks
only once. Elsewhere we have a narration of his thoughts (vv. 279-
95) with some carefully chosen words and a portrait-simile (vv. 439-
49). The technique is ingenious. From what Virgil does provide, we
learn that Aeneas' sentiments at this critical moment are confused,
almost mysterious. Extended conversations or monologues could
have served only to dissipate the intensity of those sentiments.
Secondly, Aeneas' long stay at Carthage, his debt to Dido, and his
willingness to be the object of her attentions placed the epic's hero
in a difficult moral position. There seems to me little doubt that
Virgil's rather oblique description, by leaving much unstated,
inevitably protects Aeneas. We learn enough to recognize the
elements of his struggle but not enough to condemn him for acting
in an unacceptable fashion.

Our first description of Aeneas follows Mercury's warning to
leave Carthage. Virgil calls Aeneas 'amens', 'attonitus' (IV, 279,
282), underscoring his fear of the gods, and adds 'ardet obire fuga
dulcisque relinquere terras' (he burns to take to flight and leave
these sweet lands) (IV, 281). The verse has been much discussed

because of the juxtaposition of 'fuga' and 'dulcis' which effects within the line a confrontation of the feelings that tear at the hero: to flee and obey the gods, to remain and enjoy the peace of Carthage. The juxtaposition is real enough, but the verb 'ardet', with 'amens' and 'attonitus', more than upsets the balance. It is the gods who dominate his thoughts. There may be regret ('dulcis') but nothing intimates that Aeneas seriously considers remaining in Africa. Equally revealing are his allusions to Dido as 'furentem' (IV, 283) and 'optima' (IV, 291). Dido is a problem because of *her* passion, not his and the sentiment he appears to fear betraying is his gratitude for Dido's kindness, not love.

We do not see Aeneas again until verse 333, when he makes his defence before Dido. He begins by echoing the sentiments Virgil had alluded to with 'dulcis' and 'optima': he recognizes how grateful he is to her; he will never forget Elissa. But, to the point. He never meant to hide his flight from her nor to marry her. If the first statement is contradicted by the text, the second is not. Aeneas never refused her advances but Virgil makes clear that Dido reads into their affair what she wishes. On the occasion of their adventure during the storm, Virgil writes that if Dido calls what had transpired a marriage, it is to hide her erring ways (vs. 172).

The remaining portion of Aeneas' speech revolves even more around the 'pius' Trojan who, though human and forgetful, will respond to the destiny which is his. If he had his way, he tells her, the first Troy would be his concern. But Italy must be his destination, 'hic amor, haec patria est' (vs. 347). Although the context makes us think of 'amor' in terms of Dido's wishes, the passage also embraces the loves inherent in the word 'pius': fatherland and the gods. Aeneas is denying that his sentiments toward Dido are comparable to hers. What she has poured into their relationship, he felt for Troy and now must feel for Italy. 'Hic amor' shows that Aeneas' piety extends to the point of accepting even the love the gods will and separates Aeneas' passive reaction before what destiny has offered at Carthage from Dido's wilful, egotistical wish to love, oblivious to all vows and bonds outside that passion. When Aeneas concludes his speech with 'Italiam non sponte sequor' (I do not will that I should go to Italy) (vs. 361), Virgil has insured that the reader will recognize the dilemma as one of pious duty versus the human temptation to enjoy certain quiet and luxury (Carthage) and prefer the familiar (Troy). To what degree this dilemma tries him remains unsaid. The simile of Aeneas as the oak tree buffeted by winds yet indestructable sets the tone of our final glimpse of the hero. 'Now certain of leaving' (vs. 554), he sleeps until Mercury forces him to set sail in all haste. That slight phrase seems to allude to a previous conflict but it has been passed over in silence.

Jodelle's Aeneas is dutiful but deprived of all mystery. Whereas Virgil leaves unspecified how deep are Aeneas' feelings toward Dido, Jodelle paints a portrait of caddish duplicity. There is no doubt that Aeneas loves Dido. His closing speech in Act I mentions him as 'de trahison coulpable' (f. 256^v). He would have 'vne ame estrangement cruelle', he notes,

> Si la iuste pitié qu'il me faut auoir d'elle,
> Ne me faisoit creuer & rompre l'entreprise,
> Qui la loy de l'amour infidellement brise.

(f. 257^r)

In the second act, he admits that he is not entirely 'incoulpable' (f. 266^r). He even confesses to Dido that, 'Si tel amour tu sens, ie le sens tel aussi' (f. 266^r), but, of course, the gods' will must be followed. While Jodelle's Aeneas loves Dido, he must love the gods more.

Although transforming Virgil's couple into a Dido wronged by the gods and a 'pariure Enée' is characteristic of all the members of Pléiade,[7] Jodelle's adaptation owes much more to contemporary concepts of tragedy. Jodelle did not delve beneath the words of the *Aeneid* because he did not need to examine the fourth book closely to see how it could serve as material for tragedy. Any one would recognize that the pitiful end of Dido, a powerful Queen, was a tragic subject. He could impose a simplistic narration upon the subtleties of Virgil because for him and his fellow humanists tragedy was above all an event whose depiction would provide insight into the course of human histories (what Prévost's character calls 'les affairs mondains'). The Classical dramatists work like Virgil, using love or other strong emotions to penetrate more deeply the psyches involved. Thus, in the *Aeneid* we eventually come to know the total meaning of Dido's eastern origins and gain fuller understanding of Aeneas' piety. Jodelle works differently. Love is a given that helps to accentuate the story's message. In both *Cléopâtre captive* and *Didon se sacrifiant* the characters' love comprises part of that happy state from which they have fallen. It is in many ways no different from Dido or Cleopatra's regal quality. It needs no examination and

Jodelle expends energy elsewhere, in Aeneas' debate with the chorus over religion, for example (vv. 990ff.), which predictably raises the question of divine intervention in human events.

In accentuating the humanists' lack of attention to characterization and singular distance from some of their more perceptive sources, I am not unaware of the general admiration lavished upon Jean de La Taille for his *Saül le furieux* nor of the very interesting argument put in Saul's mouth when he is reminded of his refusal to carry out certain of God's commandments. Ordered previously to destroy all the Amalekites and their goods, Saul instead spared the life of their king and preserved the finest of their cattle. The disobedience begins Saul's fall from favour and is therefore mentioned by his squire when he asks the cause of God's wrath. Saul refuses to accept guilt:

> O que sa Prouidence est cachee aux humains!
> Pour estre donc humain i'esprouue sa cholere,
> Et pour estre cruel il m'est donc debonnaire!
>
> (vv. 312-14)

The response is disarmingly modern. God's law appears to contradict the simplest human values, which are sufficiently strong to erase the notion of disobedience. Here, some might say, man has discovered man, much to the detriment of the divine.

What La Taille intended can really be answered only by La Taille; however, certain aspects of the play and of the genre should be scrutinized before we hastily identify with Saul's values. In passages where La Taille unquestionably determined to give a positive portrait of his protagonist (vv. 1099-112, 1428-9), the king is praised for his valour, conforming to the view of one of La Taille's sources, Josephus, but nothing is said to defend his act of disobedience. On the contrary, Samuel soundly denounces Saul and David prefaces his call to the daughters of Israel to lament Saul's death with this warning to Palestine:

> Garde toy bien que l'orgueil ne te trompe,
> Et qu'à la fin le sort pour ta fierté
> En ton malheur ne se monstre irrité!
>
> (vv. 1418-20)

At the very least we can note that La Taille advanced arguments both for and against Saul—the surest indication, I believe, of the context in which we must consider Saul's outburst.

I have already spoken above of how difficult it can be to discern with any certainty which point of view we are expected to adopt in the numerous debates. Saul's words are meant to rebut the squire's observation about his disobedience. Their scene together is constructed primarily of arguments and counter arguments. It remains interesting that La Taille should formulate such a violent argument for Saul, but then, Saul is accused of pride. Did not the rhetoricians urge that characters speak in accordance with their nature? Are Saul's exclamations not in keeping with the views of the defiant sinner? Mrs. Jondorf is confident that 'Saül is put firmly in the wrong throughout the play' (p. 130); Erwin Kohler sees in him 'die Freiheit des Individuums' (p. 64). The truth may lie with neither but rather with both together and the fact that in filling out the tragic event with moral observations, the humanists were as usual more concerned with style than consistency, with the interplay of ideas than with the struggles within and between personalities.

On the other hand, in innumerable ways rhetoric so combined style and characterization that we must accept as sincere attempts at character portrayal or dramatization remarks which today seem quite inadequate. Rhetoric contented itself with very simple definitions of the young, the old, and the middle aged. La Taille's Ionathe offers a particularly excellent example of humanist tragedy's perspective on behaviour. Attempting to exhort his brothers to fight, he argues:

> Vault il pas mieux mourir vaillamment à ceste heure,
> Qu'attendre les vieux ans pleins d'oisifue langueur,
> Ennemis de vertu, de force et de vigueur?
> Qu'on louë qui voudra la vieillesse debile,
> Pour son graue conseil, pour son aduis vtile,
> 'Il n'est que l'ardeur ieune, et d'auoir au menton
> 'Plustost l'or que l'argent.
> . . .
> Ie me tuerois plustost que de me veoir si vieux
> Trainner dessus trois pieds mes iours tant ennuyeux,
> Aux hommes desplaisant, fascheux, melancholique.

(*Saül*, vv. 104-10, 117-19)

Not only are the attributes assigned to youth and old age characteristic of the rhetorical tradition (e.g. 'Qu'on louë qui voudra'), but also the evident prejudice expressed by Ionathe serves to identify him immediately as a young man. Similarly, the long stichomythia between Hector and Priam in Montchrétien's *Hector* (pp. 22-6) is built upon a continuing opposition between Priam's 'graue conseil' and Hector's 'ardeur ieune'.[8] The entire exchange may appear wooden and dehumanized today, but Montchrétien's readers would have had no difficulty appreciating the appropriateness of the sentiments attributed to each character and for that reason Montchrétien can be said to have acquitted himself fully before his public.

In a genre which took pride in its moral lessons and understood human character in such simplistic terms, it is hardly surprising to find the humanists subordinating the personality of their characters to these lessons. The characters' awareness of symbolizing through their situation a truth about human events emerges in two stylistic devices, which, significantly, were also widely used in poetry of the day. The first involves the word 'fable' and emphasizes its designation of a story with moral (not improbable) content.

When Du Bellay wrote in the *Regrets*

> Sus doncques, et devant que le cruel vainqueur
> De nous face une fable au vulgaire moqueur,
> Banissons la vertu d'un exil volontaire,

(sonnet 50)

or Ronsard put in the mouth of his Clymène

> Non, ny mon sang, mon honneur, ny ma race
> Ne veulent point que fable je me face,
> Et que chacun d'un cueur dissimulant
> Flatte mon mal, et puis, s'en-allant
> Me deshonore, et tançant sa famille
> Par mon malheur face sage sa fille,

(I, 729)

it is quite clear that 'fable' designates a tale told as a moral lesson. The phrase reappears in Jacques de La Taille's *Daire* (f. 4ʳ), Chrétien des Croix' *Amnon* (p. 74), Montreux' *Sophonisbe* (p. 74), Montchrétien's *Aman* (vs. 1448—text 1601), Du Souhait's *Radégonde* (p. 24), Hardy's *Méléagre* (I, 155, vs. 6), Poullet's *Charite* (p. 65), and *Les Amoureux Brandons de Franciarque et Callixène* (p. 4), where the characters all contemplate the present or future prospect of entering the lore of common tales.

The second device I mentioned in Chapter II as a longstanding means in classical and Italian literature to call attention to the speaker or to another person as representing some particular phenomenon. Because Petrarch used the 'Qui veut voir' topos to introduce the *Rime*, French love poetry of the period did much to popularize it. Its appearance in Garnier's *La Troade* (vv. 1ff.) is most likely due to a translation from Seneca (*The Trojan Women*, vv. 1ff.) but whatever the source the device occurs often enough to show that the humanists had assimilated it to their own style and with reason. Whether the Damoiselle is inviting us to observe fortune's work in the French civil strife (Belyard, *Le Guysien*, p. 61) or Vasthi (Matthieu, *Vasthi*, p. 6) and Patron (Hardy, *La Mort de Daire*, IV, 1, vv. 81ff.) urging us to contemplate the meaning or fate of royalty in the plays' respective examples, the dramatists could not have done more to bring us closer to the heart of their intent. One might wish that they had been more subtle or left the finger-pointing to the chorus, but again we would be missing the spirit of their enterprise. Such a wish presupposes that the story must take precedence over its meaning. The humanists enjoyed the opposite technique, following their medieval predecessors and classical models to perfection. Characterization suffered most in this procedure but as with his foreshortening of the plot line, the humanist had many a device ready to use in the space acquired and did so.

By suggesting that characterization occupied little of these dramatists' time, I do not mean to imply that they left the question of motivation totally unexplained. They did not, but they also did not derive their explanations from any process that we might be tempted to see as 'psychological investigation'. Certain titles—*Les Gordians et Maximins ou l'ambition, Hypsicratée ou la magnanimité, Aman ou la vanité, Cyrus triomphant ou la fureur d'Astiages, Roy de Mede*—give an indication of one kind of characterization employed. It is readily recognizable as but a facet of rhetoric's practice of coupling behaviour with age, class, or moral trait. Another practice was to show the demons of the underworld invoked to spread evil abroad and/or to inspire criminal acts in a character. Humanists did not use this technique extensively in the early years of their involvement with tragedy but Erasmus' *Praise of Folly* shows that the concept had long been familiar to the century. Folly takes pains to distinguish between the insanity she brings and another which is

sent from hell by the avengeful furies, and as often as they unloose their snaky locks, they assault the hearts of men with a thirst for war, an insatiable greed, shameful and unspeakable lust, parricide, incest, sacrilege, or other evils of the same type. They also pursue the guilty and conscience-stricken soul with the fire of their terrible wrath.

(p. 127)

The humanists on occasion referred to the Furies' role as pursuers of the guilty. Garnier, for example, has Antoine rue the day when he first looked on Cléopâtre: 'dés l'heure vne palle Megere / Crineuse de serpens, encords ta misere!' (f. 77ʳ) In *Hippolyte* both Phèdre and her nurse at the moment of death feel the flames and serpents of hell. Phèdre sees an 'affreuse Megere' (f. [152ʳ]). Far more common are the instances where Furies or demons take possession of certain characters and lead them to crime.

One could consider these Furies a classical counterpart of Satan. The humanists had an obvious penchant for employing classical terminology or trappings even when least expected. Mercury appears in Act III of Chantelouve's *La Tragédie de feu Gaspar de Colligni* saying that Jupiter has sent him to protect the king and to guide the ball of the harquebus to warn Colligny, who thinks he can hide his designs from Jupiter. The anonymous author of a *Tragédie de Jeanne D'Arques* has his heroine accept her fate with these words:

Hà malheur inhumain puis qu'il ne reste rien,
Et qu'il faut aller voir le champ plutonien:
O Parque qui desia t'assis dessus ma teste!

(p. 44)

More important perhaps is the fact that whereas the humanists grew willing to depict more and more horrible events within the framework of tragedy, they nevertheless adhered to that simple view of human motivation expounded by rhetoric and already in practice in medieval drama.

They did this on occasion even when their source offered a slightly more modern situation. Paul and Deacon gives this description of the change of heart in Rosemund that leads to Alboin's death:

While he sat in merriment at a banquet at Verona longer than was proper, with the cup which he had made of the head of his father-in-law, king Cunimund, he ordered it to be given to the queen to drink wine, and he invited her to drink merrily with her father. . . . Then Rosemund, when she heard the thing, conceived in her heart deep anguish she could not restrain, and straightway she burned to revenge the death of her father by the murder of her husband.

(pp. 81-2)

This sequence of events did not satisfy Chrétien des Croix, however. His *Albouin* opens with the shade of Rosemund's father crying vengeance and the Fury Tisiphone's agreement to help him by spreading rage and madness although his work will mean Rosemund's death. Even Alboin sees the change of spirit which comes over him in Act III as the possible work of 'quelque Daemon' (p. 48). Similar demons and furies incite disorder or crime in Laudun's *Horace*, Pageau's *Monime*, Behourt's *Hypsicratée*, Nerée's *Le Triomphe de la Ligue*, Matthieu's *La Guisade*, Chantelouve's *Gaspar de Colligni*, Belyard's *Le Guysien*, Garnier's *Porcie*, Billard's *Henry le Grand*, and *Le Mérovée*. In Montchrétien's *Sophonisbe* and Hardy's *Alcméon*, they are merely invoked.

Other plays by Chrétien strengthen the view that these dramatists conceived of their characters as either good or evil, the reflection of a fundamental conflict between these forces within the world. *La Tragédie d'Amnon et Thamar* has the Fury Mégère and an angel vie for domination of Amnon's thoughts. The conversation is meant to take place in Amnon's mind, as in a dream, and some attempt at interiorization is evident; still, the persons selected leave no doubt as to how we are expected to interpret the episode. The accent falls not on any investigation of complex sentiments, but on a definition of the act to come as an evil one, abhorrent to the forces of good. It is for this reason that the furies proved so useful and provided another significant didactic pattern. Where direct inspiration of the furies could be shown, the moral lesson sharpened. Playwrights who gave over their characters to the furies could feel all the more certain that they had endowed tragedy with a moral lesson and fulfilled their obligation to genre and to public. This observation suggests that on other occasions the question of motivation and responsibility could be somewhat unclear, and in point of fact, it was.

Chrétien's own *Les Portugaiz infortunez* shows the Genie or demon of the Cape of Good Hope in debate with an angel. The demon rages against the increasing number of Christians sailing around the Cape. The angel assures him that he protests in vain; he will not be able to change God's will that his Word be spread. The angel reports that *he*, not the demon, caused Diaz' shipwreck, for Diaz was inspired by avarice. When the demon predicts the misfortunes to befall those Portuguese depicted in Chrétien's play, the angel counters with the idea that death is nothing but the passage to our eternal reward. The give and take goes beyond the familiar struggle between good and evil; it raises the equally central issue of dominion. The Genie feels master of the Cape's waters only to learn that the divine hand has been responsible for many events he ascribed to himself. Still, he cannot be totally impotent since the angel's remark about the play's characters concerns only the victory in their misfortune. The angel in no way takes the responsibility for their plight. The unanswered question—who, indeed, is responsible for misfortune, a moral divinity or some other force—goes to the heart of humanist tragedy's thematic structure and should properly be treated there.

2 THEMATIC PATTERNS

Whether the dramatist chose to depict those evil passions that lead to inevitable misfortune as a character's basic nature or the work of some agent from Satan, the link between comportment and misery was essentially that of the medieval theatre. When the grammarians joined tragedy to changes of fortune, they were not introducing an association that was unknown to the medieval world—Boccaccio has amply illustrated this—but they did bring into play an alternative to the motivation pattern of medieval drama that was strengthened by contact with classical tragedy and certain trends in religious thinking of the day. In the much imitated Hecuba story, for example, humanists found the tableau of a misery that befalls Hecuba, yet is neither created nor deserved by her, and the innumerable references in classical drama to fortune and destiny generally depict them more as arbitrary forces than as watchdogs for mortals' behaviour. At the same time that the humanists were absorbing the Hecuba story, a segment of their world, engaged in intense re-examination of Christian texts, was preparing the way for Protestantism, and more particularly for the theory of predestination, where God, too, took on the qualities of an arbitrary force. As a very early humanist tragedy reveals, the genre responded to the new concepts, but without deciding to adopt categorically one or the other explanation of human misery.

The early tragedy in question is *Jephthes*, by George Buchanan, a humanist with decided Protestant leanings. In its prologue, spoken by an angel, Buchanan outlines the nature of man's relationship to God. The angel speaks of man's pride and God's kindness. The more prosperous man becomes through this kindness, the more rebellious he acts. A long comparison is introduced. Man behaves like a spirited horse which rebels as soon as the groom loosens the reins and has to be brought under control again with the spur. Allusion is made to a whip ('flagrum', vs. 26) in order to fill out the comparison. If it ceases to keep man in check, man rushes to false gods. By the terms of the comparison, this whip can belong only to God and gradually the nexus between man and his Creator changes character.

The first impression Buchanan creates is one of a disobedient people, loved by their maker who is forced to punish this disobedience. Then, the image of the whip—indeed, the entire comparison—brings God into the picture *before* the disobedience as well as after. We learn through the comparison that God does more than react to man's rebellion; like the groom he is present at the very moment of disobedience and can be said to instigate it. The groom knows the horse is highspirited. God knows man is proud and rebellious by nature. Yet both relax their hold and permit the rebellion. As a result the situation in which man is wholly responsible for his punishment becomes one in which disaster derives from those forces outside man who are responsible for ordering the universe. That man remains an imperfect creature, that God may release his hold out of love for his people cannot efface the fact of God's arbitrary decision to place man once again in a position which He knows will end in the necessity for punishment.

Imposing the vagaries of fortune upon the pattern of sin and fall could mean no more than employing a particular vocabulary. In describing fortune, the humanists often used words such as 'muable', 'inconstante', 'variable' which accentuated the concept of reversal but said nothing about the reason behind fortune's actions. Occasionally the adjective 'aueugle' is coupled with fortune (e.g. Prévost, *Edipe*, p. 1), suggesting with the Hecuba story and certain examples from Boccaccio, that fortune's reversals were arbitrarily distributed among humans. Other times the humanists remained faithful to the symbol of Fortune's wheel and associated reversal with acquisition of power. Saul's groom speaks of his master as an example that 'on ne doit abboyer / Aux grands Estats' (p. 64) but again such phrases do not help the reader to understand fully fortune's procedure since they, too, leave open the question of guilt. The groom can mean only that the state of ruler is a dangerous one, not some specific fact about Saul, whom God chose to be king.

The amalgam of views becomes more complex when the dramatists go so far as to speak of destiny as a force that cannot be overturned. 'Si le destin le veut on ne le peut forcer' (p. 5), weeps Comonde upon learning in Chrétien's *Albouin* that his vengeance will be carried out but at the cost of his daughter's life as well as his enemy's.

Although Montchrétien's Hector joins his wife in hoping for victory over the Greeks, he warns her that destiny reigns 'invincible et ferme' (p. 14). In these declarations, there is more than a hint of some predestined scheme, established prior to any action by those concerned. A few, but only a very few dramatists attribute specifically to God such total dominion. Jacques de La Taille has Aristarque convince Alexander not to quit Babylon to save his life with the argument that

> Il n'y a seulement que le vouloir de Dieu
> Qui soit cause de tout, & d'autant plus qu'on pense
> Reculer son decret, d'autant plus on l'auance.

(f. 13^r)

Early in Philone's *Tragédie* Aican assures the assembled mourners of their late king that 'Rien n'aduient d'auenture. / Certain est du grand Dieu la haute prouidence' (p. 9). Jean de la Taille would probably agree, judging from his preface to his brother's play *Alexandre*. There he casts doubt on the appropriateness of the word Fortune to designate 'l'entresuitte des choses, & l'ordre certain, qu'en l'vniuers Dieu a de tout temps estably' (f. 2^{r-v}). At the other end of the spectrum, Garnier's Anthoine declares that Fortune 'N'est qu'vn euenement dont la cause on ignore' (f. 94^v) only to reveal that on reflection he must admit that in his own case the cause is clearly 'volupté'.

In a series of related discussions, the views reflect less a philosophical position than the sympathies or situation of the speaker. In Jodelle's *Didon se sacrifiant*, the chorus of Phoenician women cannot help being hostile to Aeneas and therefore to his faith in the gods. Similarly, the difference in views on the gods which opens Montreux' *Sophonisbe* reflects Scipio's victory and Syphax's defeat. Scipio sees Jupiter as guiding the Sun 'd'vne main si prudente' that the earth is never burned and calls him the author of Rome's conquests (pp. 6-7). Syphax believes that there is no law for the heavens, no order on earth and calls the gods the authors of this disorder. He shares with Jodelle's Phoenician women the feeling that the gods protect the evil, not the virtuous. Scipio points out that in overturning the king the gods were merely punishing his breach of faith with the Romans. Syphax replies that the fault was not his; he merely followed the advice of another. Lelius then rebukes him for betraying his divinely appointed role to rule, not obey. The debate is much

prolonged to expose both the appropriate *sententiae* and the necessary background for the action but its opening theme is not forgotten.
The Chorus of Africans later declares, 'Ce ne sont point les Dieux, /
Qui regissent ce monde' (p. 48), whereas the Chorus of Romans
feels confident that 'les grands Dieux en leur conseil secret / Au
iuste fer, apportent assistance' (p. 69).

Finally, perhaps because of their tendency to include as much
didactic material as possible in their plays, the humanists sometimes
exposed fully both views in the same work. Hardy opens *Alcméon*
with the shade of Eryphile. Violent in a denunciation of Alcméon,
Eryphile reflects on his career of murder. She wonders how he
dares to continue only to pivot in her thoughts and to recognize that
he is simply 'carrying out destiny's fatal sentence' (V, 202, vs. 21).
When Alcméon himself speaks of destiny in Act IV, the interpretation is quite different:

> Folie d'estimer que nos actes peruers
> Procedent d'vn destin qui guide l'vniuers,
> Non, des biens & des maux nous sommes l'origine,
> Nôtre inclination diuerse nous destine
> Le chemin des vertus & des vices offert,
> Suiuant l'vn nous conserue & en l'autre nous perd.

(V, 232, vv. 65-70)

Within the same speech which opens Garnier's *Hippolyte* Egee
blames 'le mechant destin' (f. 115^v) for the misfortunes of his city
and then predicts the catastrophe about to befall Thésée, who is to
be punished for abducting Minos' daughters.

On other occasions the humanists brought these two views into
open confrontation and made them the basis for yet another debate
pattern. In Garnier's *Marc Antoine* Cléopâtre maintains that the
gods are good and leave to men to determine what happens 'dessous
le firmament' (f. 83^v). Charmion disagrees. 'Les choses d'ici bas
sont au ciel ordonnees / Auparauant que d'estre entre les hommes
nees' (f. 84^r). When Montreux took up the same story, he gave to
Cléopâtre's other lady, Iras, the task of urging her mistress to abandon her thoughts of death. Her argumentation with respect to the
gods' influence returns us to the period's double vision. They first
appear responsible for everything. 'Que sçauez vous encor', she
asks of Cléopâtre, 'si leur main plantueuse / Apres tant le meschefs,
vous rendra bienheureuse?' (p. 17) Then Iras intimates that Cléopâtre
bears the responsibility for her situation:

Les Dieux ne sont autheurs du mal qui nous outrage,
C'est nostre seul forfait qui cause ce dõmage,
Mais quand nous le quittons, implorant leur bonté,
Ils nous aydent alors, changeans de volonté.

(p. 19)

Although here, as elsewhere, it is rather difficult to determine which side carries the author's convictions, a closer look at the thematic structure of humanist tragedy in general reveals that the playwrights responded more enthusiastically to medieval associations between sin and fall and were decidedly more interested in showing how death could be the child of sin than in depicting the simple reversal of Fortune's wheel.

To enumerate the many ways in which this moral was conveyed could only result in a tedious list of plot summaries. If, at the risk of not including all possible approaches adopted by the humanists, we ask what attitudes were operative in a fair proportion of humanist tragedies, we find them concerned primarily with the conflict between reason and passion, a conflict that was basic to the literary as well as the ethical principles of the humanist world. Quintilian calls reason 'praecipuam' (something special), given by the maker of the world to man to share with the immortal gods (II, xvi, 14). 'But', he adds, 'reason by itself would help us but little and would be far less evident in us, had we not the power to express our thoughts in speech' (II, xvi, 15). Mastering the art of rhetoric represented to Quintilian an affirmation of one's ability to make optimum use of this very special gift of reason. It is difficult to believe that the humanists did not make every attempt to respond to Quintilian's challenge since their tragedies show that pride in the display of reason went hand in hand with disapproval of or regret at its loss. La Taille's *Saül* opens its second act with the first groom lamenting the king's madness:

Mon Dieu quelle fureur et quelle frenaisie
A n'agueres du Roy la pensee saisie!
O spectacle piteux de voir leans vn Roy
Sanglant et furieux forcener hors de soy.

(vv. 221-4)

Is not the implication in La Taille's use of 'vn Roy' instead of 'le Roy' that it is pitiful to see any king in the throes of madness? And does not such a sentiment stem from expecting in one's ruler all the finest qualities imaginable, among which reason must be counted?

Although the conflict between reason and the passions had classical and Christian connotations, its implementation in humanist tragedy most closely parallels the perspective of such works as Boaystuau's *Théâtre du monde* or Belleforest's introductions to his tales translated from Bandello. There, acts leading to misery are seen to derive from two particular desires—ambition and love—the very passions tragedy chose to depict and both are conceived, to use Boaystuau's phrase, as 'vne . . . maladie & affliction d'esprit' (p. 158). The great peril in love, he says, is that the lovers will finally become 'frenetiques, & transportez de leurs sens' (p. 159). According to Belleforest, 'les effets [d'Amour] suyuis avec raison, laquelle doit regir toute action humaine, sont necessaires & honorables à nostre vie, si sont autrement disposez qu'en bonne part, & si aueuglement lon se lance és precipices d'vne folle fantasie, n'est rien tant pernicieux . . . que telle folle passion aporte à la vie des hommes' (II, 202-3). The humanists changed none of this; rather in their characteristic attempt to moralize as fully as possible they expanded the material in a variety of ways.

In no fewer than twenty-four tragedies composed by Hardy or his predecessors is ambition openly denounced. Brought into focus by the 'histoires tragiques', it proved particularly useful to the dramatists because of the evident relation between ambition and two figures—the tyrant and the would-be-tyrant seeking to capture a throne—that quickly achieved importance for a society torn by warring factions and flooded with words in disagreement over the nature of a perfect monarch.

It is not rare to find the humanists establishing an explicit parallel between their plots and contemporary events. Matthieu, in dedicating his *Aman*, suggests that this 'prodigieuse Tragedie du Schisme, du Discord, de la Deloyauté, de l'Heresie' (sig. $\pi 2^r$) is à propos. The title page for Philone's *Tragédie* calls his work a 'Vray miroir des choses aduenues de nostre temps'. Best known is Garnier's own admission that in lamenting the misfortunes of Romans and Greeks, he was 'pleurant nos propres maux sous feintes etrangeres' (Courtin, *Hymnes*, f. [4^r]). Other ties have been suggested by the critics. Mrs. Jondorf accepts Garnier's portrait of Antoine as a valiant man weakened by 'volupté' to be an implied criticism of Henry III but rejects Mouflard's theory that in *Les Juives* Amital, Nabuchodonosor, and Sédécie represent Catherine de Médicis, the Duke of Guise, and Henry III respectively. Her reasoning is sound; it also sets honest limits for what can otherwise become a complicated game of seeking equivalents. By their own words, the dramatists sometimes chose themes with contemporary parallels. How much farther they went remains conjectural.

Similarly, in a context where dramaturgy is the main concern, the differences between Protestant and Catholic playwrights can be overemphasized and the genre's involvement with *general* truths lost sight of. If, for example, Montchrétien presents Marie Stuart as innocent of the death of her husband and faithful to the Catholic cause in Scotland and France, the thematics of his final acts are only in part political. Marie relates the death of her first husband which occasions the familiar: 'O fortune volage, est-ce ainsi que ta roüe / Des Reines et des Rois inconstamment se ioue' (p. 91). She gives a detailed *récit* of the storm that drove her to England's shores and captivity and apostrophizes Freedom, which she sees as having abandoned her for ever. The conclusion—she must prepare to die— sets the tone for the remainder of Marie's speeches. 'Nous n'auon rien d'humain plus grand que le courage' (p. 93) she reminds the chorus. When Dauison brings news of Parliament's decision, Marie exhibits her preparedness—and the appropriate themes—with 'C'est vne loy certaine à qui vient ici bas, / Que tousiours la naissance apporte le trepas' (p. 97) and:

> Ciel, vnique confort de nos aspres trauaux,
> Port de nostre tourmente, et repos de nos maux,
> Reçoy donc mon esprit qui sauué du naufrage
> De l'éternelle mort descend à ton riuage.

(p. 98)

A Protestant could not have said it better.

Indeed, although Rivaudeau's *Aman* repeats the Protestant plot of a just people unjustly persecuted yet protected through their faith in God, this partisan theme, too, is permitted to engender many other commonplaces of all humanist drama. The eunuch warns Aman that 'Contre les destins durs la force rien ne sert' (p. 70). Rivaudeau characterizes Assuere as a good king in essentially the same manner used by the Catholic Garnier to describe Charlemagne in *Bradamante:* Assuere recognizes the supreme power of the gods over him and his sceptre.

As these examples suggest, the general interest in moralizing observed above was developed to a singular extent in plots involving tyrants, ambition, and the monarchy.

Pageau's *Monime* treats these themes within the pattern of a reversal of fortune. Mithridates has embarked upon a campaign against the Romans. They put his army to rout and Mithridates curses fortune for having created in him a desire to be king:

C'estoit pour m'attirer, au sang & au carnage
Et pour plus exciter, mon animé courage:
Qui trop ambitieux, felon & inhumain,
Osa bien attaquer cet Empire Romain.

(p. 131)

Other references to ambition abound. The Romans curse fortune when they learn before battle with the enemy that a consul has deserted to Mithridates, a decision which provokes the observation, 'O combien de malheurs cause l'ambition!' (p. 124) Ambition is equally linked to the subplot. Here we meet Monime, one of Mithridates' wives, who bitterly denounces her state. All the riches in her possession cannot equal her lost freedom nor efface the evils of the court: 'C'est toute tromperie, & la fraude y demeure, / Le fard, l'ambition, y seruent de pareure' (p. 105). The following scene contains a long monologue by the philosopher Tyrannion, who echoes Monime's sentiments and prepares the revelation contained in Mithridates' destiny. Whoever follows the great kings 'Se trompe, se deçoit, & contre ses desseins, / Souffre . . .' (p. 111), he warns and opposes to this thrust toward greatness the beatitude of the simple labourer, secure in his anonymity as Monime was once happy, though poor.

When the play closes, it will be with a repetition of Tyrannion's views, spoken first by the chorus and then by someone who had lived in the company of Mithridates. In the opening scene of Act V, Mithridates' sister kills herself rather than fall captive to the Romans. The chorus picks up Tyrannion's praise of the humble rustic who is 'exempt des fureurs, / Et des malheurs' (p. 173). The linking of 'fureurs' and 'malheurs' is not just for the sake of a rhyme. It goes to the very heart of the humanists' concept of man's role in bringing about his own misfortune. In the next scene, Bachilde, sent to execute his master's wives, rues the day when he entered Mithridates' service and overcome by the horror of his duty, commits suicide, crying, 'Adieu, doncques, ô Roy! ie quitte vos grandeurs, / Ie vous quitte tyrans' (p. 179).

Two other characters in humanist tragedy abandon the glories

of monarchy. In *S. Clouaud, Roy d'Orléans*, Heudon cleverly combines Christian propaganda with the general theme of vanity in
grandeur by depicting on the one hand a furious attempt on the part
of Clouaud's uncles to murder the rightful heirs to the kingdom of
Orléans and seize the crown and on the other, Clouaud's complete
indifference to his patrimony. Already in Act II the saint declares,
'Aux grandeurs d'icy bas mon courage n'aspire' (p. 29). He will not
forget his salvation for a sceptre. Subsequently he alone escapes
the assassins and at the moment when efforts to save him appear
to have carried the day, he renounces the crown to lead a hermit's
life. As we know already, Laudun's Diocletian, after presiding over
the martyrdom of several Christians, suddenly appears in the last
act 'Habille en Iardinier'. Eventually, he will be filled with remorse
for his inhuman crimes and will kill himself but Laudun keeps the
opposition between the grand and simple life so separate from
Diocletian's contrition that the chorus'

> Ores l'on recognoist bien
> Que du monde ce n'est rien
> Que d'honneur vne fumée
> Qui soudain est consumée
>
> (f. 30ᵛ)

is here as much a visual as an intellectual realization.

Vanity was the negative lesson that tragedy wished to impart
about ruling; it had a positive lesson as well: how to be a good king
and subject. Again, such points were often made within plot lines
concerned with rather different subjects. If Chrétien establishes a
distinct relationship between Amnon's passion for his sister and
Absalon's ambition to take David's crown, we would not necessarily
be prepared for the amount of political theory in the play except for
our awareness of the period's delight in argumentation. An
impromptu council is formed as Absalon seeks advice. His first
friend advises against rebellion. David is just and a subject is bound
to serve his king: 'Non, il vaut mieux perir auec vn mauuais Roy, /
Que viure bien heureux affranchis de sa Loy' (p. 35). A second
friend counsels revolt, 'Vn Royaume vaut bien de commettre
iniustice' (p. 42) and wins the day. Interesting among the arguments
used to restrain Absalon is this introduction of reason: 'La valeur
sans raison, est esclaue du blasme' (p. 40). It cements the link
between Absalon's outburst and Amnon's passionate pursuit of
Thamar and reveals to what extent the humanists were more con-

cerned with a unity in their moral perspective than in their plots.

Vasthi (Matthieu), *Les Gordians et les Maximins* (Faure), and *Adonias* (Philone) also wax eloquent on both ethical and political subjects. Unlike the other two tragedies, *Vasthi* does not concern itself with ambition and rebellion. Still, it has no difficulty in exposing many of the most familiar themes related to kingship. Assuere himself opens the play, declaring that kings are 'des Dieux la belle & viue image, / Qui reçoit de leurs mains cest vnique pouuoir' (p. 2). As the ambitious lack reason to halt their mad thrust, Assuere leaves no doubt that kings are first of all rulers of themselves:

> Mon Iupin trois fois grand tient en sa main le cueur
> Du Roy qui est de soy non des autres vainqueur,
> Qui scait de ses Espris punir la felonnie
> Auecques la raison qui tous ses faits manie.

> (p. 2)

He concludes with the observation that monarchy is the finest form of government.

Once Assuere has served his role as political theorist, Matthieu transforms him into the braggart tyrant, vaunting his exploits and comparing himself to the gods. The author's intent is made immediately obvious by an ensuing stichomythia between Assuere and his queen, who reminds him that rulers, unlike the gods, are mortal: 'Et iamais on n'a veu estre exempt vn Monarque / Des iniures du sort, du temps, & de la Parque' (p. 7), another striking example of structure and characterization dictated by didacticism.

When we reach the next scene, it becomes clear that we are also dealing with an example of those many first acts which exist at a certain distance from the remaining four. Here the separation is hopelessly great and only by verbal gymnastics could we find a thematic bond between Matthieu's introduction and the action proper. The first act opens with general remarks on the monarchy and will not leave the subject. The century often condemned unscrupulous flatterers for leading their royal masters astray, so Matthieu introduces the Princes, who assail evil courtiers. They insist that virtue, justice, piety, clemency are as important to a king as strength and valour and appear to decry the popularity of wine and 'volupté' at the court. This last point could conceivably have had implications for the main plot where the drunken Assuere sends for

his wife and repudiates her when she disobeys. However, the condemnation of the wine comes before Vasthi's disobedience and the
Princes at no later time seek to upbraid the king or to justify the
queen. *Sententiae* and plot were rarely so detached as in this tragedy.[9]

Faure and Philone were more concerned about transforming the
concept of ruling by reason into a structural as well as a didactic
principle. In *Les Gordians*, subtitled *L'Ambition*, political theory is
first brought out by the elder Gordian in a way that immediately
implicates reason. Urged to revolt against the tyrannical Maximin,
he replies:

> La Foy, fille des Dieux, doit estre inuiolable,
> Noz folles passions ne la rendent muable,
> Par la seule raison il la faut mesurer,
> Et la raison ne peut ses reigles alterer.

(f. 9ᵛ)

Moreover, if Maximin is a traitor, he accepts this fact as the gods'
will. In the second act, Gordian debates the same subject with his
son, who claims that the gods are with them. The father maintains
that the gods alone can punish the monarch. Once chosen, the
monarch must be upheld, for such is the basis of the constitutional
system at Rome. All Gordian's views, as well as those of his opponents, were most familiar to civil-war France. The elder Gordian is
dissuaded from pursuing the thoughts he expresses, joins the
rebellion, and is defeated. The defeat may mean only—as other
tragedies of the period tell us—that the gods are with no one. However, another scene in *Les Gordians* suggest that Faure sought to
justify through defeat the principles which Gordian expressed but
abandoned.

In keeping with the pattern of preaching reason to the rebel and
conceiving of kings as guided by the same faculty, Faure shows the
tyrant in Act III confronted by Modestin just after this faithful
counsellor has made clear his master's fatal error, 'Il falloit Maximin,
pour mieux fonder ta gloire / Sur toy premierement rapporter ta
victoire' (f. 44ᵛ). This idea he reiterates in diverse forms to Maximin.
He condemns the emperor's faults and urges him henceforth to be
less concerned with 'le nom, que l'honneur d'estre Roy' (f. 48ʳ). Set
together, the elder Gordian's concept of a subject's 'Foy' and
Modestin's definition of a ruler's obligation approximate well the
dominant French views on kingship and rebellion and if perchance
Faure was not expressing his own sentiments through these charac-

ters, there can be no escaping the realization that he enjoyed the spectacle of so many contemporary themes put to verse.

Philone's *Adonias* relates the story of an attempt by Adonias, oldest son of King David, to take the throne from his father before the dying monarch can guarantee its passage to Salomon. The play succeeds fully in a dramatization of the contrast between reason and fury by opposing the acts of Adonias to those of David and Salomon. Adonias opens the work by consulting with two friends. As in other council scenes, the protagonist's advisors disagree. One favours seizing the throne immediately; the other urges patience. 'Sage est celui, qui telle ardeur reprime / Par la raison' (sig. [A6ᵛ]). The supporters of Salomon quickly obtain from David a renewed promise that he, not Adonias will be proclaimed the new king. Adonias feigns obedience to Salomon but soon recommences his plotting.

> Depuis que l'aueugle desir
> De Regner vient le cœur saisir,
> C'est fait; la Raison plus n'y entre

(sig. [C7ᵛ])

comments the chorus. Next we see David on his death bed. He counsels Salomon to obey the Lord's law, advice praised by the prophet Nathan. In the final act, Salomon answers God's request to ask of Him what he wishes by seeking wisdom. Adonias reappears, scheming again, but Salomon decrees that he shall die. The judgment is recognized as just by the chorus and is certainly calculated to be the first example of Salomon's wisdom. A wise king grown wiser yet, a rebellious subject condemned for his temerity and folly: a fitting end to *Adonias* and to our study of patterns in the humanists' treatment of ambition.

Although the humanists wrote a significant number of plays constructed wholly or in part around the subject of love—that favourite topic of the Classicists—they did so without leaving the didactic perspective under examination here. In humanist tragedy the study of love leads not to any revelations about the human psyche or conflicting *devoirs* but to commonplaces on women and passion. Taken as a group, these plays resemble each other more markedly than do the works on ambition. This uniformity may be related to the intense interest of the period in love poetry and to the patterns of thought established early in that genre. They were faithfully imitated by French humanists, who very quickly associated the diction of Italian love verse with tragedy's elevated style.

E

When treating love, the playwrights of the humanist tradition divided their attention somewhat equally between depicting love as a furious rage and as a noble devotion. In the former instance, the plays follow an almost prescribed development. The lover speaks of the fierce emotion that has taken possession of him. There is no sign of an internal struggle; rather, the poet concerns himself with describing at length the lover's state in imitation of contemporary love poetry. A particularly interesting example comes from Matthieu's *Clytemnestre*, Act II. Although the play deals with the murder of Agamemnon by his wife and her lover Egiste, the lover alludes to the impending crime only at the end of an interminable monologue, composed primarily of heterometric quatrains, not the traditional *rimes plates*. He tells of once having laughed at others in love. He does not understand the fury which clouds his mind.

> Ie suis semblable au Phœnix qui consume
> Sur l'odorant bucher
> Ses os sacrez, & sa chair, & sa plume,
> Pour le repos chercher.
> . . .
> De froids glacons au lieu de fleurs se pare
> De Flore la saison,
> Le ciel pour moy se monstre trop auare
> Le monde m'est prison.
> Que ne suis-ie vn Hibou Timoniste
> Que n'est il tousiours nuict,
> Le plus clair nuit m'est nebuleux & triste,
> Le plaisir m'est ennuict.

(p. 11)

After such a description of the lover's state, the dramatist usually shows him in discussion with a friend or servant who urges use of reason and abandonment of the passion. (Where incest or infidelity are concerned, the lover's interlocutor also brings to bear the moral enormity of what is being contemplated.) These debates are predictably to no avail. Pyrrhe, in Percheron's study of the Greek's unhappy love for Hermione, offers an apt description of the perspective from which love is viewed in these plays:

> Celuy n'ayme poinct qui ayme sagement.
> Le malade qui porte en l'ardeur de sa fiebure
> Le feu dans sa poictrine et la soif sur la leure,
> N'attend impatient, se sentant embrazer,

Qu'on vienne chichement ses leures arroser,
Il boit à plein hanap . . .

(p. 22)

So Clytemnestre thirsts for Egiste, David for Bethsabée, Amnon for Thamar, Phèdre for Hippolyte, while their confidents and the chorus denounce passion's ability to supplant reason. The lovers traditionally respond that it is easy for those unafflicted with passion to speak of simple solutions. Sometimes they are confronted by what appear such invincible impediments to their desires that death seems the only issue. The confident relents and agrees to help rather than witness that misfortune. The play then develops according to the particular givens of the plot.

The portrait of passion's evil ends can occupy no more space than is left following the episodes just outlined. In *Clytemnestre*, Agamemnon returns in the fourth act. Billard's version of the Alboin story devotes so much space to Rosemund's passion for Elmechyde and Elycie's love for the same man that Alboin is killed in the last act and all the violent aftermath depicted in Chrétien des Croix' treatment of the subject falls away. Since Chrétien and Billard published their plays within two years of each other, it would be otiose to translate the differences in technique into trends away from violence and toward love. It would also be unnecessary. In Billard's long introductory scenes on love, while we find an habitual interest in exploiting the poetic possibilities of the theme, the ethical material leaves its mark. It *says* what Chrétien *shows* but the message does not change: love as rage and fury knows no law and all behaviour that places fury above reason leads to crime.

Significantly, both Billard's *Le Mérovée* and *Alboin* mix the themes of ambition and love. The concluding chorus for Act IV of *Alboin* first discusses a discovered attempt by Alboin's nephew to seize the throne. The boy is put to death:

Mais quel malheur! he quel dommage!
De perdre vn si braue courage,
Si le ver de l'ambition,
Ou bien ie ne sçay quoy de flame
N'eust trauersé cete belle ame
Seul lustre de sa Nation:
Dont le fer se deuoit venger
Non ailleurs que sur l'estranger.

(f. 156ʳ)

The next line begins 'Ce maudit amour'. Is Billard referring to the nephew's ambition or to Rosemund's passion, the subject which closes the passage? I cannot say with certainty and will merely reproduce the verses in question to show how closely related were love and ambition in conception at this time:

'Ce maudit amour ne nous donne
'Que les feus d'vne Tysiphone:
'Ne couue que meutre, & malheur:
'C'est le bris de nostre esperance,
'D'où le Ciel de nous prent vengeance,
'Eternise nostre douleur:
D'amour on ne peut rien sentir,
Que par le sens du repentir.
  La miserable Rosemonde
Ne serre de sa tresse blonde,
N'anime au fer de ses beaus yeux
Rien que ruine, & que misere,
Son œil ne nous est moins contraire
Qu'vne comete dans les Cieux:
'Malheureus don que la Beauté
'Qui s'oppose à la chasteté.

(f. 156ʳ)

It was doubtlessly inevitable that this genre, so concerned with depicting examples of human behaviour, would find inspiration in the Greek novel, its adaptations, and in the pastoral. Here, however, a more positive view of love was stressed. Neoplatonic purity and virtue sustain the lovers of the novels while the pastoral's heroine fiercely protects her chastity until her lovesick, yet purely inspired suitor wins the day. Bellone's *Amours de Dalcméon et de Flore*, Chevalier's *Philis*, and Troterel's *Tragédie de Sainte Agnès* all owe moments in their development to the pastoral, notably the scenes in which Saint Agnès and Flore disdainfully repel their importunate lovers. Chevalier's work also has ties with the Greek novel. Though Philis loves Florisel, she can exclaim that 'La femme par amour se monstre vne impudente' (f. 30ʳ). Love leads to vice:

De toutes les vertus la prudence est supreme,
L'homme qui est suiect à tous pas tresbucher,
Des obiects dangereux ne se doit approcher.

(f. 30ᵛ)

The pastoral influence may explain why Saint Agnès' suitor remains for some time a sympathetic figure. Afflicted with the familiar invincible passion, ready to die of her rebuff, Martian initially recoils in horror before the friend's suggestion that force be used. Only with time and frustration will he attempt force (Act IV).

Bellone and Chevalier offer completely sympathetic protagonists and sterling examples of love's positive portrait. After Flore has put down Dalcméon for his declaration of love, she feels herself struck by 'le feu de l'enfant de Cypris' (p. 28). Her confident urges Flore to put away this emotion and to think of her social rank. But Flore responds that Dalcméon's 'vertu' constrains her. In Act III they swear eternal fidelity. Unfortunately, Flore's father has promised her to another. The lovers flee, aided by the shade of Flore's grand-father. 'Possede la tout seul comme seul tu es digne', he says to Dalcméon, 'Pour ta belle vertu, pour ta beauté insigne' (p. 50). They are caught. Dalcméon is executed and Flore takes poison. Her father cries 'ô subit changement: / Helas que de malheurs venus en vn moment' (p. 58), before being struck down for his heartlessness.

Philis and Florisel overcome parental opposition, religious differences, and despair only to face misfortune after marriage. When Florisel dies of battle wounds, Philis languishes long enough to remind us that life is but 'vanité', that their 'Saint Amour' will not die and to be reminded that her behaviour will bring her the renown of Porcie and Cornélie. Yet fidelity is not the only distinction of these lovers. Dalcméon and Flore reject any thought of murdering her father's choice of bridegroom. Philis and Florisel refuse to consummate their love when marriage seems an impossibility. The separation of character types is quite absolute. The villains are portrayed as loving without exercising any control over their actions; the heroes love, yet prove capable of using their reason to distinguish between good and evil. At the same time, the reminder of 'vanité' and cries of 'subit changement' prove that such variety in the treatment of love does not eclipse tragedy's prime message. In fact, exposing the effects of passion often proved an equally opportune means of discoursing upon some of tragedy's favourite subjects.

In *Sichem ravisseur*, part of the confident's attempt to turn the Prince from his amorous thoughts concerns princely behaviour. 'Tousiours le forfait d'vn Prince abandonné / Retombe sur le chef du peuple infortuné' (p. 12), he warns, but in vain. When the Prince later offers marriage to the object of his passion, she refuses, repeating the leitmotif: 'Ie n'ayme les Palais, les biens, ny la grandeur: / (Certes l'estat plus bas est tousiours le plus seur)' (p. 29). Phèdre's discussion with her nurse in Act II of Garnier's *Hippolyte* covers some sixteen pages, of which very few actually treat of the immediate question of Phèdre's situation vis-à-vis Hippolyte. They discuss whether the gods excite us to incestuous love or not, whether a wife or husband may love outside of marriage, whether Thésée's absence suggests infidelity and would permit Phèdre to follow his example. The nurse pleads for the repression of Phèdre's love and Phèdre answers with the usual description of love's invincible powers. Only two pages from the close of their scene does the nurse allude to Hippolyte's refusal to love and to Thésée's possible return. The proportions speak for themselves. We are expected to find the general problems of love and gods, licence and marriage every much as engrossing as the situation at hand.

Since humanist tragedy in general enjoyed depicting the vanity of this life through kings' loss of power, it was predictable that some playwrights would introduce their lovesick protagonists as already powerless, undone by a mere child and Heudon in *Pyrrhe* and Montchrétien in *David* both found the device quite appropriate. Similarly, the century which revived the Querelle des Femmes found it appropriate to use the love theme to expose its negative view of women. When Garnier's Hippolyte speaks of Phèdre's 'sexe odieux' (f. 136[r]), he echoes not only his classical counterparts but also contemporary ones. Roillet's 1577 tragedy of *Philanire* depicts the heroic attempt by a wife to save her husband. She is tricked by the local magistrate who agrees to return the husband after Philanire has slept with him. He does not state, however, that the man will be returned alive. Philanire brings her case before the Vice-Roy. He orders them to be married, hears Philanire tell of her happy wedding night, and then sentences the magistrate to death. Philanire now pleads for her second husband as passionately as she had once done for the first, but to no avail. The double portrait of heroism and inconstancy well suits the genre's attitude toward women. Next to Porcie and Cornélie stand Marcé's Jesebel, who prompts these lines at the opening of *Achab*:

O quatre fois heureux celuy, dont la prudence,
Ne se laisse empestrer, aux lacets d'inconstance,
De ce sexe subtil . . .

(f. 4[r])

Billard's Fredegonde (*Le Mérovée*), who brings her own lover to fear for his future, since 'Ce faux sexe est leger, se repaist d'aparence'

(f. 80ʳ), and Chrétien's Rosemund (*Albouin*), used to exemplify that women are a 'sexe abominable orfelin de raison' (p. 62).

Faithful to their didactic calling, the playwrights also did not hesitate to use the love theme to exhibit the required command of style. Selections from Hermione's lament in Act III of Percheron's *Pyrrhe* give a fair impression of the vocabulary, tone, and conceits involved:

> Nourrice, dictes moy, suis ie pas malheureuse?
> Helas! ne suis ie pas malheureuse amoureuse?
> Ie suis ce qui me fuit, j'ayme mon desplaisir,
> Trop pauure d'esperance et riche de desir.
> Mon malheur est de fer, et mon bien est de verre;
> Ie cherche le repos, et sy me fais la guerre.
> Ie hai ma guarison, tout mon contentement
> Ne gist qu'au souuenir qui cause mon tourment.
> Et bref, rien de moy mesme à moy mesme il ne reste
> Que la hayne de moy pour aymer mon Oreste.

(p. 45)

Oreste was about eleven when she first saw him.

> Ton poil frizé crespu d'vn or fin jaunissant,
> Sembloit vn beau soleil sur le matin naissant,
> De tes yeux doux riantz les amoureuses flammes
> Dardoient vn feu sacré, douce fiebure des ames,
> La blancheur de ton teint honteusement vermeil
> Ces pommes ressembloit, qu'vn meurissant soleil
> Vermeillonne sur l'arbre, et ta bouche pourprine
> Promettoit le baiser et le ris de Cyprine.

(p. 4)

When Montchrétien produced his first version of *Aman*, Assuere was made to describe Ester in these terms:

> Vraiment ie ne croy pas que les rays de ses yeux
> Ne facent deuenir le Soleil enuieux;
> Et que, honteux d'auoir vne moindre lumiere,
> Souuent il ne se cache en l'onde mariniere.
> Ce ne sont yeux aussi, mais deux Astres luisans
> Et l'heur & le mal-heur en mon cœur produisans,
> Qui d'vn trait seulement me font mourir & viure,
> Et qui d'vn seul attrait me forcent à les suiure.

(vv. 1233-40)

The passage disappeared from the second version of *Aman* but lest we conclude that such language had become unacceptable, let me quote from Hardy's *Méléagre*. Atalante arrives for the hunt. Méléagre espies her:

Mais, quelle Deité maintenant nous vient voir,
La trousse sur le flanc, à Diane pareille?
Ce poil d'or crépelu, cette face vermeille
Figurent Atalante . . .

(I, 146, vv. 72-5)

She announces that she has come to show what experience has taught her. Here is Méléagre's reply:

Non certes ton secours amene dans ces yeux,
Le vaincœur enchainé du Monarque des Cieux,
Amene de renfort les amours, & les graces
Auec leur moindre effort le monstre tu terraces,
Tu charmes sa manie, & ne faut autre dard,
Autre chasse, autres rets, qu'vn amoureux regard.

(I, 147, vv. 87-92)

All these patterns of theme, style, and construction illustrate not only the playwrights' commitment to didacticism and rhetoric but also the consequences of that commitment. Composition became a process of moving out from the basic plot line, endowing it with as many themes of general interest as possible and embroidering its language with as many topoi as possible. The plot is periodically expanded, forgotten, transformed but rarely developed in order to bring into focus those tensions and forces that explain the story as it was found by the playwright. Instead, we are treated to examples of irrational behaviour and its consequences, depicted as such, with the plot serving primarily as a convenient framework, not an inspiration. It is in this perspective on plot that we can understand why love shares with ambition the interest of the humanists. One proved as satisfactory a vehicle as the other for transmitting the lessons of importance to them. Although Petrarchist love poetry told of inner struggles between reason and love, the humanists were more concerned with the victory of love and its effects. Early in Berthrand's *Pryam* Paris confesses that

vne folle erreur qui va iusqu'à l'extréme,
Qui sans sortir de moi me rend hors de moy-mesme,
Esgare ma raison, & ie ne sçay plus rien.

(p. 14)

This description of Paris' state is given to explain the impending abduction of Helen and by extension, the whole tragedy of Troy, which is related in the play to the moment of Pryam's death. Extreme in its sweep from the judgment of Paris to the fall of Troy, *Pryam* remains very characteristic of the genre in its simplistic approach to motivation and emphasis upon the result (not the determination) of emotion.

This general perspective has something to tell us regarding the most famous of the tragedies written in the early seventeenth century, Théophile's *Pyrame et Thisbé*. Lancaster held that 'A certain *gaucherie* is . . . displayed in the structure. Each of the first three scenes consists of a conversation between an important person and an attendant. No effort is made to weld them together' (*French Dramatic Literature*, Part I, 174). However, welding scenes together never constituted a preoccupation of humanist tragedy and in that each scene reveals information central to the plot, Théophile ought to be credited with more achievement than failure in the first act. At the same time, it is interesting to contemplate how Théophile develops scenes II and III along traditional lines.

The second scene takes place between Pyrame's parents. The father opposes his son's love for Thisbé, but we must wait some time to learn that Pyrame has chosen the daughter of a mortal enemy. Instead, Narbal commences by reminding his wife that when he was young and subject to love's flame: 'Tousjours mes desseins estoient avec licence, / Et mes justes desirs pleins d'heur et d'innocence' (vv. 95-6). To which his wife replies: 'On ne sçauroit dompter la passion humaine, / Contre amour la raison est importune et vaine' (vv. 107-8). Scene III shows the king who loves Thisbé incensed at her preference for Pyrame and resolved to kill his rival. 'L'aymez vous jusqu'au poinct de violer la Loy?' (vs. 193) asks Syllar. Justice is beneath kings; kings should follow the example of the gods, venting their anger at will, is the king's retort. The question, 'Le temps et la raison pourroient-ils point oster / Ces violens desirs?' (vv. 221-2), produces assurance that time and reason can only increase his desires. Since nothing can divert the king from his plan, Syllar agrees to help him.

I shall not insist upon the obvious relation between Théophile's procedure and that of his predecessors or upon this further evidence of tragedy's fascination with a plot that permits inclusion of thoughts on kingship and passion. Instead, I would point out that Théophile continues this tradition even in the absence of a chorus. It had greatly facilitated the multiplication of themes by breaking down tragedy into several small units (the chorus was used after scenes as well as acts) for which an immediate commentary was provided. To be sure, the humanists could also endow their plays with a leitmotif. Odette de Mourgues has demonstrated that it is possible to find unity in Garnier's *Hippolyte* in the orchestration of two major themes. But unity of action and thematic unity are not synonymous. The symbolism of 'bords', repeated at crucial moments in *Phèdre*, will never suffice to explain why the plot contains an ineluctable chain of events. Similarly, although Corneille enjoyed many of the humanists' techniques, especially opposing concepts, he never permitted the opposing views to exist for the sake of rhetorical display alone. They are subsequently made to interact, to establish a dialectic without which the dénouement cannot be reached. Some would say that Corneille's practice was superior since the interaction it fostered gave a dramatic sweep to the plot which we cannot find in humanist tragedy. By now, however, we should have ceased to inspect early French tragedy for dramatic traits and recognized that its energies were expended elsewhere.

Not unexpectedly, these energies were also expended with varying degrees of skill and intensity. The preceding analyses, offered under rubrics both using the word 'patterns', describe the anatomy of a genre and accentuate this aspect to the exclusion of any discussion of the relative artistic merits of each individual dramatist. The exclusion was conscious. It is in the anatomy of the genre that we observe most graphically what we have been seeking: the nexus between the genre and its public. Moreover, without prior appreciation of these very basic and widespread patterns, comparing one dramatist with another can mislead.

Mrs. Jondorf appreciates Garnier over other humanist playwrights because 'he intends his plays to provoke some serious reflections on serious problems' (p. 135). She finds no such concern in Montchrétien, whose primary concern is seen to be skilful use of language. By way of illustration, she contrasts *Les Juives* and Montchrétien's *La Reine d'Écosse*, 'where Marie Stuart's "constance" in the face of death is displayed for admiration without any complete examination of whether it is right or wrong for her to be executed' (p. 135). In truth, all these playwrights were fascinated by language. All felt that their works touched on serious problems. Montchrétien's handling of the story—depicting the vicissitudes of monarchy in Elizabeth and strong religious faith in Marie—fully responded to contemporary practice. The particular bipartite structure mirrors a debate and overlooks the question of whether Marie should have been executed in favour of the moral to be learned from each woman's dilemma. Perhaps mere words to us, the moral truths exposed furnished serious substance for innumerable humanist tragedies.

What Mrs. Jondorf ably demonstrates is that Garnier uses the patterns we have discussed in a different way from Montchrétien. In Garnier, she argues, language, tone, and moral lessons interact consistently. In Montchrétien, these elements appear in a more random, inconsistent fashion. If the distinction is valid, Montchrétien would be particularly characteristic of the genre in question; Garnier, more exceptional. Can we also say that Garnier was considered 'better'? Just as I have no doubt that Garnier's command of language surpasses his contemporaries, and that such superiority was destined to make him stand out in his own time, so I feel certain we cannot prove conclusively that Mrs. Jondorf's preference for the consistency in Garnier's technique was shared by his public. The very uniformity of perspective on tragedy in the sixteenth century that helps us to appreciate the importance of the patterns outlined above also places limits on our ability to detect the period's preferences. Basic to an understanding of the genre, these patterns are no less fundamental to a formulation of our approach to it and of the line of demarcation between its canons of excellence and ours.

3 VARIETY

In discussing theme and plot we have already seen how extremely varied humanist tragedy could be. A glance at form will reveal that here, too, the humanists' technique was scarcely uniform.

At its inception, humanist tragedy followed two rather distinct forms. One, used by Théodore de Bèze in *Abraham sacrifiant*, did not employ the term act, saw no need to divide its plot into five episodes, had choruses which spoke and sang, but did not serve to separate the main blocks of the action. These divisions were indicated by printing the word PAUSE at the appropriate moment in the text. Des Masures, Le Coq, and Bretog imitated this procedure with further variations. The other technique corresponds to Horace's outlines in the *De arte poetica*. Horace required five acts, a chorus that was also an actor, singing between acts what contributed and kept to the play's theme, favouring the good, praying that fortune might return to the unhappy and leave the proud (vv. 189-201). Buchanan, in his ever-popular *Jephthes*, adapted the precepts much as they would appear well into the seventeenth century. He used a five-act structure, permitted the chorus to speak occasionally as a character but employed it principally to signal the break between acts and to underline the moral truths contained in the preceding events.[10] Jodelle, La Péruse, La Taille followed Buchanan's example.

The subsequent history of the genre reveals an overwhelming victory for the Buchanan pattern, at least with respect to a five-act structure. Chevalier's *Philis* (1609), written in three acts 'à la mode des Italiens' (sig. ẽi^r), offers one of the rare exceptions. (The impression given by the text of Du Souhait's *Tragédie de Radégonde* that the play contains only four acts may be misleading and due to a printer's error on page 44, where the indication of a final act was omitted. The length of the preceding chorus and the blank space after the chorus' words on page 43 certainly signify a break comparable to those between the other acts.) The victory is impressive not only because of the number of tragedies to follow this pattern but also because of the nature of some of these plays. Roillet's *Tragédie françoise de Philanaire* (1563) prefigures the more romanesque plots to come but still divides its action into five parts. The *Tragédie* of Josias, published in 1566 by an unidentified Philone, who has been thought by some to be Des Masures, belongs in content to the kind of religious tragedy produced by Bèze and Des Masures, yet maintains the five-act pattern, with, it must be admitted, two indications of a PAUSE within the fourth act. Rivaudeau, too, shows the early ascendancy of this structure for religious subjects in his *Aman* (also 1566). Even Heyns' *Le Miroir des Vefues* (1596), one of the most elaborate religious works of the period, contains five acts. At the same time, Rivaudeau's choral parts are each specifically entitled 'chant', reminiscent of the 'Cantiques' to be found in Bèze and Des Masures. Heyns' *Le Miroir* is written in prose, not verse and in fact, as soon as we seek any conformity beyond the use of five acts, we fail.

For the playwrights coming after Jodelle and Des Masures, use of the chorus remained almost as diverse as it was for the earliest French humanists. There was some regularization in that a blanket refusal to use the chorus between acts did not appear again until the seventeenth century but if Heudon, Garnier, Pageau, Chrétien des Croix, Godard, and Montchrétien employed the chorus as Jodelle had done, Montreux, Billard, Le Breton, and Poullet thought nothing of occasionally omitting the chorus between acts.

This element of variety has bearing on more than one aspect of the genre's history. The disappearance of the chorus from tragedy has long been considered a step forward in the evolution toward Classical drama. Rigal gives the decision by Hardy to suppress the chorus as one of the two important reforms accomplished by the dramatist and insists that the choruses of *La Mort d'Achille* and *Coriolan* 'n'ont rien de commun avec ceux de l'antiquité; ils parlent, contribuent à l'action, remplissent des rôles de personnages' (*Alexandre Hardy*, p. 256). But Hardy was not alone in abandoning the chorus. There is none in *Sophronie* (1600), in Virey's *La Machabée* (1603), or Troterel's *Sainte Agnès* (1615), works that can have little claim to bringing humanist tragedy closer to Corneille or Racine. Hardy's use of the chorus within the acts as defined by Rigal offers nothing new since the chorus participated in dialogue at the very beginning and does so to a significant degree in such later plays as Garnier's *La Troade* and *Antigone*. Absence of the chorus does not of itself equal presence of a dramatic action. Appearing rather irregularly, the chorus, when used to close a scene or act, always served to underline the moral lessons in play. The chorus aided playwrights in their favourite enterprise—rhetorical display and moralizing—and its elaboration is but another indication of the humanists' concern for those aspects of their plays. The disappearance of the chorus may logically be related to a change of attitude regarding rhetoric and moralizing and through that review of tragedy to questions of structure and presentation but the chorus was otherwise too subordinate, too expendable an element to stand between the humanists and dramatic action.

Of no less consequence is the fact that this extensive variety within humanist tragedy enables us to look with a more critical eye at several pronouncements made about the genre in general and about its relationship to the Baroque in particular. Some views are best discarded. Loukovitch's insistence that 'Tout le long du XVIe siècle, la lutte se serait poursuivie entre le théâtre traditionnel né sur la place publique et soutenu par le peuple, et le théâtre human-iste né dans les collèges et entretenu dans les écoles et les hôtels des grands' (p. 27) creates a distinction which, as far as tragedy is concerned, the texts do not uphold. Whereas some tragedies are distinctly more akin to Seneca or to medieval drama, a larger number cannot be conveniently categorized and show that in this particular context the period's thinking was characterized by tolerance rather than strife.

Other views require some qualification. Dabney points out that during the reign of Henry IV the playwrights 'were seeking to exploit new material' (*French Dramatic Literature*, p. 449). This is exact but we would be committing an injustice to the decades before 1589 if we believed that experimentation came late to the genre. The difference in approach among works by Bèze, Bretog, Des Masures, Garnier, and Chantelouve—all written well before 1589—indicates that the early playwrights roamed quite broadly in search of inspiration. Lanson's 'Après 1580, le mélange de deux courants devient plus fréquent' (*Esquisse*, p. 31) is true only in so far as tragedies themselves become more frequent in number; the mixture of medieval and classical inspiration has a longer history.

This fact adds an interesting dimension to certain statements made by the humanists themselves. Such general diversity, coupled with the vagueness of theoretical writings of the century discussed in Chapter I, suggests that the period was somewhat at a loss when it had to refine the definition of tragedy offered by the authorities. In 1561 Grévin wrote about tragedy and comedy that he had no intention of claiming to be the first to write them in French, 'Car je sçay qu'Estienne Jodelle . . . a esté celuy qui les a tirées des Grecs et Latins pour les replanter en France. Mais aussi je diroy ceci sans arrogance, que je suis encores à voir Tragédies et Comédies Françoises, excepté celles de Médée et d'Hécuba, lesquelles ont été faictes vulgaires, et prises du Grec d'Euripide' (p. 5). Lanson argued that Grévin must have meant *printed* plays ('Etudes', p. 191). What should be our reaction, however, when Jean de La Taille says the same thing some eleven years later: 'Or parce que la France n'a point encor de vrayes Tragédies, sinon possible traduittes, ie mets ceste cy en lumiere' (p. 16)? Lanson's argument will not suffice here and even he admitted that the lack of printed texts was 'un peu moins vrai en 1572' ('Etudes', p. 191). We can, perhaps we must, conclude that one or both of these humanists possessed a specific definition of tragedy to which the others did not conform. *De l'art de la tragédie* gives us some hints as to why, in La Taille's eyes, Bèze or Des Masures were unacceptable but after analysing these hints we are still confronted by the realization that the sixteenth century produced no thorough definition of tragedy.[11]

Despite what the manuals intimate, an interest in classical letters did not insure the creation of one 'pre-classical' mould for tragedy. It took no special genius to observe that Seneca's *Hercules oetaeus* or Aeschylus' *Eumenides* ends happily and both Grégoire de Hologne (*Catharina*, sig. A2ᵛ) and Scaliger (III, 96) said as a consequence that tragedies did not always have to end in misfortune. Vauquelin maintained the same point, citing Euripides (pp. 109-10). Beaubrueil's preface to *Regulus* countering the idea of a twenty-four hour rule has been identified with the breakdown of the form established by Jodelle. But Beaubrueil's dedication and preface are perhaps even more striking because they firmly relate the author to the leaders of French humanism. We learn that Beaubrueil studied with Dorat and admired the eloquence of Muret. Moreover, he claims—quite properly—that 'doctes' writers have also broken the twenty-four hour rule (sig. [A5ʳ]). No conflict here between a popular and a humanist tradition, just another view of how best to execute tragedy. It will appear heretical if French Classicism is our point of reference but the humanists had no such perspective. Since the evidence continually suggests that style and moralizing occupied their thinking on tragedy, we may appreciate how very undaring from that perspective was Beaubrueil's preface. Like the Jesuits, who maintained in their *Ratio studiorum* that tragedies should be pious, or Laudun, who echoed his views on the twenty-four hour rule, Beaubrueil proposed nothing which conflicted with the prime concerns of humanist tragedy.

Although Rigal very early associated the rise of irregular theatre in France with a weakening of 'l'esprit classique' (*De l'établissement*, p. 13), the concept has gained in importance since literary criticism became infatuated with the Baroque. R. A. Sayce specifically defines the Baroque in terms of such a weakening: 'It involves the distortion (with no pejorative connotation) of classical forms in order that something different may be exposed' (p. 251). Recently, use of the Baroque to explain diverse aspects of French letters has come under heavy fire. Terence Cave is disturbed by its effect on the study of lyric poetry (pp. ix-x); Mrs. Jondorf has little praise for those who have seen Garnier as a Baroque writer (p. 2ff.).

Doubrovsky rejects Rousset's interpretation of change as a Baroque element in Corneille (p. 524, n. 30). I applaud their good sense and feel certain that just as we now have cause to wonder if it is possible to trace the distortion of a genre which was extremely varied from its earliest years, so our ongoing investigation into the nature of humanist tragedy will help us to evaluate certain 'Baroque' traits of that drama in a broader context.

While there remains considerable disagreement over what constitutes the Baroque, some characteristics often mentioned are also prominent in humanist tragedy. However, if a sense of instability, change, and illusion defines the Baroque, then *all* humanist tragedy is related to the Baroque. All plots constructed upon the reversal of fortune theme sought to convey the observation that life, its riches, and its glories were transitory. The intent of the play could not be achieved without showing or alluding to change or describing the unhappiness derived from change in fortune. Moreover, if we attach the term Baroque to these themes, then Boccaccio, too, is Baroque as well as Seneca and much medieval literature. The theme of change and instability was inseparable from the humanists' moral intent, the definition of tragedy that was available to them, and their source material. We do not need to postulate a Baroque sensibility to explain the theme's presence in humanist tragedy.

The Baroque has also been linked to a taste for irregular genres, such as the tragi-comedy and the pastoral, which unquestionably came into prominence after 1580. Although these genres lie outside the scope of this study, some critics, like Lanson, have spoken also of a 'tragédie irrégulière'. I have already warned against believing that all tragedy before 1580 was regular. By the same token, it would be a mistake to believe that all tragedies thereafter ceded to the lure of the irregular. Lanson lists as traits of this 'tragédie irrégulière qui se multiplie entre 1580 et 1615' both '*Vie de saints*' and '*sujets romanesques*' taken from Tasso, Ariosto, and short stories (*Esquisse*, pp. 31-2). Still Montreux' *Isabelle* (1595), taken from Ariosto, or Jean Heudon's *Saint Clouaud* (1599) are as regular as most humanist tragedies, whereas such classical subjects as Faure's *Les Gordians et Maximins* (1589) or Berthrand's *La Tragédie de Pryam* (1605) are allowed to move quite freely through time and space. (Berthrand opens with Paris' decision to give the golden apple to Venus and closes with the sack of Troy!) Subject matter can be a very deceptive gauge for determining technique in this period, just as the regular quality of humanist tragedy can be exaggerated or misunderstood.

The humanists never executed a tragedy in the manner of Racine. Drawn from the outset toward moralizing and rhetoric, they might imitate George Buchanan, who added the long debate between Jephthah and the high priest to the Biblical account, or Des Masures, who inserted in *David triomphant* a monologue of some eighty-nine lines spoken by the lovesick Michol and modelled on Dido's opening lines in the *Aeneid*, Book IV. Neither piece was essential to the action but each could easily have been justified at the time. Critics have long been dismayed by Jodelle's scene between Cléopâtre and Seleuque, which degenerates into the scolding of a servant in an almost farcical vein. But did not Jean de La Taille himself decree that tragedy should be 'bien entre-lassee, meslee, entrecouppee, reprise' (p. 11)? The basis for a Racinian plot was laid by much theoretical writing of a sort unknown to the humanists. In its place they possessed comments primarily on subject, language, and intent. These were their principal interests and there is every reason to believe that the simplicity of many humanist plots derives from an imitation of Seneca or the nature of their sources, not some conscious attempt to preserve the aesthetic superiority of the rules whenever possible.

A final Baroque trait to examine is the presence of violence. Here the statistics are all on the side of the Baroque. Although Goliath's head is held high by David in Des Masures' *David combattant* (1568), only well beyond 1580 do we find a trend toward displaying the bodies (Soret, *La Céciliade*, 1606), head (Heyns, *Le Miroir des Vefues*, 1596, Heudon, *Pyrrhe*, 1598), or heart of the dead (*Sophronie*, 1600). Interest in the details of torture also comes later (Laudun, *Dioclétian*, 1596; Virey, *La Machabée*, 1598) as do rapes on stage (Hardy, *Scédase*, 1624 and *Timoclée*, 1628) and plays with an accumulation of murders and suicides (Chrétien des Croix, *Albouin*, 1608, Du Souhait, *La Tragédie de Radégonde*, 1599, Bellone, *Les Amours de Dalcméon et de Flore*, 1610, Billard, *Le Mérovée*, 1610, Hardy, *Méléagre*, 1624, and *Lucrèce*, 1628). In addition, we find Billard justifying his subject matter against those who feel it is not of a tragic nature with the remark, 'où il y a effusion de sang, mort, & marque de Grandeur, c'est vraie matiere tragique' (sig. [ã8ᵛ]), a phrase seized upon by Adam to demonstrate a transformation in tragedy, characterized by that 'goût de l'horrible et de l'extrême violence qui apparaît dans la peinture du temps' (*Histoire*, I, 182).

It is unfortunate that Adam and others have felt inclined to derive this conclusion from the above-mentioned facts without concerning themselves further with the wider context in which Billard's remark or the new wave of violence appeared. The equation of tragedy with frightful events was hardly new in Billard's time. Senecan tragedy includes several atrocious acts occurring on stage. Scaliger mentioned 'terrible' (atroces) things as proper for tragedy and included incests in his list of precise subjects. Laudun's list, very similar to Scaliger's omits incest but includes 'viollement de filles & de femmes'.[12] There is every reason to believe that the substitution derived from simple observation rather than from a Baroque sensibility. Incest had not figured in any French tragedies composed before Laudun's *Art poétique*. However, Filleul's *La Lucrèce* (1566), Perrin's *Sichem ravisseur* (1589), and Montreux' *Isabelle* (1595) all deal with the theme of rape although the act is either avoided or not shown on stage. Even the most classical of Billard's predecessors, Jean de La Taille, linked tragedy with terrible things. Where Scaliger spoke only of 'iussa Regum' in his list, correctly rendered by Laudun as 'les commandements des Roys', La Taille gives as an example of tragic material, 'execrables cruautez des Tyrans' (p. 10). That he actually produced no work that depicts rape, torture, or blood baths must not obscure his ability to speak of tragedy in broader terms.

I am not unaware that La Taille also adapts in his *De l'art de la tragédie* Horace's dictum that the author must 'not show on the stage actions suitable for the wings and keep from the eyes [of the spectators] many things which eloquence will soon narrate in their presence' (vv. 182-4). La Taille says that one must 'se garder de ne faire chose sur la scene qui ne s'y puisse commodément et honnestement faire, comme de n'y faire executer des meurtres, et autres morts' (p. 11). There is a longstanding view that Horace and his influence account for a restraint in the dramaturgy of the early humanists which the Baroque aesthetic overturned. Lebègue specifically refers to 'l'abolition de la règle *multa tolles ex oculis*' as one of the innovations of irregular tragedy (*La Tragédie française*, p. 88). Yet Horace is very vague about which acts are to be kept to the wings. He prefers to offer a few examples—Medea killing her children, Atreus cooking human parts or the metamorphosis of Procne—and gives a clue to his sentiments only when he calls himself 'incredulus' (vs. 188) before such sights. Thus, the *De arte poetica* does not reject violence; it rejects acts which cannot be conveyed convincingly. La Taille demonstrates an excellent understanding of Horace with the adverbs 'commodément et honnestement'. When he explains himself further, he maintains that such acts should not be permitted 'car chascun verra bien tousiours que c'est, et que ce n'est tousiours que faintise' (p. 11). Secondly, even when we understand more fully what Horace's words contain, it can be asked to what degree these details bound the humanists. If Horace's word was law to the early humanists, how to explain the unwillingness of La Péruse to spare us Medea's frightful crimes in one of the first French tragedies (1566) or Scaliger's choice of a metamorphosis to be the basis of his exemplary five-act plot? And what to think of this statement by Bénigne Poissenot, friend of humanists, author of liminary poems in their praise and of a volume of *Nouvelles Histoires tragiques* (1585)? He defends the excessive acts in his and other short stories by noting, 'Les vices y sõt blasmez, on y loüe la vertue' (p. 12) and by reminding the reader that even the story of Thamar and Amnon is to be found in the Bible. It is the same problem presented by Beaubrueil and the twenty-four hour rule. In agreement over the necessity to moralize and to write in accordance with rhetoric's principles, the humanists were very varied when actually confronted with the problem of execution.

Every allusion to violence does not herald the arrival of Baroque innovation. Garnier explained in his preface to *Porcie* (1568) that he had added to Porcie's death the suicide of her nurse in order to wrap the play in more 'choses funebres et lamentables & en ensanglanter la catastrophe' (sig. A3^v). A Iosue Gondovin praised Bousy in 1582 for having learned from the Muses how to 'ensanglanter le Cene [*sic*]' (*Méléagre*, f. [4^r]). Yet in this play, fraught with potential scenes of violence, all terrible acts are narrated and only Althée's suicide appears on stage. Two suicides will not make a new aesthetic and Garnier's complete phrase shows him working within a perspective no different from that of Donatus or Scaliger.

It is equally important to recognize that many tragedies composed after 1580—sometimes by those very playwrights who amassed bodies or depicted rape in their plays—differ little from the basic approach of earlier decades. I refer, for example, to Hardy's *La Mort de Daire* and *La Mort d'Alexandre* and to Jacques de La Taille's *Daire* and *Alexandre* or to Billard's *Henry le Grand* and Belyard's

Le Guysien. Variety remains with us to the end; it reminds us that we are seeking to understand not some radical reorientation of attitude but the appearance of violence and plots involving multiple deaths.[13]

A significant clue has already been provided by Dabney, who amply documented the other characteristic of tragedy in the century's closing years and thereafter: new sources. Prominent within the new source material are the French novels and tales, for of the six plays listed above with multiple deaths in their plots, no fewer than four can be shown to derive from such material. (No specific source has been offered by critics of Billard's *Le Mérovée* and Hardy's *Méléagre* was drawn from Ovid.) I say 'such material' because only *Radégonde* and *Les Amours de Dalcméon et de Flore* are specifically listed by Dabney as taken from French novels and tales. Hardy's *Lucrèce* was, in Rigal's opinion 'emprunté à quelque nouvelle italienne' (*Alexandre Hardy*, p. 243, n.). *Albouin* by Chrétien des Croix comes principally from Paul the Deacon's *History of the Langodards*, which Dabney classified under French history. In truth this source material is only superficially varied and only superficially distinct from previous sources.

As an earlier part of this chapter has demonstrated, the moral concerns of humanist tragedy coincide dramatically with those of the 'histoires tragiques'. Yet from reading Boccaccio, Boaystuau, Tahureau, or Le Roy, we know also that the association between a 'tragedy' and the effects of love or ambition existed long before 1580. Consequently, it is possible to argue that the multiplication of sources which Dabney has documented is no departure from established techniques but the natural exploitation of that very large body of *exempla* already recognized as containing tragic material but not yet exhausted. Forsyth lists exactly twenty-six original tragedies published between 1550 and 1580, hardly enough to represent a norm. We could say that the earliest plays showed a distinct preference for Greek and Roman subjects but it is just such an observation that leads us astray.

The humanists sought above all stories with a moral. When a popular tale had the outlines of tragedy, the moral was superimposed (Virgil's Dido) but more often the moral lines appeared in the source. I do not think that Jodelle chose to write about Cleopatra, Montreux and Montchrétien, about Sophonisba simply because they were women of antiquity who had met with a sad end. Jodelle and Montreux read of their characters in Plutarch; Montchrétien read Livy, where narration and moralizing were almost as common as in humanist tragedy. In editing Jodelle's *Cléopâtre captive*, Lowell Ellis affords important evidence to suggest that Jodelle's play owes much to Claude de Seyssel's abridged translation of Plutarch's life of Marc Anthony. Ellis gives innumerable details from the Seyssel text which appear in Jodelle; however, it is equally possible to show that Jodelle was sensitive to Plutarch's moral portrait of Anthony and Cleopatra. The long monologue which opens *Cléopâtre captive*, in particular, reproduces the perspective on the lovers contained in Plutarch. Anthony's irresponsible treatment of Octavia and his own men (vv. 106, 114) Plutarch, too, underscored (f. 434^{r-v}, f. 435^v, f. 437^r), as well as Anthony's ambition (ff. 435^v-436^r) and lack of judgment resulting from love's blinding powers (f. 439^r, f. 441^{r-v}). In telling the story of Scipio the African, Plutarch alludes to the meeting between Massinissa and Sophonisba which sets in motion the tragic love affair but Montreux preferred to begin elsewhere. Sophonisba never appears in his first act, devoted, as we have seen in another context, to a discussion between Scipio and Syphax. In Syphax' first speech he characterizes himself as an example of the gods' unjust treatment of men—a particularly piteous example because as kings are meant to savour more happiness than their subjects, so the more cruel is their fall from greatness. The two then discuss the reasons for Syphax' misfortune, touching eventually on the role of Sophonisba, who turned Syphax against the Romans. Syphax even dares to warn Scipio that Sophonisba may do the same with her new husband.

Montreux has opened his play with chapter XXVII of Plutarch's life of Scipio. The defeated Syphax is to appear before the Roman general.

Du commencement tous furent joyeux, quand il leur fut dit qu'on amenoit Syphax prisonnier au camp: mais après quand ils le veirent lié & garroté, tous furent esmeus à pitié le voyans en si piteux estat, pour la memoire qu'ils avoyent de sa grandeur & majesté. Car il leur souvenoit combien grande avoit esté un peu auparavant la renommée de ce roy, combien grandes avoyent esté ses richesses, & la puissance d'un si grand royaume: mais le voyans puis après tumbé de si hault estat en ceste misere, ils en avoyent pitié.

(IX, 551)

Syphax confesses to Scipio his wife's influence over him, a remark which leads Plutarch to remind the reader that Sophonisba has now married Massinissa. 'Ces choses furent bien tost signifiées à Scipion, dequoy il fut grandement troublé', (IX, 552), fearing that Massinissa's action had already showed some disrespect for the Romans and repulsed by what Plutarch calls Massinissa's 'orde paillardise' (IX, 553). Within a few more lines, Scipio has upbraided Massinissa and Sophonisba is dead.

To say the least, there is nothing dramatic about the way in which Jodelle and Montreux begin their tragedies. Their practice does follow closely the unfolding of their source material, however, and we are doubtlessly witnessing another indication of the humanists' interest in moralizing, not dramatizing.

Livy's description of the Sophonisba-Massinissa story has much in common with Plutarch. If he adds a speech by Sophonisba to Massinissa and some comment regarding her effect upon the hero (XXX, xii, 17-18), he, too, indulges in accentuating Syphax' changed state and the political side of Massinissa's marriage. Scipio's eloquent plea to Massinissa to abandon his new bride was certain to catch the attention of the humanists.

But of those virtues on account of which my friendship might seem to you desirable there is none on which I might have prided myself so much as on self-restraint and continence. This virtue I would have you also, Massinissa, add to your other remarkable excellences. There is no danger—believe me, there is none—so great to our time of life from armed enemies as from pleasures all about us.

(XXX, xiv, 5-7)

Massinissa weeps, reminds the general of his promise to Sophonisba, and sends off the poison. The accent falls precisely on those elements of interest to a humanist: two grand speeches, a defeated king, the death of a queen. Montchrétien, like Jodelle and Montreux, follows his source closely, including all these themes. The result is not a love story either, but a rendering of Livy faithful to source and genre.

The sources for the so-called violent plays and especially those which amass a fearsome number of deaths offer the very same guidelines. Rigal is quite right to point out that although Hardy identifies his source for *Scédase* as Plutarch's life of Pelopidas, this account is far too brief and Hardy's real source can be found in a shorter work by Plutarch, entitled in the Amyot translation, *Estranges Evénemens advenus pour l'amour*. I see no reason to belabour the obvious import of such a title for Hardy or his predecessors or to explain why Hardy might have felt a tale so entitled worthy of the tragic genre. Bellone's source is an almost predictable *Histoire tragique des constantes et fidelles amours de Dalchemion et de Flore*, by a J. Philippes (1589) and Dabney's 'A Sixteenth Century French Play Based on The *Chastelaine de Vergi*' established that Du Souhait's *Radégonde* was inspired by Marguerite de Navarre or Belleforest. Very near the beginning of Marguerite's adaptation of the story, Parlamente speaks of the duchess' love as 'oultre raison' (p. 401). In Belleforest's version, too, the moral is stated immediately: 'De là pourront apprendre hommes & femmes, à ne soumettre le col au dangereux ioug d'amour si librement, qu'ils en demeurent enchainez, de façon qu'ils ne puissent apres rompre ni deslier l'entrelacé lacqs du fils de Venus' (V, 178).

Paul the Deacon likewise judges amply the characters who figure in the story of Alboin. Not only is Alboin praised for his deeds and bearing and Rosemund denounced for her wickedness, but also Book II, xxix adds to the death of Helmechis and Rosemund: 'thus these most wicked murderers perished at one moment by the judgment of God Almighty' (p. 85).

The plays enjoy making comparable pronouncements. The very first speech by the chorus in *Radégonde* reminds us of the strength of love: 'Que l'Amour à de force / Grands & petits il force' (p. 17). Later it calls our attention to the changing sentiments of the duchess, 'Voyez comme ceste Dame, / En rage changea sa flamme' (p. 35) and closes the play with this observation: 'Rien ne peut se celler: Le grand Dieu irrité / Aux despens des meschans monstre la verité' (p. 48). The Lombard soldiers praise Albouin (Chrétien's spelling) as Paul the Deacon had done: Longinus echoes Paul's final words by associating the fate of the regicides with that of all 'perfides' who wish to 'trahir les Rois oingts du Seigneur, / Qui les maintient tousiours en leur Royal honneur' (p. 108). The community of perspective appears in F. M. P.'s 'Stances' to Chrétien which summarizes the play's message with 'L'honneur suit la vertu, le peché le suplice' (sig. A4ᵛ) and in Montreux' calling Rosemund and Alboin 'Miroirs de la sainte Iustice' (*Amnon*, sig. ãɪᵛ). Iphicrate, confident of the two Spartans who will commit the rape and murders in Hardy's *Scédase*, shows that Plutarch's message about love was not lost on the playwright. Reacting to the haste of the Spartans to reach Scédase's house, he comments:

Ainsi court à la voix de l'hyene homicide,
Le pasteur que nommé deuore la perfide,
Ainsi le chant mortel des filles d'Achelois,
Les compagnons d'Vlisse a perdus autrefois,
Ainsi la volupté (iaçoit qu'on me le nie)
Exerce sur tous deux sa libre Tyrannie:
Ce mal desesperé les remedes passant,
Cette erreur en fureur mania que croissant,
Que funestes effets ne peuuent plus produire.

(I, 75)

Perhaps more important still, these plays depend upon the familiar *sententiae* of all humanist tragedy for their development. It is one thing to observe that more deaths occur here than elsewhere; another, to recognize that these deaths bring about no marked change in the way the plot is handled. Iphicrate's presence in *Scédase* has no function other than to provoke a discussion about the nature of love. Du Souhait's first act has no equivalent in the Châtelaine's story but a debate between a lovesick mistress and her rational nurse conjures up not only classical models but humanist patterns already discussed. The following act employs the principle of opposites, juxtaposing the evil duchess and the faithful lover in a way that incites the chorus to engage in a detailed comparison of vice and virtue. Act III shows the duchess falsely accusing the virtuous Floran and is glossed as an example of the effects of anger. The final act dispatches all the deaths within the last thirty lines. Its accent is elsewhere, on the principle of opposites again, comparing the violent feelings of the duchess with the constancy of Floran and his beloved. In Chrétien des Croix' *Albouin*, the conspiracy against Albouin does not begin until Act IV, although his impending death is the main concern of the prologue. What transpires in Acts I, II, and III derives its importance from the many opportunities to discuss the vagaries of fortune: Narcez's fall from power, warnings to Albouin about to make war again, fears of Rosemund and of Albouin himself about his future. If Chrétien was fascinated by the the carnage to come, would he have waited so long? Moreover, even when Rosemund's evil scheme begins to take form, the action is periodically halted for those stylistic (and moral) excursions the humanists adored. We are treated, for example, to a touching scene between Peredée and Barcee, who occupy part of the fourth act with lyric praises of constancy and declarations of their mutual love. After Peredée is tricked into helping murder Albouin, he engages

Almachide in a protracted debate on the potential outcome of the regicide. Peredée fears the people: 'De tout peuple mutin la prompte émotion, / Aporte bien souuent grande confusion.' Almachide answers, 'Vn peuple preuenu à domter est facile', to which Peredée opposes 'Apaiser vn tumulte est chose dificile' (p. 80).

Two conclusions appear reasonable from the above. Whether we talk of conception or execution, it is less easy to separate the so-called Baroque phase of French tragedy from its earlier years than has been thought and secondly, when judging the importance of certain late tragedies, it is debatable to what degree we should separate the many murders and suicides from the moral framework into which they fit. These observations may not suffice to assure every reader of the shaky ground on which the Baroque approach is based. Nonetheless, they derive from facts and offer an interpretation of French humanist tragedy that is consonant with the contemporary material we possess regarding its aims, its effect, its importance, its nature.

Nothing has been said yet about the remaining manifestations of violence—the exposed corpses, heads, and scenes of torture. Of the first phenomena, excepting the display of Goliath's and Holofernes' head, I offer no explanation other than the realities of the French Religious Wars. Decades in length, staggering in their horror, they brought the French nation into daily contact with death. By 1600 the horrible had truly become the familiar. With respect to Des Masures' *David combattant* and Heyns' *Le Miroir des Vefues*, it is impossible to read Des Masures' Biblical source or the *Apocrypha* account in Judith, chapter 14, without realizing that the head of the enemy was displayed not out of pleasure in violence, but to signal victory. It is also impossible to read the two plays and to believe that the authors were concerned with the macabre.[14]

The torture scenes in Virey's *La Machabée* have achieved some prominence because of Rousset's discussion of the play in his *La Littérature de l'âge baroque en France*. Comparing *La Machabée* to Garnier's *Les Juives*, Rousset concludes:

Virey, comme Garnier, veut exalter la résistance, l'intégrité d'âmes écrasées sous le malheur, mais il fait porter tout l'accent dramatique sur le malheur, un malheur physique, visible, sanglant et spectaculaire. La mort n'est plus la substance secrète de la tragédie . . . elle est arrachement à la vie, long cri haletant, agonie déchiquetée en multiples fragments.

(p. 84)

If Rousset cannot be challenged for finding Virey's work different from *Les Juives*, a Baroque obsession with death does not offer the only way to distinguish between the authors. Garnier could present the physical horror of death when he chose to. I think of this portrait of Astyanax in *La Troade:*

> Son corps est tout froissé, tout moulu, écaché,
> Rompu, brisé, gachy, demembré, dehaché,
> Sa teste par morceaux, la cervelle sortie,
> Et bref vous ne verrez une seule partie
> Qui n'ait les os broyez plus menu que le grain
> Qu'on farine au moulin pour le tourner en pain:
> Si qu'il semble plus qu'une difforme masse
> Confuse de tout poinct, sans trait d'humaine face
> Ny d'humaine figure, et puis le sang, qui l'oint,
> Fait qu'en levant un membre on ne le cognoist point.

(vv. 1939-48)

La Machabée and *Les Juives* are different plays because the role of torture in 'exalting the resistance' of the characters, as Rousset phrases it, varies markedly and because the situation between torturer and tortured also varies. The respective sources help to point out these differences.

Only one of Garnier's Biblical sources (II Kings 25:7) even refers to the murder of Zedekiah's sons and the putting out of his eyes. Jeremiah 29:21 simply prophesies the death of the children. Yet all three (Kings, Jeremiah, and II Chronicles 36) make clear that Zedekiah has sinned against the Lord, who will punish Zedekiah through Nebuchadnezzar. As Garnier himself tells us, Josephus Flavius relates Zedekiah's story in greater detail. The king's wrongs are cited, his punishment revealed and justified through these words by Nebuchadnezzar: 'Le dieu est grant qui ta [*sic*] prins en sa hayne pour ta mauuaistie et assubiecty a noz cõmandemens' (f. xciii). In the *Apocrypha*, II Maccabees 7, Virey found an extended description of the torture inflicted by Antiochus, replete with his commands and the proud words of the Maccabees, who prefer to die rather than eat flesh forbidden by their law. One dramatist thus possessed an ample source centred on torture; the other only the outlines of a tragedy, centred on sin, punishment, and the ways of God.

Torture is belaboured in *La Machabée* because without it the story cannot make its point that the heroes are ready to die for their religion, that, in the words of one of them to their mother,

'Madame, du tyran l'insatiable rage / N'amolira iamais nostre ferme courage' (p. 29). If the play makes us endure the seven individual deaths, so does the *Apocrypha*, allowing the faithful to appreciate the defiant response of each martyr before he dies. Because Garnier chose to portray the misfortune of a sinner, one who had already suffered much before the murder of his sons, *Les Juives* could not indulge in the stark black and white drama Virey created. The play shows that Garnier was very sensitive to Zedekiah's mistakes, but sensitive more to the complexities inherent in God's choice of the tyrant Nebuchadnezzar to punish Zedekiah. An *étalage* of Nebuchadnezzar's cruelty could only underscore an established fact—the black heart of the Babylonian—and no amount of torture could wash away Zedekiah's faults. Appropriate to a work about martyrdom, torture and death were peripheral concerns in a study of God's acts. Despite Rousset's judgment, it is the divine will which emerges from *Les Juives* as the frightful secret of tragedy. There may be cries and agony in *La Machabée* but they are sweet to those who know that God will give them everlasting life. Every misfortune —even captivity—is agony to Garnier's Sédécie, who for so long does not understand why he chould be punished by a man more wicked than he.

Before leaving the Baroque question, I think it valuable to quote two students of other tragedies about the place of violence in those works. Mendell says this about Senecan drama: 'In each of the cases cited of horror enacted on stage the action is far from clear and of course has to be inferred from the spoken word' (p. 93). Miss Bradbrook observes that in Elizabethan tragedy 'the style was thought of as something apart from, and imposed upon the material. . . . In *The Spanish Tragedy* and *Titus Andronicus* the atrocities are quite cut off from the sober and sententious speeches of the characters; there is no vital connection between the bloody acts and the moral dialogue' (pp. 77-8). Both quotations appear to me germane to French humanist tragedy. We know some were acted; we know little of how this was done or particularly of how much an effort was made to render realistically the battles, let alone the rapes or tortures called for. That the humanists placed style most high among their concerns remains, however, an indisputable fact and the distance between moral and means in their plays can be oftentimes no less great than in the examples of Elizabethan drama mentioned by Miss Bradbrook. Added to the material already presented in this chapter, these final considerations offer still more reasons to rethink the role of violence in humanist tragedy.

If the intent of our words on variety has been to question the theory of a gradual evolution in French tragedy after 1580 away from the form used by Jodelle, this does not mean that changes are impossible to detect over these years. It means rather that 'irregularity' or 'Baroque' may not be the best words to indicate such change. Tied from its inception to moral concerns of the day, humanist tragedy continued throughout its history to reflect such concerns which, not unexpectedly, knew changes in emphasis over the years. Buchanan and Théodore de Bèze remind us in their tragedies of the religious ferment of the day; Garnier and Pierre Matthieu echo the contemporary discussions on political theory. The debate on astrology in Behourt's *Esau* may reflect the fact that astrologers were often the object of criticism in a period that believed man could not presume to know the intent of the divine.[15] Humanist tragedy of the early seventeenth century culled from its surrounding culture a pronounced Stoic tone, fascination with a thirst for glory, and unending praise of chastity. The rise of Stoicism at the close of the sixteenth century has been too well documented to require any discussion here. With respect to the interest in glory and chastity, it will be recalled that these themes were also prominent in the fiction of the day.

Humanist tragedy incorporated these new concerns easily, since, probably through Seneca, it had always had a Stoic bent and expressed admiration for the miserable soul who bore heroically his misfortune. The traditional debate between distraught protagonist and confident normally included a good Stoic injunction to face difficulty with constancy, to oppose emotion with reason. But only in a 1599 tragedy, Du Souhait's *Radégonde*, do we find the duchess' confident replying to 'On ne peut aisement dompter sa passion' with 'Mais telle passion ne surmonte le sage' (p. 15). The same sage inspires another character in the play, Duke Ferdinand, who resists the effects of anger with 'Vn homme sage doit moderer son courroux' (p. 29). The play repeatedly accentuates the wages of strong emotion. The hero Floran thrusts at Radégonde:

L'Amour cause la mort des hommes les plus braues
L'Amour par ses effets rend les libres esclaues.
L'Amour fait renuerser les plus riches citez,
L'Amour est cause en fin de nos aduersitez.

(p. 21)

The chorus claims, 'Iamais vn homme vertueux / Ne peut estre voluptueux' (p. 25) and says with respect to Radégonde's acts: 'Voyez combien le courroux, / A de pouuoir dessus nous' (p. 35).

Similarly, although the main lines of Alexander's story remain the same in the tragedies written by Jacques de La Taille and Hardy, certain details are present in the Hardy play to give it a more pronounced Stoic cast. The earlier work has Alexander initially resist the notion of flight from Babylon for fear of 'soiling his honor' only to cede to the prophet's argument that his army would be lost without him. When the philosopher appears to condemn Alexander's decision, the ensuing debate takes place between the philosopher and the prophet. Alexander merely admits to the validity of the philosopher's ideas. Hardy never takes the spotlight from Alexander and does not permit any consideration of flight, however temporary. Alexander alone deals with the prophet saying,

> Craignent, craignent la mort ceux de qui le tombeau
> La memoire engloutit ne laissant rien de beau,
> Mes gestes immortels chez la race future,
> N'ont plus qu'apprehender de pareille auanture.

$$(IV, 52-3)$$

When the Mage (Hardy's name for the prophet) persists, Alexander calls him 'importun' and orders him to retire and not trouble his 'repos' (IV, 53). Hardy may have meant by 'repos' some superficial state of calm enjoyed at Babylon now that Alexander has conquered his enemies. I would rather think, in view of the previous quotation and the lines just preceding 'repos' ('Tes superstitions, tes menaces friuoles / N'étonnent qui ne craint, non la cheute des poles'), that Hardy speaks of a more spiritual repose, one achieved partly by certainty of renown and partly by victory over the fear of death. Both represent singularly *active* achievements and contrast in that way with the Alexander of La Taille's play, where acceptance to stay derives from the hero's realization that he must accept what fate decrees.

Concern with renown appears even in Alexander's enemies as depicted by Hardy. While plotting the assassination they are moved to speak these lines: Iolas—'La gloire du sujet recompense ma vie, / Si le destin permet qu'elle me soit rauie.' Cassandre replies, 'Partageons le peril & le los à moitié, / L'honneur me le commande ainsi que l'amitié' (IV, 56). There is nothing comparable in La Taille. The high-sounding words are not out of character either. Inspired to oppose the great general by many of the reasons also found in La Taille, they are not content with a simple enumeration of Alexander's evil deeds. Cassandre finds emperor worship rebarbative because it is a 'Spectacle intolérable à un courage fort' (IV, 55). Late humanist tragedy has a large share of men and women with such a 'courage fort' and even some plays devoted exclusively to them. Did not Billard himself designate as tragic material 'effusion de sang, mort & *marque de Grandeur*' (sig. ã8ᵛ, my italics). Death and blood were parts of the oldest definitions of tragedy available to the humanists. Grandeur had been related to style, to the social rank of the protagonist but not to subject matter. It is of course possible that Billard intended his phrase to repeat the commonplaces about tragic style. If he did, the plays he and others wrote in the early 1600's leave no doubt, nevertheless, that 'signs of Grandeur' were important for the material as well as the style of tragedy.

Prévost's observation when dedicating *Edipe* that 'Le vertueux pourtant du desir est espris / D'acquerir du renom' (sig.[ã2ᵛ]) might serve to define the mentality in question. Earlier dramatists had shown awareness of an ethic that placed great emphasis on honour. Jacques de La Taille's Alexander feels dishonoured to die poisoned instead of struck down in battle and the chorus in Garnier's *Porcie* asserts that

Il n'est trespas plus glorieux
Que de mourir audacieux
Parmy les troupes combatantes.

(f. 23ᵛ)

But, as Prévost's verses suggest, later plays concern themselves with characters so eager for glory that they actively seek it out. An interesting sign of shifting sentiment appears in Chrétien des Croix' *Les Portugaiz infortunez*. André Vaseo begins a long monologue praising the simple life free of ambition, avarice, or pride. Before the familiar theme has been fully exploited, however, Vaseo changes perspective:

Mais vne ame hardie altierement desdaigne
Ce qui d'oisiueté laschement s'accompagne,
Sachant que dans les cœurs de plaisirs abatus
Ne reluist iamais l'honneur, ni les vertus.

(p. 13)[16]

When the women of Coriolanus' family discuss going to dissuade him from attacking the Romans, Thierry has one argue that they have the means to 'grauer [leur] gloire / Immortelle à iamais au temple de memoire' (p. 51). Billard's *Guaston de Foyx*, Montchrétien's *Hector* and *Les Lacènes* deal almost exclusively with a thirst for glory. *Les Lacènes* is the most extreme case and the most revealing. The play relates in the manner of *La Machabée* a series of heroic deaths. A group of prisoners agrees to risk death rather than continue their unhappy state. Release is not their only aim. As Agis declares before he and two others attempt their plan: 'Chacun de nous trois hazardera sa vie, / Pour rendre son renom plus grand que toute enuie' (p. 178). When the attempt fails and the men have met death, their women resolve to follow their example.

This fierce will to achieve fame is also reflected in the various chaste women of humanist tragedy. Imitating their Greek novel ancestors and cousins of the Italian pastoral, Chrétien's Thamar, Troterel's Sainte Agnès, Montreux' Isabelle and Du Souhait's Constance all express themselves in absolute terms. The context may vary—Agnès wishes to be faithful to her heavenly spouse, Constance upholds her faith in 'vn parfait mariage' (p. 42), a sentiment which recalls Marguerite de Navarre's 'parfaite amour'—yet each agrees that life itself cannot outweigh the value of her honour.

Important as these developments are for establishing further links between tragedy and other didactic literature of the day (or demonstrating that all in Corneille is not new), I believe that their major significance resides in their ties with the violent, romanesque, drama of the same period. Still very concerned with moralizing, plays like *Radégonde*, Billard's *Le Mérovée*, Chrétien's *Albouin*, or Hardy's *Méléagre* break with the majority of earlier French tragedies in portraying the actively evil and their downfall within a non-Biblical context. Porcie, Cornélie, Cléopâtre, Didon, while not always above reproach, furnish in essence the portrait of fortune's passive victims. The interpenetration of tragedy, romanesque tales, and Stoic philosophy encouraged the dramatists even more to moralize through the portrait of disobedience or its opposite, yet brought them also to depict the character who heroically seized glory in misfortune or who ignominiously wallowed in vice.

Because the perspective is one of fascination with the will to act, it is rather different from the religious conviction that produced earlier tragedies on a Biblical subject. There, not only are we expected to abhor the evil characters, but the author lavishes his talent on stripping them of any grandeur while painting his hero in glowing terms. In later humanist tragedy energy and fierceness are divided among the good and the bad, proving that long before Corneille's Médée or Cléopâtre, a French dramatist might expend as much skill depicting the vicious as he did the virtuous. And why not. One was but the moral reverse of the other. When Radégonde's confident points out that 'Le blasme pourra nuire à nostre renommee, / Ainsi que vous viurez ainsi serez nommee', Radégonde replies by turning inside out the principles that sustained the more chaste women of tragedy: 'Mieux vaut viure trois iours en son contentement, / Que de viure tousiours en renom seulement' (p. 17).

Interest in the active portrait of vice and virtue over fortune's passive victims could not help but produce more dramatic plays, if by dramatic we mean 'possessing scenes of violence and confrontation'. Whether such was the intent or not would be difficult to prove in the absence of any contemporary documents on the subject. We can point with assurance only to a correlation between the ever-widening spectrum of subject material—novelle, Ariosto, Tasso, Greek novels—and evolving literary tastes in France over the same period. It would have been truly exceptional if tragedy had remained closed to these works, especially since certain ones approached their subjects from a didactic angle comparable to that already used by the humanists. Personally, I am inclined to believe that the primary attraction remained the themes to exploit, that the subsequent filling out of the plot was a by-product, not an aim. The genre had flourished and developed through exploitation of themes. It was long before a public without the question of a more dramatic presentation having been raised. But if I am mistaken, we must yet contend with the fact that such an expanded plot line of itself could not break the tradition of rhetorical language, overt moralizing, episodic construction, and symbolic, one-dimensional characters. I have already pointed out that simple reversal of fortune plots satisfied few humanists and whereas their presentation of fortune varied to the end, in these stories of shining virtue or murky evil, the moral lesson came through unequivocally. When one thinks that in 1610 a friend of Billard, Motin, characterized the content of his tragedies as 'Des Princes l'estat lamentable' (sig. ã5^v) and that La Péruse, writing in 1556 to Saint Gelais, praised tragedy for putting 'deuant les ïeus les exemples de l'humaine vie' (*La Médée*, sig. A2^r), it is clear that more than Aristotelian rules would have to come into play in order to prepare the way for Classical drama. The chapter to follow discusses which broader questions concerned the early 1600's and how directly or indirectly they affected the future of the new century's humanist heritage.

NOTES TO CHAPTER III

[1] Compare this remark by Ellis, introducing his edition of Jodelle's *Cléopâtre captive*, 'Jodelle uses the facts of the story [by Plutarch] but without translating them into dramatic action. He does not begin *in medias res* but so conceives his plot that Anthony is already dead as the play opens' (p. 22), with Marie Delcourt's observation regarding play and source: 'Hécube est malheureuse sans avoir été coupable. L'enseignement essentiel de son histoire c'est *ne quis fortunae magnae nimium confidat*. Jodelle comprend de la même manière la destinée de Cléopâtre: Plutarque l'achemine à l'intelligence du tragique tel que le comprenaient les anciens. On saisit donc dans *Cleopatre captive* le lien qui unit les deux articles de la poétique humaniste sur la tragédie à sa renaissance: c'est parce que le sujet est emprunté à l'histoire qu'il donne une idée frappante de la fragilité du bonheur' ('Jodelle et Plutarque', p. 52). I am certain that Miss Delcourt is correct to see the nexus in an example of fortune's work and to leave out any judgment of Jodelle's handling of the potential plot.

[2] See above, p. 40.

[3] See my 'The Place of Garnier's *Bradamante* in Dramatic History', *AUMLA*, 26 (1966), 260-71.

[4] See above, p. 86.

[5] Let me give one example from the last act of Rivaudeau's *Aman*. The act opens with a long monologue by Harbone. He describes the magnificence of the banquet prepared for the king and hints that this dinner may well prove fatal to Aman. The scene is well set but before retreating, Harbone pronounces thirty-six more verses on the power and nature of beauty. His 'Ie tarde trop icy' (p. 121) would probably appear slightly comic in a modern performance of the play. Its presence assures us that Rivaudeau and his contemporaries had a rather different concept of dramatic action, one that always permitted delay when moral points could be made.

[6] The theme appears in Heyns' *Miroir*, p. 37, Amboise's *Holoferne*, f. 23^r, Faure's *Gordians*, f. 1^r, Billard's *Le Mérovée*, f. 85^r (for 83), Matthieu's *Aman*, p. 34 in its traditional form. Montchrétien uses it in *La Reine d'Ecosse* to convey Elizabeth's weariness of the trials of ruling, p. 71, and in *Sichem*, p. 16, it becomes a lover's complaint against love's dominion.

[7] See my article 'Dido and Aeneas, Theme and Vision in the Third Book of the *Franciade*', *Neophilologus*, XLIX (1965), 289-96.

[8] See also Jacques de La Taille, *Alexandre*, f. 13^r; Percheron, *Pyrrhe*, p. 33; Garnier, *La Troade*, vv. 1397-8; and Hardy, *La Mort de Daire*, IV, 13, vv. 23-4.

[9] Another example of this separation can be found in the Princes' denuncia-

F

tion of women in Act II, followed after Vasthi's defiance by their attempt in Act III to convince the king not to judge all women by his wife.

[10] Horace's translator in the Loeb Classical Library series, H. Rushton Fairclough, gives for verse 195 'which does not advance and fitly blend into the plot'. I find this a somewhat misleading translation of the noun propositum. The Latin word for plot was argumentum, not propositum. The humanists, already conditioned to appreciate above all tragedy's message, would have been quite justified in pointing to this verse and to Horace's choice of propositum as further evidence that effort was to be expended in the direction of the play's theme rather than its story.

[11] Compare also Billard's confession about the subjects of his plays: 'tel les voudra dire peu tragiques, au moins quelques vns' (sig. ã8ᵛ), when in truth they offer little to distinguish them from the works of other humanists.

[12] See p. 9.

[13] Adam recognizes the close relationship between the 'violent' drama and earlier tragedy but prefers to see the coexistence of didacticism and violence as something 'étrange' (Histoire, I, 182), heightening thereby (but perhaps unintentionally) the impression of some incompatibility between the two.

[14] See above, p. 88, for Heyns' own description of his intent.

[15] See [Andrea Alciati,] Livret des Emblemes de maistre Andre Alciat, [trans. J. Le Fèvre] Paris, 1536, sig. H1ᵛ; [Barthélemy Aneau,] Picta poesis Lyons, 1552, p. 113; and [Gilles Corrozet,] Hecatomgraphie Paris, 1541, sig. K6ᵛ.

[16] Compare the tone and vocabulary of Chrétien with an earlier appearance of this theme in Beaubrueil's Regulus. Attilie remarks that all of his ancestors were content with anonymity, 'S'estimantz plus heureux en leur estat champestre / Qu'aux Villes où l'Enuie ha dequoy se repaistre', yet, 'celuy gaigne vn los magnifique / Sur les aultres humains, qui de la republique / Les affaires epouse (pp. 1-2).

IV THE FATE OF THE HUMANIST AESTHETIC

I   AN HYPOTHESIS

For generations, there has been little doubt that one could pinpoint the creation of French tragedy:

> Jodelle . . . avait vingt ans lorsqu'il fit jouer devant la cour sa *Cléopâtre captive*, notre première tragédie. L'événement fut célébré avec enthousiasme par Ronsard et les autres poètes de la Pléiade. Aujourd'hui la pièce nous paraît longue et lente, et nous y trouvons fort peu d'action dramatique. . . . Il en sera de même de toutes les tragédies du XVIe siècle. Cependant, cette œuvre annonce le théâtre classique par sa composition en *cinq actes* . . . et par l'apparition des trois unités. La rupture est complète avec la tradition médiévale.[1]

Such an analysis has thrived because it combines a concern for form with the opportunity to make of the sixteenth century France's Renaissance. Supposedly grounded in the rules and models of antiquity, French Classicism appeared the obvious culmination of humanist activity, and given the undisputed quality of Classical literature, there could be no shame in rendering the sixteenth century a preparation for France's Classical moment. There could be little error as well. Did not the Pléiade specifically call upon poets to abandon the medieval genres and to turn toward antiquity for inspiration; did not *Cléopâtre captive* prove markedly different from medieval plays? The difficulty with a theory based on the evolution of form is mirrored in the fact that we cannot answer this last question by a simple 'yes'.

All the evidence of the preceding chapters has demonstrated that despite the changes in form which occurred during the sixteenth century, in purpose, characterization, even concept, tragedy did not undergo radical change. By the same token, were we to reflect a moment, would we not admit also that it is impossible to reduce the essence of Corneille or Racine to their form and that the qualities we admire in Corneille and Racine are as absent from Jodelle and Garnier as from Marguerite de Navarre or the *Mistére du Viel Testament*? Resemblances in form create one pattern of affinities; resemblances in concept and intent trace a different one in which the sixteenth century appears far closer to the period that preceded it than to French Classicism. The chapter on humanist dramaturgy has brought out some of the principal reasons for making such a statement. Yet there are others.

Some insist that humanist tragedy was not closet drama. Lebègue calls it a 'sottise' to think any other way (*La Tragédie française*, p. 34), and even Mrs. Jondorf believes that 'The sixteenth-century French dramatists, although they were imitating closet drama, seem clearly to have been thinking in terms of stage performance' (p. 15). The discussion may prove a rather otiose one. If we accept the full import of our observations in the preceding chapter, we must admit that humanist tragedy was enjoyed first and foremost in much the same way as the didactic literature that often inspired it.

It is not fortuitous that in his *Théâtre du monde* (p. 65) Boaystuau relates the Amnon and Thamar story to David in terms that prefigure the works of Chrétien des Croix and Thierry. When Noël du Fail's *Propos rustiques* accentuate the felicity of pastoral life and by-gone days much as tragedy did, the similarity stems from a common fund of moral lessons and a common aim to teach which cut across genre lines somewhat in the manner that rhetoric's principles cut across all the varieties of literary expression.

I am not unaware that Lebègue has shown certain adjustments which were made by Garnier and Baïf with a staging of their works in mind (*La Tragédie française*, p. 34). Yet an author's effort to adapt his plot to a stage situation is not synonymous with an effort to create dramatic action and these instances of accommodation must be weighed against the mass of material offered by the humanists' plays to suggest that the moral purpose, not the development of character and plot occupied the playwrights. It is a simple but all-important fact that the coming of French Classical drama is accompanied by discussions about performance which at no time surrounded humanist tragedy.

In yet another instance we can find rhetoric's hold over humanist practice creating a fundamental distinction between sixteenth-century and Classical tragedy. The concept of vraisemblance was hardly unknown to the humanists. Amyot, translating Heliodorus in 1547, specifically claims that fictions 'qui sont les moins esloignées de nature, & ou il y a plus de verisimilitude, sont celles qui plaisent le plus à ceux qui mesurent leur plaisir à la raison, & qui se delectent auecq' iugement' (sig. A2ᵛ). Pierre de Courcelles' *La Rhétorique* (1557) states that 'Trois choses principales principalement la narration doit auoir, qu'elle soit breue, clere, & vray semblable' (f. 24ʳ). Jean de La Taille begs his reader in *De l'art de la tragédie* to recognize that if the play departs somewhat from the Biblical text, he did not 'tant desguisé l'histoire, qu'on n'y recognoisse pour le moins quelques traicts, ou quelque ombre de la verité, comme vraysemblablement la chose est aduenue' (p. 15). The quotations are all the more impressive because they appear to designate essentially what the seventeenth century understood by the term and other writers of the period strengthen that impression. Laudun is certain that in tragedy 'L'argument ne doit point estre feint, mais vray, & clair & distingué par actes, & personnes. Outre La Tragedie, ne reçoit point de personnes feinctes, comme auarice, . . . ny mesmes dieux ny deesses comme tesmoigne Horace en son art' (pp. 279-80). A detailed comparison of Homer and Virgil by both Scaliger and Peletier—much to the praise of the Latin author—reads like a preview of the Querelle du *Cid*. In the fourteenth book of the *Iliad*, Scaliger finds that Homer calls Sleep 'Lord of all gods and of all men'. The critic is shocked. Who indeed would say that the Prime Mover sleeps. (V, iii). Later he is indignant to hear Juno promise Sleep a Grace for his wife if Sleep will do her bidding. Nonsense! 'It does not please me', says Scaliger, 'to have the Graces given in marriage to Sleep, for grace never needs to sleep' (V, iii). And when Juno uses a particular word here to designate marriage, Scaliger declares this shameful since the word can also be used for the sex act and is so employed by Homer in another passage of the *Iliad*. Peletier praises Virgil for not repeating Homer's many epithets and for avoiding Homer's 'redites' in the various messages and harangues. Virgil wisely did not follow the *Iliad*'s practice of having the gods take part in battles or showing them lamenting their fortune 'like mortals'. On the other hand, Peletier cannot appreciate Virgil's remark that Turnus threw at Aeneas a stone which, according to the poet, twelve strong men could not have moved. This is to Peletier a 'thing difficult to believe'.

If, however, the concept was so widespread, it can be asked why humanist tragedy created innumerable situations in their works that do not in the least conform to the principle of vraisemblance. I have already pointed out examples of grave inconsistencies in characterization. Matthieu's *Aman*, Berthrand's *Pryam*, Chantelouve's *Colligni* are but a few of the tragedies in which the passage of time exceeds months, even years. As for any kind of vraisemblance in the setting, Hardy's immediate shift from Daire's camp (III, ii) to Alexander's camp (III, iii) provides but one instance of a common practice in the genre. The explanation for this curious juxtaposition of concept and execution lies in the humanists' source of thought on vraisemblance.

The dates of Amyot's translation or of Courcelles' *Rhétorique* show that one did not have to know Aristotle to talk about vraisemblance. Rhetoric, by insisting on the principle of appropriateness (*propria*), too, espoused vraisemblance. Courcelles' definition of narration is but a translation of the three qualities of *narratio*, established by the Isocratean school and repeated by Quintilian (IV, ii, 31). His use of the word in this precept 'si tu ne narroys de la dignité & capacité de la personne: elle ne seroït aucunement vray semblable & approchante de verité' (f. 28^r) exposes a principle fundamental to rhetoricians. Likewise, Badius' introduction to Terence's comedies provided the sixteenth century with not only an amalgam of Donatus and Diomedes but also a theory of drama whose inspiration was profoundly influenced by rhetoric. In each of the various paragraphs which discuss *decorum* (De decoro [et] primo personarum, De rerum decoro, De verborum decoro, De decoro totius operis), Badius reveals that his understanding of the term does not extend beyond rhetoric's already unsophisticated notion of *propria*. *Decorum* in matter will be observed if important personages and eloquent speeches are omitted from comedy. *Decorum* in style requires clarity and uniformity. The whole work will observe *decorum* if all, not just some, of its parts are well done. Not only is this a far cry from unity of action, but when Badius repeatedly mouths the rule that words and acts must conform to the characters in question, we quickly learn that he means little more than the view of human character propagated by rhetoric: women are inconstant and fickle and so on.

As a result, vraisemblance proves a far less important concept to the sixteenth century than the necessity to teach and to embellish.

Significantly, in the same translation, Amyot chastises early French fiction not only for its lack of all 'vraysemblable apparence' but for the fact that 'il n'y a nulle erudition, nulle cognoissance de l'antiquité, ne chose aucune (à brief parler) dont on peust tirer quelque vtilité' (sig. A2ᵛ). Heliodorus, on the contrary, is recommended for his 'beaux discours tirez de la Philosophie Naturelle, & Morale: force ditz notables, & propoz sentencieux: plusieurs belles harengues, ou l'artifice d'eloquence est tres bien employé' (sig. A3ʳ). Laudun no sooner makes his pronouncement about the characters unfit for tragedy than he excuses the use of a Fury in one of his own plays in order to show that the misfortunes which befall the players are justified. The perspective is all too familiar. It also introduces a certain irony into the question of tragedy's evolution. For, most of those who avoid accentuating changes in form when explaining the rise of Classical tragedy speak not of the disappearance of this perspective but of the gradual appearance of drama, unities, and rules.

Antoine Adam derives from the fact that in seventeenth-century tragedy 'Des batailles se déroulent maintenant sur la scène' (*Histoire*, I, 183) a clear sign of change from the old form of tragedy. Marsan upholds the traditions of eighteenth-century scholarship by maintaining that Mairet's *Sophonisbe* established Classical tragedy: 'Avec la *Sophonisbe*, . . . toutes les promesses de *Sylvie* et de *Silvanire* semblent se réaliser: sobre, puissante et humaine, la tragédie française est née' (p. 390).

In truth, battles were to be depicted long before 1600. Beaubrueil's *Regulus* and Des Masures' *David combattant* both include specific indications of battle scenes, and yet no one would be tempted to associate these plays with the coming of Classical drama. Of Marsan's three adjectives, 'sobre' hardly distinguishes *Sophonisbe* from earlier tragedy. 'Puissante' and 'humaine' are not necessarily more helpful. They could apply as well to Théophile's *Pyrame et Thisbé* or to Garnier's *Les Juives*, plays conceived and executed along lines established early in the history of humanist tragedy.

How can we be so confused? My personal feeling is that for many critics such lines did not exist or somehow did not matter. Miss Kern's belief 'that the principle of the unity of action represents the most striking contribution which the rediscovered treatise of Aristotle made to modern criticism' (p. 42) contains much truth but the establishment of Classical tragedy depended not only upon the introduction of new principles but also upon the disappearance or challenging of old ones. We have had innumerable occasions to see that characterization and structure in early tragedy derived as much from specific intents as would their Classical counterparts. The desire to teach—overtly and incessantly—must share the limelight in this connection with an intense fascination for words. When Chamard described the evolution we are discussing in terms of an effort to eliminate all poetic elements of classical drama in favour of dramatic ones (*La Tragédie*, p. 30), he proved one of the few to sense the change in the relative values of language and action between humanist and Classical tragedy.

Two other distinguished scholars of the French theatre have given us reason to believe that a significant change took place *between* these two varieties of tragedy. H. Carrington Lancaster's article 'The Introduction of the Unities into the French Drama of the Seventeenth Century' is a model of common sense at work on a complex problem. Cutting through the many theories to the essential facts, he establishes that there was no discussion of the unities by French dramatists between 1607 and 1629, when Mairet, quite independent of any remarks by Balzac or Chapelain, decided to write a play according to these rules. By Mairet's own admission, he responded to encouragement from a group of nobles to compose a pastoral in the Italian mode and upon studying the Italian pastoral, he 'found that the secret of their success lay in their following the rules of the Ancients' (p. 209). Just as Mairet set about to achieve similar success for himself, so, argues Lancaster, the other dramatists soon began composing regular plays 'to gain the same success that had been won by Tasso, Mairet, and Corneille' (p. 216). In conclusion Lancaster is brought by his own argumentation to pose the all-important question: 'But why, one may ask, were the regular plays more successful than the irregular?' (p. 216) His reply remains on the level of intelligent guessing—the economy forced dramatists to rely on psychology, not spectacle and psychological investigation and unity in form were in tune with the taste of the period. Despite the vagueness of the reply, Lancaster has made quite clear that the success of regular drama must be sought within the period which created it, that there is no evidence of some inevitable evolution in French literary mores from Jodelle to Corneille.

Octave Nadal's 'La Scène française d'Alexandre Hardy à Corneille' examines a different problem but arrives at conclusions similar to those of Lancaster. Nadal finds that the first thirty years of theatre in the seventeenth century can be characterized by an evolution which he terms 'la désaffection puis l'abandon du sacré' (p. 209). The 'sacré' is replaced by 'l'humain', that is, through the theme of man's passion for glory, the theatre returns to a purely human sphere. Nadal sees signs of the change appearing already in *Pyrame et Thisbé*, thanks in part to Théophile's naturalism, 'purgé de toute angoisse religieuse' (p. 214). But the moment has not come and the drama marks time until Corneille writes *Le Cid*. The observation is interesting because Nadal is not echoing Fontenelle or the Frères Parfaict. He states bluntly that the regular or irregular nature of a play cannot determine the evolution he has in mind. 'Mairet élabore une *Sophonisbe* régulière (1634) mais ne fonde pas, pour cela, notre tragédie' (p. 215). Again, then, we find Classical tragedy separated from what preceded and associated not with the rules so much as with a new perspective that the unities may help to convey but can scarcely be said to create.

As a consequence, I believe that the changes which took place to discredit the old humanist principles were fully as important for the establishment of Classical tragedy as the introduction of a five-act form in 1552. Nadal effects a series of bridges from humanism to early seventeenth-century theatre and then to Classical drama by seeing in that enthusiasm for the romanesque and the heroic which characterizes literature at the close of the sixteenth century an 'étape décisive' (p. 213) in humanism's development and the seed of Classical theatre's concerns. The pastoral in particular opened new and essential horizons for the theatre and we have seen for ourselves a rise in the number of plays devoted to acts of heroism. However, tragedy had on good authority also devoted its energies to style and moralizing. To recast love and valour within such a framework would not have brought about Classical tragedy. Only by profiting from increased interest in the romanesque or the heroic *and* by redefining an acceptable tragic style as well as an audience's expectations was such a change to come about.

The pages to follow discuss the many ways in which I believe it is possible to chart France's reaction to the concepts that supported humanist tragedy. Although there is considerable evidence that a re-evaluation of such concepts took place, it is perhaps significant to note how little appears in a context of sustained commentary on tragedy. In conception and aim humanist tragedy has proved to be inevitably related to other sixteenth-century genres as well as educational theory; so, certain changes that effect the nascent Classical drama come to light in works of literature, manuals of social behaviour in addition to the more obvious treatises on theory and language. Classical drama, no less than humanist tragedy, reflects the period that created it.

Because we can deduce from a variety of texts that humanist techniques did suffer re-evaluation, I do not mean to say that such writers as Montaigne, Faret, or Sorel intended their words as commentary on theatre; I do not wish the evidence presented below to be equated with the total definition of how Classicism was established in France. I suggest only that parallel to, indeed, often underlying many aspects of the coming of Classicism studied by other critics there exists a marked shift in attitude toward style and toward representation of the human condition without which we cannot explain adequately France's evolution from the tragedies of Garnier to *Phèdre*.

2 THE EVIDENCE

It is not possible to look at the bulk of writings on rhetoric in the seventeenth century without recognizing that certain earlier principles had been seriously rethought. The *Logique de Port Royal*, for example, openly questions whether an individual passes from the various *loci* to eloquence. Believing that eloquence comes rather from 'la nature, la considération attentive du sujet, la connoissance de diverses vérités (p. 234), the authors cite four lines from the *Aeneid* which Ramus had glossed to point out that the development contained a *locus*. The *Logique* refuses to believe that Virgil was thinking of *loci* when composing the verses; he had suspended his knowledge of the rules and was attempting to render the emotion in question. The passage is particularly outspoken; its perspective on the creative act, the very opposite of what sixteenth-century manuals taught. Although the sixteenth century and especially the Pléiade did insist that the poet had to be inspired as well as erudite, it was much easier to describe the erudition needed. This is what their treatises did and the mass of sixteenth-century poetry shows that the artists definitely prided themselves on their ability to manipulate mythology and *loci*. In the *Logique*, the work accompanying inspiration is quite detached from erudition. It is expended within the confines of the subject's needs and the example from Virgil implies that the presence of a *locus* must be explained by the poet's unconscious pool of images rather than by an express wish to decorate his style.

In no longer accenting the use of rhetorical figures to insure great style, the *Logique* proves part of a general trend that led on the one hand to negative evaluation of rhetorical display and on the other, to an impressive number of remarks that quite divorce the notion of eloquence or art from the *loci* of Aphthonius and Fabri. The 'Discours de M. Le Grand', which precedes Bary's *La Rhétorique française*, refuses to associate eloquence with 'cette habitude déclamatoire des Seneques & des Quintiliens, ny de cette science Progymnastique des Theons & des Apthones . . . qui employe le fard & les couleurs pour couurir des taches' (sig. ã5ᵛ). Racan wrote Chapelain in 1654:

Comment établissons-nous des règles générales à un art où la pratique et le jugement en forment tous les jours de nouvelles? Et par où commenceray-je à vous escrire mes sentimens du poème épique, moy, qui ne say pas seulement le nom des choses dont je veux traitter. . . . Ainsi, encore que je me serve quelquefois assez heureusement des figures de rhetorique, dont je ne say pas le nom, c'est plus par hazard que par science.

(I, 347)

Pascal's familiar phrases 'La vraie éloquence se moque de l'éloquence' and 'Quand on voit le style naturel, on est tout étonné et ravi, car on s'attendait de voir un auteur, et on trouve un homme' (pp. 75, 79-80), if I understand them correctly, would have us realize that true eloquence is something other than *narratio*, *fabula*, *sententiae*, or *laudatio*. Pascal says nothing to suggest that true eloquence does without *loci* or figures and his own writings certainly do not. There is a definite denigration, however, of style patently based on the mechanical implementation of rhetorical principles— the very style in which humanist drama indulged repeatedly.

When La Mothe le Vayer quotes Cicero's 'Nihil est aliud eloquentia, quàm copiosè loquens sapientia' (Eloquence is nothing but wisdom speaking copiously) (I, 446) to uphold his conviction that it is impossible to be eloquent without the aid of philosophy, we begin to see a return to that complexity of views on rhetoric which is to be found in Cicero and Quintilian but did not impress the sixteenth century. Again, other examples are not lacking. The *Logique de Port Royal*, negatively disposed toward *loci*, quotes

Quintilian to prove that even the master did not think that the orator needed to know all the *loci* (p. 234). La Mothe le Vayer, sharing a basic view with the *Logique*, quotes Quintilian as well to introduce his contention that 'ce n'est pas le propre de ceux qui conçoiuent les belles choses, de ce soucier si fort en quels termes ils les enfanteront' (I, 422). Perhaps no part of this same work reveals better the shift in thought than the following quotation: 'Mais ie soustiens aussi que les mesmes qui nous ont donné ces regles, nous ont enseigné de ne nous y asseruir que de bonne façon, et qu'ils nous ont laissé des exemples de les mépriser, autant de fois qu'elles pourroient preiudicier au bon sens' (I, 431). The perspective on *loci* and *figurae* has been reversed; where Aphthonius saw a fund of principles, La Mothe le Vayer appreciates all the exceptions and the distance that permits, encourages even, a disdain for the same principles when our common sense protests.

Why such a return to the complexity of views in Cicero and Quintilian came about touches on the most essential elements in the evolution that separates humanism from Classicism. The same rhetoricians provide a variety of clues. For example, when Bary has nothing good to say about the pedants with their 'langage des écoles' and lack of precision which he finds rather in the purists of society (p. 224), we can appreciate to what degree the seventeenth century had an alternative to erudite style not to be found a century before. From the outset the humanists were drawn to imitate antiquity's grand style because it contrasted so violently with the poverty of the vernacular. It seemed the only path to linguistic perfection whereas Bary believes that the 'vulgaire' sins against those cardinal virtues of rhetoric—elegance and clarity—*'faute d'auoir leu les bons Liures, & frequenté les beaux esprits'* (p. 224, my italics).

Bary begins his work by calling eloquence the art of speaking 'polyment' (p. 1). The adverb may seem to betray the high moral and aesthetic principles of a Quintilian, but, as the Querelle du *Cid* showed, the seventeenth century could endow its concept of acceptable behaviour with very high standards and linking rhetoric with politeness proves every much as serious a statement as associating elegance with 'les beaux esprits'. How serious it can be is best exemplified by M. Le Grand's definition of eloquence as 'cette habitude imperieuse qui regne absolument dans les cœurs, qui exerce vne puissance, legitime sur les volontez' (sig. ã5ᵛ).

Superficially, he is not saying more than Quintilian did when he associated excellence in oratory with excellence in morals but the simple fact that he says this after generations had read Quintilian and come away defining rhetoric as the art of speaking well, that is, with much use of *copia* applied to moral questions, shows that the seventeenth century had yet another basis for separating rhetoric from *loci*. The *Logique de Port Royal* integrated subject and rhetoric; M. Le Grand integrates speaker and rhetoric. His definition intimates that we will know a character by his words, but in a fashion that far outdistances the superficial traits required by *propria*. Words are linked rather to what I would dare to call, using modern parlance, the character's personality. For, is not Le Grand suggesting that the more noble the personality, the more eloquent the speech? What an innovation if we compare this concept with the reasoning behind the grammarians' requirement that tragedy consist of elevated style and grand personages.

Donatus and Diomedes were, first of all, merely synthesizing the evidence of classical tragedy. The presence of these two elements in the tragedies they had read was a fact. Secondly, they upheld the formulae of the most venerable authorities. Did not Horace specifically describe tragedy as 'scorning to babble trivial verses?' (*De arte poetica*, vs. 231) In theory and practice the sixteenth century made no attempt to contradict such a principle. Not interested in its characters beyond the level of moral exempla, humanist tragedy applied rhetoric across the board to prove its seriousness and its elegance. Variation was predictably by theme. Love poetry, tyrants' tirades, these contexts provided the perceptible shifts from one set stylistic pattern to another. Le Grand gives eloquence an entirely new basis. It comes from no manual but from an 'habitude' that regulates the emotions and the will. It is not some traditional characteristic of the grand but a means of revealing the grandeur that lies deep in their personality, waiting to be challenged or denied before it can be fully exhibited. The net result may be that Le Grand says nothing to change the elements of tragedy as defined by the grammarians, but he does change the relationship of character to speech and so did Classicism. If Emilie opens *Cinna* with an elegant monologue in which she weighs the relative strength of the desires within her, Corneille has done far more than pay lip service to a stylistic requirement for tragedy; he has given us an essential insight into Emilie's personality. It, too, is structured, if complex, endowed with the 'habitude' of reflection and dialectic. Racinian characters trace different patterns when they speak but again revelations regarding 'cœur' and 'volonté' are generally inseparable from the information Racine wishes to communicate. The very fact that so many Cornelian characters speak alike yet differently from the several Racinian characters whose rhetoric is similar, whereas all humanist characters tend to speak in the same fashion, may be the simplest means to recognize rhetoric's new-found role of character portrayal —our first concrete sign of tragedy's shift from the sacred to the human. These clues only begin to tell a story which also includes the particular positions of those humanists who have been termed ahead of their time and of one man who definitely was.

In studying the evolution of French prose style over the sixteenth and seventeenth centuries, critics have traditionally selected the works of Erasmus, Ramus, and Muret as harbingers of the kind of change just observed. Personally, I am less convinced that we can feel confident about understanding rhetoric in the seventeenth century after reading Erasmus' or Ramus' *Ciceronianus* or Muret's 'Conversation with Darius Bernardus on the Folly of some who call themselves Ciceronians'. Quite the contrary, while responding more sensitively to the complex questions of style and imitation, these men had other concerns that help us understand rather why their century did not see rhetoric as its successor did.

All three deplore restricting one's vocabulary to that of Cicero. Ramus and Erasmus insist that to follow Cicero means to imitate as he did, that is, borrow from all the finest authors, not from just one person, and certainly not from Cicero alone since he was far from perfect in everything he wrote. Also it is noted in the Dutchman's work that Ciceronian eloquence no longer has a major role to play. Absent from the courts, it is replaced in the councils by the vernacular and would be incomprehensible to the people in any public forum. There is evident common sense at work here and in the same piece that good sense appears to wax philosophical when Bulephorus, Erasmus' spokesman, remarks, 'if you wish to express Cicero exactly, you cannot express yourself' (p. 78). Although this is the sort of phrase that has made Erasmus a modern man for some, the *Ciceronianus*, read in its entirety, has quite a different thrust from encouraging a development of the self. This thrust is well summarized by Bulephorus' observation that 'Cicero, if he were alive today, would not consider *God the Father* less elegant than *Jupiter*

Optimus Maximus or *Jesus Christ* less pleasing to the ear than *Romulus* or *Scipio Africanus*. . . . The body is baptized in sacred water but the mind is unwashed; . . . we profess Jesus with our mouths, we wear Jupiter Optimus Maximus and Romulus in our hearts' (pp. 71, 73). Erasmus' quarrel with Ciceronianism is fundamentally religious. He sees in it a cult of the classical which receives the attention that should go to Christianity and worse, it establishes a hierarchy of values that places Cicero's vocabulary above the Christian. All in all, Erasmus' document attacks not eloquence or rhetoric or erudition but a preference for classical over a religious Latin and the ethical overtones of that preference. One of Bulephorus' parting remarks could not be clearer in this regard: 'That belief in sacred things which is truly worthy of a Christian must first be gained. When this is accomplished, nothing will seem more ornamental than the Christian religion, nothing more persuasive than the name of Jesus Christ' (p. 129).

Muret's orations, too, criticize only to uphold a concept that will not take us to the *Logique de Port Royal* or La Mothe le Vayer. His 'Cum interpretari inciperet epistolas Ciceronis ad Atticum' repeats the idea that eloquence has lost its ancient place but in recognizing that eloquence now serves principally in letters only, he is registering regret, not approbation. That regret bursts forth earlier in the oration as Muret sadly observes that in all Italy only a bare handful of old men could be found who sustain a once great tradition in use of the Latin tongue. When he admits that in deliberations the listeners heed what one says, not how elegantly one speaks, he adds, 'This is all together correct and cannot be rejected; nevertheless, in this way a good deal of material is taken away from eloquent men. Having, so to speak, attained retirement by virtue of its age, eloquence has been told to content itself with our academic, dusty debates, the sacred assemblies held before the people, and congratulatory or funeral speeches made to princes' (*Scripta selecta*, p. 176). This is no request for a reassessment of eloquence, but a woeful calling to mind that things are unfortunately not as bright as they once were.

Similarly in 'De via et ratione ad eloquentiae laudem perveniendi' Muret argues against the Ciceronians mainly because (to invoke a familiar sentiment), he feels that they are incorrect to limit their source of inspiration to Cicero. When he refuses to call eloquence learning 'the kinds of cases, the names of the figures and certain commonplace precepts concerning shaping the parts of a speech and dreary things of this kind and putting together little words culled from Cicero and fashioning from them as from little building blocks a jejune and scrawny speech, busily guarding against saying something that Cicero had not said before' (*Scripta selecta*, p. 71), we perceive a more fruitful tack, especially since it is accompanied by an echo of Erasmus' argument: 'That is the eloquence of magpies and parrots to iterate and reiterate utterances [already] heard and never to say anything that is truly and properly your own' (pp. 71-2). Yet when Muret gives his own definition of eloquence, it is not clear whether we have advanced beyond the usual sixteenth-century views or not: 'The ancients called eloquence something else. They called no one eloquent unless he was able to speak about civil matters in an ornate and fluent fashion, bent the feelings of his listeners with his speech, evoked admiration, and now brought forth applause, now struck the assembled multitude dumb with wonderment' (p. 72). If Muret had in mind here the distinction between 'la vraie éloquence' and the Ciceronians' verbal exercises, his definition fails to state what the works of the seventeenth century quoted above are so intent on communicating: that the eloquence favoured lies outside the humanists' traditional practices. Muret devotes most of his definition to the effects of eloquence, not its content, and when he does once allude to content, his 'in an ornate and fluent fashion' would hardly discourage a writer from pursuing Aphthonius. For these various reasons we can appreciate why, in Croll's words, Muret 'has been held up to the admiration even of school-children as the modern Cicero' (p. 107).

Croll's own view is more complex and brings much evidence to light to suggest that Muret became ultimately an admirer of Attic style. Still, what is apparent to a scholar, exploring the works of a writer's lifetime, need not have been apparent to the contemporary who read the occasional oration. Muret and Erasmus wrote these pieces out of reaction to a specific trend within the humanist movement and this fact would have been paramount to their readers. That their position on Ciceronianism brings them closer to us in perspective does not mean that they were automatically instrumental in effecting a change in attitude among their contemporaries. On closer investigation we even find that they were moved to write out of motives quite foreign to the aesthetic of Bary or the *Logique de Port Royal*. Erasmus worries about paganism; Muret sighs at the decline in use of good Latin. Croll transforms this regret into the first sign of a shift from a *genus grande* to a *genus humile* but not without admitting that Muret's statement is perhaps just a 'cynical observation' (p. 64).

I do not see how regret can be made to sound like a positive programme of reorientation. If in another oration, 'De auctoritate & officio judicum', Muret distinguishes between two styles ('I shall speak not in our oratorical fashion but in our instructional, private, and calm style which is suitable not for stirring the mind but for teaching it, not for evoking applause but rather for obtaining quiet and attention'—*Orationes*, 1592, p. 193), one would like some statement of preference or at least of realization that this teaching style is now the only valid style since the oratorical tone has been excluded from the councils and public fora. The remark is all the more disconcerting because the ancients recognized fully such distinctions and always related teaching to a simpler style.

For a radical re-evaluation of rhetoric that points ahead we must look elsewhere—to Michel de Montaigne, who, interestingly enough, has also much to say that bears on other areas of change affecting the theatre.

Michel de Montaigne. There is much in the *Essais* to link Montaigne to his own century. In another book I attempted to sketch the similar lines of thought between Montaigne and contemporary developments in historiography and law'[2] The well-known study by Pierre Villey of Montaigne's sources and evolution shows conclusively that the earliest essays in particular owe much to moral literature of the day not unlike the sources of many humanist tragedies. At the same time, Montaigne stands apart from his contemporaries in a number of truly significant ways.

He enjoyed disguising his erudition: 'Ez raisons et inventions que je transplante en mon solage et confons aux miennes, j'ay à escient ommis parfois d'en marquer l'autheur, pour tenir en bride la temerité de ces sentences hastives qui se jettent sur toute sorte d'escrits. . . . Je veux qu'ils donnent une nazarde à Plutarque sur mon nez, et qu'ils s'eschaudent à injurier Seneque en moy' (pp. 448-9). He enjoyed even more deflating the reputation of rhetoric.

Montaigne's thoughts on rhetoric are not as numerous as those he expresses on the wider subject of pedantry and philosophers but they are just as blunt. The essay 'De la vanité des paroles' (I, 51), though short, is devoted exclusively to this one question which Montaigne views from a variety of perspectives. He seeks to discredit rhetoric first through the words of one of its own practitioners, then through a historical evaluation, and finally through a mocking of its terminology.

An ancient rhetorician had said that his vocation was to make little things appear big. Montaigne enlarges upon this statement to brand rhetoric as an 'art piperesse et mensongere', worse than the art of makeup because the rhetorician deceives not our eyes, but our judgment. In the original text of 1580 Montaigne moved directly from that observation to the historical perspective by equating the reign of rhetoric with periods of unrest, periods when orators used their skills to sway the masses. In concluding, he contrasts the vocabulary of architects ('pilastres, architraves, corniches') with what is actually designated—his kitchen door. The contrast does not contain a direct slap at rhetoric and for that reason, perhaps, he added for the 1588 edition a similar comparison between rhetorical terms like 'metonomie, metaphore, allegorie' and the chatter of a chambermaid.

The very title of Montaigne's essay contains an important new approach to rhetoric. To consider words vain and empty is already to part company with the rhetoricians. For this reason alone Montaigne represents a significant progression in thought over the anti-Ciceronians, who quarrel within the framework of possible styles and necessary imitation without raising the basic issue that Montaigne faces squarely. He obliges his readers to reconsider the art about which their early education revolved and to perceive it in a light that imposes upon that art more serious limits than the realization that forensic oratory had no place in modern society. By attributing to rhetoric the adjectives 'piperesse' and 'mensongere', Montaigne expresses a firm refusal to accept *copia* and ornamentation as inherently positive. Where centuries of predecessors found rhetoric's beauty, Montaigne found only verbal trickery, verbal veneer, which hid, not enhanced, the reality in question. All this, and more comes through in the paragraphs on jargon.

In the case first of the kitchen door, then the chambermaid, Montaigne specifies what the jargon evokes in him. The architectural terms produce in his imagination the 'palais d'Apolidon', the figures, 'quelque forme de langage rare et pellegrin'. Then he discovers the truth. Montaigne's words show that he is not insensitive, but perhaps too sensitive, too imaginative to accept the distance between the euphony of the jargon and the simplicity of a door. From this dist-ance is born the reaction conveyed by his adjectives 'piperesse' and 'mensognere' and it is surely to make us feel such a distance that Montaigne composed the essay. Yet, as the work closes, he associates fascination with this jargon with the use of Roman titles for con-temporary offices, a practice Montaigne calls 'une singuliere ineptie de nostre siecle' (p. 345), and in the initial paragraphs of another essay, 'De la phisionomie' (III, xii), we find that he gave some thought to why man enjoyed being deceived by an 'art piperesse'.

He begins 'De la phisionomie' with a few words on authority. So great is its weight, he implies, that were Socrates' story to be re-enacted in the sixteenth century, no one would give it importance, for 'Nous n'apercevons les graces que pointues, bouffies et enflées d'artifice. Celles qui coulent soubs la nayfveté et la simplicité eschapent ayséement à une veuë grossiere comme est la nostre' (p. 1162). The aesthetics of rhetoric are confronted openly and now the full distinction between pilaster and door, metaphor and chatter emerges. There is not only a prejudice in us for an overblown and 'deceitful' style, but we are incapable of appreciating the art and beauty in the simple reality that lies beneath the jargon. 'Elles', he continues, referring to 'la nayfveté' and 'la simplicité', 'ont une beauté delicate et cachée; il faut la veuë nette et bien purgée pour descouvrir cette secrette lumiere' (p. 1162). The shift in taste is complete. The beauty denied to the high style is unhesitatingly attributed to the natural object. And as if to reassure us that he knows well what he is about, Montaigne asks, 'Est pas la naifveté, selon nous, germane à la sottise, et qualité de reproche?' (p. 1162) He thinks otherwise. He had once even sketched the thought in a short passage from 'Des cannibales' (I, 31), where he mentions 'nostre grande et puissante mere nature': 'Nous avons tant rechargé la beauté et richesse de ses ouvrages par nos inventions, que nous l'avons du tout estouffée' (p. 243). The parallel between our 'in-ventions' and our jargon is patent. There should be no surprise, then, when Montaigne affirms that where the purity of nature's works shines forth, the shame of human labour is manifest: 'Tous nos efforts ne peuvent seulement arriver à representer le nid du moindre oyselet, sa contexture, sa beauté et l'utilité de son usage, non pas la tissure de la chetive araignee' (p. 243).

In 'Des livres' (II, 10) the perspective changes somewhat.

Montaigne's basic distinction between the natural and the artificial is applied to two subjects which have a distinct bearing on the future of French tragedy: style and characterization. Employed as a canon for aesthetic judgments, the distinction becomes one between the beauty of simple elegance and the triteness of affectation. He observes that 'les bons et anciens Poëtes ont evité l'affectation et la recherche, non seulement des fantastiques elevations Espagnoles et Petrarchistes, mais des pointes mesmes plus douces et plus retenues, qui font l'ornement de tous les ouvrages Poëtiques des siècles suyvans' (p. 453) and contrasts the steady soaring of the *Aeneid*, always moving toward its point, with the movement of the *Furioso*, hopping 'de conte en conte comme de branche en branche' (p. 454). Reminiscent of the difference between the graces that are 'pointes, bouffies et enflées d'artifice' and 'la nayfveté et la simplicité', Montaigne's preference for the *Aeneid* also makes clear that when applied to literary texts, 'natural' and 'restrained' are relative terms, just as they will be for Classicism. It is not new to say that much of the particular quality of French Classical writing derives from the subtle wedding of the elegant and the natural; yet we have to bear this in mind continually when studying tragedy. The evolution from humanist to Classical concerns is to be found in a re-evaluation of rhetoric's use, not in an abandonment of rhetoric.

'Des livres' makes one further observation about style. Affected and contorted, it can lose its effectiveness. Much of Cicero's fidelity to rhetoric's principles in works of moral philosophy Montaigne finds boring and incompatible with the function of such literature: 'Car ses prefaces, definitions, partitions, etymologies, consument la plus part de son ouvrage; ce qu'il y a de vif et de mouelle, est estouffé par ses longueries d'apprets. . . . Pour moy, qui ne demande qu'à devenir plus sage, non plus sçavant ou eloquent, ces ordon-nances logiciennes et Aristoteliques ne sont pas à propos' (p. 455). Thus, to his questioning of rhetoric's ability to render the 'natural', Montaigne adds his doubts concerning rhetoric's function in works that do not teach the reader to become 'plus sçavant ou eloquent'.

Within the context of 'Des livres' Montaigne is saying only that books from which he seeks to learn more about himself and other men are spoiled by rhetorical 'longueries d'apprets'. In the context of our study, Montaigne speaks out against a number of cardinal assumptions behind humanist tragedy. The very dichotomy between 'becoming wiser' and 'more learned or eloquent' went against the humanist grain. Humanist tragedy belonged to a cultural current that prized a 'docte' style and used it constantly to enhance the didactic impact of its literary works. More serious still, Montaigne separates 'sage' and 'sçavant'. Why he did so and what meaning he attributed to each adjective are questions so fully answered in such essays as 'De l'institution des enfans' and 'Du pedantisme' that we need spend no time with them here. Of greater importance is Montaigne's evident preference for 'sage' over 'sçavant' which is linked with rhetoric, that is, rhetoric becomes undesirable not only by how it teaches but also by what it teaches.

Further statements made in 'Des livres' shed considerable light on Montaigne's preference and, significantly, the more we learn about the essayist's prejudices, the less attractive rhetoric becomes. Although moral literature such as Boccaccio's *De casibus* tended to take the public face of the great as the most important and humanist historians, imitating the Latins, felt confident that real or imagined public speeches laid bare the essential facts of history, Montaigne, musing on Brutus, remarks: 'Je choisiroy plustost de sçavoir au vray les devis qu'il tenoit en sa tente à quelqu'un de ses privez amis, la veille d'une bataille, que les propos qu'il tint le lendemain à son armée; et ce qu'il faisoit en son cabinet et en sa chambre, que ce qu'il faisoit emmy la place et au Senat' (pp. 456-7).

Many themes of the *Essais* come together in such an observation. Montaigne believed that education should aim at creating a critical faculty in us, our 'jugement', and at building for each man a philosophy of life, not cultured ignorance. So, it is not surprising that Montaigne precedes the passage on Brutus with the general remark, 'j'ay une singuliere curiosité, . . . de connoistre l'ame et les naïfs jugemens de mes autheurs' (p. 456). But as the presence of 'naïfs' suggests, the quotation also participates in the *Essais*'s long-standing contrast between what is natural or true or private and what is affected, public, and misleading.

I do not think it is excessive to discern in such a contrast the single most important stimulus behind French Classicism's preoccupation with the theme of appearance versus reality (if we add the final dimension of Montaigne's own encouragement of a division between the public and private self). In the essay on custom Montaigne asserts that 'le sage doit au dedans retirer son ame de la presse, et la tenir en liberté et puissance de juger librement des choses; mais, quant au dehors, qu'il doit suivre entierement les façons et formes receues' (pp. 147-8). The full schema of thought thus comes even closer to the world of Classicism: acceptance of external forms of behaviour mixed with intense curiosity about the private self and distrust of a recognized, yet cultivated façade. Naturally, Montaigne's ideas would have to be embellished and related more directly to literature and drama but time would provide just such a development.

The manuals of behaviour. That Montaigne was widely read by the seventeenth century is an established fact. Alan Boase, in his *The Fortunes of Montaigne,* has well documented the enduring and profound influence of this man. Mlle de Gournay and Sorel felt strongly the newness of Montaigne's portrait of the human personality. F. Grenaille's *L'Honneste Garçon* (1642) insists that Montaigne 'par vne liberté naturelle de composer s'est acquis plus de reputation que n'ont peu faire les autres auec vne contrainte artificielle' (p. 9) and agrees with Du Perron that the *Essais* should be called 'le Breuiaire des Honnétes-gens' (sig. ã3ʳ).

It is significant to find Montaigne so highly regarded in a manual of social behaviour. The work belongs to a very old tradition that includes the famous sixteenth-century titles *Il Galateo* by Giovanni della Casa and Castiglione's *Il Cortegiano.* In France the genre came into its own in the early decades of the seventeenth century. Descotes mentions the manuals in his study of the French public but because they 'lacked charm' he agrees with Magendie that the novels were the important instruments for 'l'épuration des mœurs' (p. 63). The sheer number of these manuals takes much away from such a theory and I think that it is always dangerous to underestimate the impact of a period's didactic literature, however devoid of charm it may be. Moreover, even if the novels made a greater impression, the manuals are important to us if only for the sentiments that the authors expressed and circulated among the reading public.

In particular, they reinforce Montaigne's dichotomy between 'sage' and 'sçavant'. Della Casa's judgment of Dante is withering, but quite consistent with the courtier's concept of polite conversation: 'Dante à cause de sa science fut vn peu presomptueux, mesprisant, dédaigneux, il vivoit grossierement à la maniere des Philosophes, & ne sçauoit pas comme il faut s'entretenir auec les honnestes gens' (p. 116). The manual gave specific advice to avoid speaking in verse and above all to flee 'la pompe des harangues' (p. 134).

Where acceptable style is defined, we discover rhetoric being metamorphosed into a handbook for polite social conversation. The courtier must make himself pleasing to the ladies, writes Nicholas Faret in his *L'Honneste Homme ou l'art de plaire à la cour* (1630), 'car la premiere chose qu'elles considerent en vn homme, c'est la mine & l'action exterieure, que Ciceron nomme l'Eloquence du Corps. Il ne la diuise qu'en deux parties, le geste, & la voix' (p. 228). Cicero is not misquoted, but he has been interestingly misrepresented. The lawyer's poise and enunciation are transformed into a courtier's rule for social conquest. A similar transposition takes place regarding the creation of *bons mots*. 'Il faut observer des reigles, & se retenir dans plusieurs considerations, sans lesquelles ils perdent souuent toute leur grace. Il faut regarder qui nous sommes, quel rang tient celuy que nous voulons picquer, de quelle nature est la chose sur laquelle nous voulons exercer nostre esprit, en quelle occasion c'est, en quelle compagnie, & en fin quelle est la chose que nous voulons dire, & si l'on peut esperer auec aparence qu'elle doive passer pour bon mot' (p. 208). No rhetorician would quarrel with the criteria in general. Speaking requires rules to insure its excellence; the audience, the propriety of the subject must be considered. But Faret's inclusion of the rank of the individual addressed betrays the entire transposition from law court to salon with the intent of 'speaking well' now seen exclusively within the confines of a social situation. It is this sort of transposition which forms the indispensable link between humanist interest in rhetoric and works of seventeenth-century writers on rhetoric like Bary, who dedicated his *Rhétorique françoise* to the Comtesse de Ryeux because he loved 'les beaux sentiments, & les belles expressions, le bel esprit, & la belle science' (sig. ã2^r), all associated with the Comtesse.

It also represents an essential embellishment of certain ideas in the *Essais*. Whereas Montaigne's discussions of rhetoric tend to bring into play an absolute opposition between affectation and simplicity, his portrait of the sage nobleman occupies an intermediate position between the unlettered peasant and the unfortunate pedant.

In their reworking of rhetoric's principles, noticeably directed at Montaigne's new social hero, the manuals bring language and the 'honnête homme' together in a way that supplies an important intermediate style between affectation and simplicity. Faret's allusion to Cicero is serious enough; he is not recommending for the courtier a chambermaid's 'babble'. However, just as Montaigne warns that 'Toute estrangeté et particularité en nos meurs et conditions est evitable comme ennemie de communication et de société et comme monstrueuse' (p. 201) and circumscribes our actions by society's norms, so the manuals' association of rhetorical canons with social concerns establishes a new context in which to employ and judge language.

Appended to Fouquelin's *La Rhétorique françoise* (1557) is a summary of rhetoric's constituent parts, all grouped within brackets that serve also to relate the parts to one another. Father Ong describes this configuration as characteristic of the separation between logic and life given the way in which Fouquelin and others conceived of rhetoric. Humanist tragedy is not an unimportant example of that same separation. As a discussion of its 'patterns' has shown, the development of many works derives from an interest in debate, stichomythia, *narratio*, that is, from contrasting concepts and from linguistic display. The plays meet life only at the point where an imagined situation becomes recognizable as a potential human predicament.

The manuals do not permit language to enjoy such an independent existence. Although classical rhetoricians had always urged the orator to consider the disposition of his audience and the nature of human passion, their own discussion of these topics is highly schematized and abstract.[3] In his *Traicté de la cour*, Du Refuge devotes chapters XIII through XXVI to a very similar discussion of the passions but when Du Refuge speaks of how to ingratiate oneself, the ties between speech and reality become very strong:

En la personne que nous voulons induire a faire quelque chose, outre que nous deuons considerer son aage, son rang, sa profession, . . . quelles sont ses façons de faire ses passions & affections plus ordinaires, la capacité de son entendement, son accortise ou prudence: il faut considerer la disposition vers la chose que nous voulons persuader, les respects ou esgards que ceste personne peut auoir à diuerses choses ou personnes, qui la peut faire pancher plus d'vn costé que d'autre.

(pp. 145-6)

It remained for the theoreticians to bring this development to bear on tragedy but before we contemplate that last step in the new thoughts on style, some attention should be paid to the world of letters in the early seventeenth century.

Poetry and the novel. This dimension of our subject has already been studied at great length by other critics. It is a well-documented fact, for example, that by the end of the sixteenth century the negative reaction to 'docte' poetry which had pressed Ronsard as early as the publication of his *Amours* of 1552 was beginning to carry the day.

If very 'doctes' works were printed well into the seventeenth century, they were produced by milieux that cultivated the past. When the Valois dynasty came to an end, the literati found refuge among figures such as Marguerite de Valois, Henry IV's first wife, and the Maréchale de Retz, who attempted to preserve in their salons the culture which they had known before the accession of Henry IV. Claude Billard was attached to the Maréchale's household. He also frequented the court of Queen Margot along with another writer of tragedies, Garel, and Claude Garnier, who wrote a continuation of Ronsard's *Franciade*. Pindaric odes were still fashionable in this group.

They and other supporters of the humanist aesthetic argued for the older ways. Billard defended the lack of rich rhymes in his plays through preference for 'quelque belle senteence [*sic*]' (sig. [ã8ᵛ]). Hardy insisted that 'quiconque au surplus s'imagine que la simple inclination dépouruûe de sçience puisse faire vn bon Poete, il a le iugement de trauers' (III, 5). But all were eventually brought to the conclusion that the moment had passed when erudition commanded respect. Desportes intimated as much; Hardy, Mlle de Gournay, and Claude Garnier confessed it and so did one of Hardy's admirers.[4]

There can be no single explanation for these developments. The evolution of the French language alone gave the humanist's works a singularly archaic quality. Mlle de Gournay makes this very clear:

Ie sors d'vn lieu où i'ay veu ietter au vent les venerables cendres de Ronsard & les Poetes ses contemporains, autant qu'vne impudence d'ignorans le peut faire: brossans en leurs fantasies, comme le sanglier eschauffé dans vne forest. Or apres que tels ieunes discoureurs ont dechiré de cent sortes, & parmy tout ceux qui les veulent escouter, l'art et les conceptions de ces Poetes, qu'ils croyent aisément preceller teste pour teste; leur grand & general refrain butte sur leur langage, allegans: On ne parle plus ainsi.

(pp. 565-6)

Claude Bachet published a translation of Ovid in 1626 and justified his new effort with a poet whom Saint Gelais and Charles Fontaine had already rendered into French in the preceding century by noting that both wrote 'en vn siecle assez grossier, & auquel nostre langue estoit bien esloignee de sa perfection' (sig. *3^v). The next year there appeared an anthology of poetry in which the editor included ten poems of Ronsard 'pour faire voir la difference du stile du passé au present' (Katz, pp. 66).

What other possible ingredients discussed in this chapter suggest is that the negative effects of a changing language or Montaigne's more philosophical preference for 'la nayfveté' go hand in hand with increased concern to define both behaviour and speech of the 'honnête homme', a concern that culminates in the recognition of polite society (not Cicero or Quintilian) as the arbiter of taste.

Observe signs of this double evolution in Deimier's *L'Académie de l'art poétique* (1610). On the one hand, he remarks on difficult passages, 'Quelques vns se trompans en la chimere du grand sçauoir qu'ils s'imaginent en l'obscurité d'vn Poëme, estiment que les passages plus obscurs de Du-Bartas sont les plus beaux, & tout au cõtraire ce sõt ceux qui le sont le moins, & où les vers sont les plus desagreables pour les periphrases & metaphores impropres dont ils sont chargez' (p. 271); on the other, 'Cette façon d'escrire ainsi, auec telle abondance de propos figurez, & d'allegation de fables, auoit faict haïr aux Seigneurs & aux Dames de la Cour, les Poësies qui portoyent les noms, & les discours de ces Deitez antiques' (p. 281).

Deimier's attack on enjambement and faulty syntax, his attempt to disparage poetic licence and upbraid Ronsard for sanctioning certain liberties have caused many critics to link the *Académie* with Malherbe. Yet in the same work Deimier called Montaigne 'vn des plus beaux esprits de France' (p. 230). By holding to the principles of rhetoric only to mistrust the verbal and creative extravagance of humanist style and to suggest that public response is a means for establishing literary canons, Deimier reveals that he belongs to a cultural movement that includes Malherbe, but also outdistances him in time and scope. The many facets of the *Académie*'s aesthetics are also those of a new French society coming into being.

Elevated to unprecedented heights as a judge of good taste, that society became predictably more interested in itself. What an unmistakable indication of change that Billard, no proponent of Malherbian reform, should defend his long monologues not by referring to the beauty of words but by calling them 'la *naifue* representation de *nos* pensées, *nos* esperances, & *nos* desseins, qui bien-souuent nous entretiennent plus long temps qu'ne [*sic*] simple tirade de cent, ou deux cents vers' (sig. [ã8ᵛ], my italics). Moreover, even before Saint Amant flaunted his ignorance of Latin and Théophile spoke disparagingly of classical fables, there are signs of a growing desire for portraits of contemporary life.

In his *The Genesis of Corneille's Mélite*, G. L. van Roosbroeck hypothesized that Corneille was influenced by just such a movement. He cites an impressive number of prefaces dating from the end of the sixteenth century to the 1630's—to which might be added Rosset's *Histoires tragiques* (1615)—where the authors call attention to the truth of their stories because they have gone to their own times and not to antiquity for their material. The feeling of having thereby exchanged fiction for authenticity is well expressed by Camus in his 'Proiet de ce Tableau de la perfaitte Amitié' (preceding *Le Cléoreste*, 1620). He insists that between his story and that of Orestes and Pylades there is all the difference between East and West 'car ce que nous lisons de l'ancient ORESTE est meslé de tant de feintes que s'il y a quelque rayon de vérité, il demeure prisonnier sous l'iniustice de tant de nuages qu'il ne se peut faire voye à trauers tant de broüillars' (sig. ¶6ᵛ-7ʳ).

The Bishop's views sound somewhat like prejudices of the early Protestant humanists[5] and may have similar religious underpinnings. Sorel's *Le Berger extravagant*, on the other hand, leaves no doubt that the period was experiencing a distinct and general concern over the issue of vraisemblance. Novelists should not write things, he states in the preface, 'qui ne sçauroient estre, ny celles que l'on ne doit pas faire' (sig. ã5ʳ⁻ᵛ). To accentuate the silliness of the opposite, he creates his 'extravagant shepherd' Lysis who believes all he has read about pastoral life and decides to seek out the country in which *l'Astrée* is set.

Lysis' sureness about the reality of *l'Astrée*'s world and all the literary conventions he has encountered provides the needed foil. The conventions, continually on his lips, permit Sorel's spokesman in the novel to observe that the image of the Fates' weaving the thread of our life is absurd because 'il y a cent mille vies qui durent en mesme temps' (I, 27). Echo is not a person; 'C'est nostre voix mesme qui retentit en quelque concauité' (I, 29). It is absurd to call a woman's breasts 'boules de neige' or 'deux globes'; they are in reality only 'deux demies boules' (VII, 20, 21). To such scientific precision must be added a certain philosophical and psychological sophistication that prevents Lysis' friends from treating the pastoral golden age as anything but a ridiculous travesty of reality: 'Nous ne sommes pas assez loin de l'ambition & de l'auarice pour mener vne si innocente vie' (I, 54; see also VI, 393).

A considerable number of barbs are directed at the traditional metaphoric language of love poetry. An engraving appears in the book with the inscription 'La belle Charite' (Lysis' beloved) but instead of the natural features, the picture reproduces the metaphoric equivalent—bows for her eyebrows, roses for her cheeks, and so forth. Mythology, too, is mocked. Lysis courts Charite with this argument: '& encore que ie sois Berger, ne me desdaignez pas, veu que la belle Cytheree à bien aymé Adonis & Anchise, qui n'estoient que Pasteurs', which produces the authorial comment: 'Charite qui n'entendoit rien à tout cecy estoit fort importunee de cét entretien' (III, 215, misnumbered 197). The slight is repeated in a later comment to the effect that what was already blameworthy in the ancients is even so in modern writers who are not pagans yet cannot do without the old false gods. The same writers are accused in the sixth book of using such allusions to show how 'bien doctes' they are (VI, 400-1). The phrase has little positive connotation here and if we needed an explicit denunciation of the old humanist poet, Sorel provides one. In the tenth book, the characters examine a series of portraits of French poets. 'Ce qui estoit de plus ridicule estoit le portraict d'vn Poëte Aduocat, qui au lieu de sa longue rabe [sic] auoit aussi vne casaque à l'antique; ainsi qu'vn heros de medaille, encore qu'il eust la mine la plus pedantesque du monde' (X, 211).

As in the *Essais*, rejecting pedantry meant rejecting the façade of pretension and the style of inflated minds, not the 'fruit' of the truly wise. Early in the second book Anselme (Sorel's *porte-parole*) gives Lysis some works to read in the hope that they will turn him from his pastoral fantasy. Naturally they are rejected but the list ('Senecque, Plutarque, du Vair, Montaigne & Charron'—II, 63) makes the point. Sorel has not broken with antiquity or many of its ideals, especially the Stoic ones. It would not even be fair to say that he has broken with rhetoric. He ridicules the *copia* that embellishes to embellish. He shares with Montaigne a sentiment that such decoration detracts from the true business of becoming educated. The sentiment is in some respects a veritable reversal of humanist thinking. Embellishment, particularly in the form of analogies, was conceived to teach us surely as *sententiae*. Some of Sorel's criticism seems based on illogical use of analogies but the novel as a whole indicts the very process of seeking to enhance reality by means of analogy. The portrait of Charite as depicted in the book demonstrates to what degree Sorel does not respond to the expanded significance of the woman seen through the simile of the bow and the roses. Thus, although schoolboys could still study Aphthonius, edited in 1623 by the Jesuits and in the following year by Heinsius, although Martin Del Rio, a Jesuit, published in 1619 at Paris a *Syntagma tragœdiæ latinæ*, which offered this familiar distinction between tragedy and comedy, 'In tragedy are displayed Heroes, generals, kings; in comedy, lowly people, unconnected to State affairs; in the former laments, exiles, murders; in the latter, love stories and the abduction of maidens' (p.3), and although his analysis of Hippolytus and Phaedra ('In Hippolytus you see depicted the character of a chaste, rigid, austere young man; in Phaedra, the portrait of a shameless lover, debasing herself excessively'—p. 11) belongs to the line of thought that convinced the sixteenth-century pedagogues of tragedy's usefulness, we have amassed several reasons to believe that at the same moment a wider public with very different views on style had gained prominence. It was then that the theoreticians transformed these new views into literary canons.

The theoreticians. There should be little need to reiterate the importance of Guez de Balzac or Jean Chapelain in establishing literary standards between 1620 and 1640. Tallemant des Réaux said of Balzac's first volume of letters: 'Il est certain que nous n'avions rien veû d'approchant en France, et que tous ceux qui ont bien escrit en prose depuis, et qui escriront bien à l'avenir en nostre langue, luy en auront l'obligation' (II, 42). Jean Chapelain was an essential figure in the drafting of *Les Sentiments de l'Académie française* on Corneille's *Le Cid*. Even if Lancaster is right to discount the immediate impact of Balzac and Chapelain on Mairet's first venture with the rules, it will be remembered that we are concerned here with the growth of a new perspective on literature. Balzac and Chapelain offer invaluable evidence of such a new perspective, whatever the specifics of their relationship to Mairet may have been.

It is traditional to explain the thrust of their writings in terms such as these used by René Bray. 'La génération de Chapelain allait doter la France de tout un arsenal de règles, qui pendant près de deux siècles régiront impérieusement toute la production poétique. . . .

Son rôle littéraire est d'assurer le triomphe de l'autorité sur l'indépendance, de la discipline sur l'insubordination. . . . C'est la génération de l'ordre' (p. 358). The preceding pages would suggest, however, that order or authority were only partial concerns and the participation of Balzac and Chapelain in the currents of thought just analysed accentuates their ongoing importance for the society that formulated the new Classical tragedy.

Balzac's impact on seventeenth-century style, for example, can only be understood in the context of that long debate over imitation which passed through the Ciceronian controversy and Montaigne, even if, since the time of Voltaire, it has been fashionable to mock the success of Balzac's epistolary style and to underline the quantity of bombast and rhetoric it contains. Voltaire did not err in pointing out these elements in Balzac's letters. They exist. The danger lies in concluding on the basis of *our* dissatisfaction with these works that Balzac's success should be minimized and his partisans spanked for their shortsightedness. Voltaire judged Balzac from the vantage point of eighteenth-century prose; Balzac's contemporaries judged him with respect to their predecessors who, as we have seen, pleased less and less.

Ogier's *Apologie pour Monsieur de Balzac* offers a very precise discussion of Balzac's merits as they were understood in 1628. To the charge that all of Balzac's ideas derive from Greek and Latin sources, Ogier retorts: 'il faut . . . considerer, non si vne chose est ancienne: mais si elle est iuste ou raisonnable' (p. 18). The defence reflects not only the general attitude of the *Essais* toward books, men, and ideas, but also Montaigne's own treatment of the ancients. We have seen above that Montaigne hid from no one the pleasure he took in transposing into French the classical writers he enjoyed. What appears in Montaigne as an idiosyncrasy Ogier makes a veritable literary principle: 'il est permis de prendre les conceptions des anciens, pourueu que ce soit auec vne telle addresse qu'on ne soit point surpris sur le fait, c'est à dire qu'on y aporte vn tel déguisement, que la chose change de face, & ne puisse mesme estre reconnue de ceux à qui elle appartient' (p. 22). The reasoning culminates in an observation that those who reveal Balzac's sources only contribute to his glory by showing the superiority of the French rendering to the source. While the wisdom of antiquity has hardly been slighted, Ogier upholds Balzac for having taken antiquity and made it French. The implications here are most significant. Just as

Montaigne urges wisdom but not pedantry and the manuals of behaviour warn against extravagance, so Ogier enjoys Balzac because the learning remains disguised. Behind the nuance lies all the difference between Grosnet's compendium of Senecan *sententiae* and Montaigne's essays. French society had grown less patient with the scholar's pastimes. It wanted its ideas to be like its courtiers: intelligible and attractive.

At the same time, we continue to find a not surprising acquaintance with rhetoric and appreciation of its accomplishments, 'Car les choses extraordinaires exprimees en termes magnifiques ne persuadent pas seulement, mais estõnent les escoutans' (p. 72). But Ogier too, recognizes that the day of forensic oratory is over and that eloquence must of necessity take refuge in the epistolary form (p. 196). The mixture of views is all the more interesting since it appears in Balzac's own writings.

Balzac could be devastatingly negative when speaking about rhetoric. 'Quant à moy', he wrote to Chapelain in 1632, 'je me mocque de la Rhetorique & de ses figures, & n'ay que faire d'vn Art, qui m'a fait tant de procés' (*Recueil*, p. 196). Some years earlier he told BoisRobert that if he could not praise the King without the aid of Alexander the Great and Plutarch's famous men, BoisRobert would be justified in blaming him 'de faire venir les sotties de loin' (*Lettres*, p. 250). Of course such 'sotties' were common practice in the humanist theatre and it is not unexpected, therefore, to hear Balzac lash out against the tragic style of his day: 'Vous n'ouïstes jamais tant de Bravades contre la Fortune, vous ne vistes jamais estimer si hautement la Vertu ny mespriser si genereusement les choses humaines. . . . On les nomme Acteurs improprement; ce sont de veritables Recitateurs; ce sont des Enfans qu'on a chifflez pour vn jour de ceremonie, et non pas des Hommes qui traitent ensemble dans la conversation ordinaire' (*Œuvres*, I, 306). When Balzac continues, we receive a fuller (and more accurate) definition of his sentiments. 'Il se peut encore, Monsieur, que ces sortes de Poëtes enseignent. Ie ne m'y oppose pas; mais je soutiens que leur methode d'enseigner est vicieuse sur le Theatre. Ils veulent instruire directement et sans artifice, par la voye commune des Preceptes, au lieu qu'ils devroient instruire avec adresse, par le moyen de l'imitation' (I, 307).

The quotation provides an excellent summary of the trends of the period at work. Tragedy's moral usefulness remains intact but the directness of tragedy's didacticism—once its pride—now proves unacceptable and through the kind of transposition of terms we have already observed, 'artifice', 'imitation', and 'adresse' cease to define style as the sixteenth century conceived it. Whereas the humanists vaunted their skill in reproducing the devices of rhetoric, Balzac applies to tragic style the same principle that Ogier praised with respect to his epistolary prose—artful refurbishing. The dramatist now teaches best whose art displays an ability to absorb the wisdom in question and communicates it without the crudity of recitation. We might be tempted to see parallels here with the novel as well. The phrase 'des Hommes qui traitent ensemble dans la conversation ordinaire' recalls the shift to contemporary portraits. Yet I think that we would be in error to believe that Balzac understood by the phrase a theatre of realism.

Balzac and his admirers had no doubts as to the superiority of rhetoric's grand style over all others. Ogier said as much in his *Apologie* (p. 71) and Balzac made the same point in a letter to Racan, dated 3 September 1633. It begins with praise for *Les Bergeries*. But Balzac also had reservations. 'Il faudra neanmoins, si vous me croyez, casser bien tost cet equipage champestre, & chercher les sceptres & des couronnes. Le puissant esprit qui vous agite, a trop de force pour les petites matieres' (*Recueil*, p. 38). Balzac belongs to that distinguished line of Frenchmen like Etienne Pasquier who loved rhetoric's art too well to see eloquence in the inconsequential and the lowly. The sixteenth century's indulgence in the rhetoric of recitation and 'mignardise' thrust these men toward a middle ground, within rhetoric's possibilities, not outside them.

Balzac's position does not depend entirely on stylistic considerations. He has some familiar remarks to make about the human personality. In particular Balzac minces no words when denouncing the concepts fortune, destiny, and 'la force des Astres'. If we are willing to look elsewhere for an explanation, he says, we shall find the answer in man, in 'vn transport de passion, qui sort sans raisonnement de la partie animale, et s'arreste au premier objet qui plaist et à la premiere satisfaction de la volonté' (*Œuvres*, II, 180). This disabused view of fortune leads both to heightened awareness of human nature, and, as with the *Essais*, to a heightened sense of the natural and the artificial, that is, back to style.

Like Montaigne, Balzac found fascinating the thought of knowing the great Romans *en privé*, for he, too, was convinced of the distinction between the public and private self:

Ie ne doute point qu'apres les avoir veû tonner et mesler le Ciel et la Terre dans la Tribune aux harangues, ce ne fust vn changement de plaisirs tres-agreable de les considerer sous vne apparence plus humaine, estant desarmez de leurs Enthymemes et de leurs Figures, ayant quitté leurs Exclamations feintes et leurs Choleres artificielles, paroissant en vn estat où l'on pouvoit dire qu'ils estoient veritablement eux-mesmes.... Il estoit là le vray Ciceron et se mocquoit souvent en particulier de ce qu'il avoit adoré en public. C'estoit là où il definissoit les hommes et ne les embellissoit pas.

(*Œuvres*, I, 235-6)

Here we begin to understand what Balzac meant by a 'conversation ordinaire'. Is it not the language which instead of conveying a sense of the artificial suggests what we are 'veritablement'? Balzac's ideas grow even more precise when, in an analysis of a Latin poem on the tears of St. Peter, he confesses to a M. Girard: 'Il me semble . . . qu'il dit trop de poinctes pour vn veritable affligé. La Nature ne parle pas de cette sorte, ni les passions non plus, qui sont les filles de la Nature, comme les poinctes sont les jeux de l'Art' (*Recueil*, pp. 217-18). 'La douleur', he adds, 'ne doit pas estre estudiée, ou au moins . . . l'estude ne doit pas paroistre' (pp. 218-19). The final qualification is the essential one. Humanist tragedy did nothing to hide its studied approach to transcribing emotion, convinced that the embellished description presented the finest rendering possible. Balzac now affirms that rhetoric's task is to be discreet, not blatant. Too obvious a presence makes the portrait the opposite of forceful and credible. The change may be related to an increased acquaintance through the pastoral and the pastoral novels with more sober portraits of passion but it is also, I believe, a reflection of the crisis in language's ability to be self-sufficient or creative. Montaigne felt obliged to hold up door to cornice, chatter to metaphor. In a less extreme, yet comparable fashion, Balzac will not forget the nature of passion when he experiences its literary transcription. An interplay between the real and the literary must now be considered where once language created its own reality. Is it any wonder that within a framework which could not do without the real as a point of comparison tragedy and its style should evolve from the 'sacred' to the 'human'?

If many of Corneille's heroes do not seem to fit Nadal's terminology, Balzac helps to explain that the period, like the sixteenth

G

century, sometimes had particular definitions of what constituted human behaviour. In an essay called *Consolation à Monseigneur le Cardinal de la Valette*, Balzac speaks very harshly of the heroes in Euripides and Sophocles. 'Mais quelle apparence de voir . . . des Heros infirmes et miserables; qui crient encore à present et se tourmentent . . . qui remplissent les Theatres de leurs longs et importuns gemissemens, qui ayant eu plus de fougue que de fermeté, sont tombez en des foiblesses, qui ont deshonoré leur affliction? Ils enervoient et effeminoient la douleur, au lieu de l'aguerrir et d'en tirer du service' (*Œuvres*, I, 315). There is an element of flattery here because the Cardinal is held up as someone who knew how to contain his grief. But the compliment rests on a principle: 'vous faites bien voir la difference qu'il y a entre la Vertu sauvage, et la Vertu cultivée; entre les forces aveugles de la Nature, et l'adresse advisée de la bonne Institution' (I, 314). By signalling his preference for the 'Vertu cultivée—the act that is more praiseworthy because it is not spontaneous or unconscious—Balzac ushers us into Corneille's tragedy and explains his inability to appreciate the Greek heroes. They lack 'apparence' (credibility) because heroes to Balzac do not break down under stress. They stand up to their difficulties. Thus, the 'reality' of Corneille's heroes is affirmed whereas a standard character type in humanist tragedy loses its importance and meaning.

For partisans of the rules-and-order theory of French Classicism, Balzac also has an interesting view of the Court. As early as 1624, he agreed with BoisRobert that 'c'est la voix de la Cour qui approuue les hommes, & qui les condamne, & que hors de sa lumiere les belles choses ne paroissent point' (*Lettres*, p. 230).In discussing the crude language of Montaigne's time, he remarked that the Court was then as indulgent as it is now rigorous (*Œuvres*, II, 407). Yet what does Balzac really mean except that at Court one finds the etiquette of which he approves and that the Court sanctions an aesthetic different from the one in vogue at the time of Montaigne. There may be those who feel that the entire period fell in love with the abstraction called order but the hegemony of the Court that is alluded to here also corresponds to the growing agreement on behaviour, both social and linguistic, whose manifestations we have been studying. That such agreement should stimulate a feeling of distinctiveness is nothing new in history. The remarkable element in French Classicism lies in the wide success of the new aesthetic, not in the Court's sense of superiority, just as the story of its origins is the story of those changes which brought about a definition of 'les belles choses' Balzac mentions, not of the principles employed to preserve such an aesthetic.

Vraisemblance is just such a principle and it, too, has been discussed as if it were some abstract concept cherished by abstract thinkers when the evidence suggests that the seventeenth century simply endowed the old concept of *propria* with its observations about human nature and social behaviour as the observations grew in number and importance. An interesting example of how vraisemblance has been dissociated from its roots in contemporary mores is provided by Lanson's 1901 article on Corneille's *Discours*, in which he touches momentarily on Jean Chapelain.

While recognizing Chapelain's sincerity in the *Sentiments*, Lanson insists that 'sa critique est pleine de naïveté' and gives as an example: 'Il a fait un reproche à Corneille de ce que Rodrigue n'a pas dit son nom au portier en entrant dans la maison du comte!' (p. 122) If Chapelain is naïve here, then he belongs to a long line of naïve critics such as Scaliger, Peletier, and Deimier, whose criticisms of Homer and Virgil were cast in the same mould. Lanson lost sight of the fact that to a society which now held art up to reality there could exist a very real conflict between feeling the drama of Rodrigue's appearance before Chimène and recognizing that in real life the scene would probably not be possible. The conflict cannot be taken lightly and the argument—much used in Corneille's own time—that Chapelain's objection is out of order because *Le Cid* pleased those who saw it, begs the question. Corneille's opponents never contradicted his ability to entertain the public successfully.[6] But some could not share easily in the illusion created on stage and their criticisms attempted to suppress those traits which stood between them and Corneille's genius. When Chapelain called vraisemblance 'l'essence de la poésie dans le particulier du poème tragique' (*Opuscules*, p. 120), he left no doubt about the importance of that concept in his own eyes and unless we do it justice, we have not understood fully his quarrel with *Le Cid*.

The catalogue of Chapelain's library reveals not only his vast reading but also his ties to many of the currents mentioned above. He possessed an edition of Aphthonius, Erasmus' work on *copia* as well as the classical texts of Aristotle, Cicero, and Quintilian, Garnier's tragedies, Del Rio's *Syntagma*, Montaigne, Casa,

Castiglione, and Faret on moral philosophy and preparation for public life. Like Balzac or Montaigne, he made a sharp distinction between the pedantry of the colleges and the discourse of the Court.[7] Like Théophile, he regretted in Ronsard 'cette affectation de paroistre sçavant', 'cette servile et désagréable imitation des anciens' (*Lettres*, I, 632), yet had great respect for the poet's genius. He deplored Ronsard's language and use of mythology but confessed regarding Malherbe: 'ceux là ne luy ont guères fait de tort qui ont dit de luy que ses vers estoient de fort belle prose rimée' (*Lettres*, I, 637). Chapelain was neither insensitive nor imperceptive. He saw more in Ronsard than Malherbe probably did; he read and enjoyed to some degree the romances of earlier centuries but he was also of his time.

Chapelain's justification for long *récits* in tragedy ('le soliloque s'admet sur la scène comme pour le discours intérieur qui arrive tous les jours à tous les hommes qui ne sont pas absolument stupides' —*Opuscules*, p. 125) brings to mind Billard's justification, where there is a comparable absence of the word rhetoric or of any of its appropriate figures. The romances pleased Chapelain most in the high sense of honour felt by the knights—not surprising in a society imbued with the Stoic ideal. Their conversations and gallantry, on the other hand, aroused Chapelain's interest without meeting his entire approbation. For, on both counts the romances lack a trait that Chapelain's society had come to consider essential. Their conversation he termed moral but not urbane, 'en un mot, peu galante et fort solide' (p. 26). The manuals had done their job so well that Chapelain could distinguish between gallantry then and now because Lancelot 'ne sait que c'est de se mettre bien auprès de sa maîtresse par les paroles étudiées ni par le soin de la suivre en tous lieux' (p. 30). I accentuate these views not only because they demonstrate the wider context of Chapelain's so-called 'naive' statements, but also because they show how much the evolution of society had endowed vraisemblance with new implications.

We recognize today to what degree the prominent commentators of Aristotle in the sixteenth century fell short of capturing the sense or spirit of his *Poetics*. Later theoreticians like Heinsius proved to be more faithful to the master than Castelvetro or Scaliger. Heinsius did not make pleasure the end of poetry as the former did and through long paraphrases of Aristotle's discussion of the proper magnitude of tragedy, he gave to the concept of unity of action an aesthetic

connotation quite different from Scaliger's emphasis on verisimilitude alone. When we examine the work of Chapelain, we discover
that he, too, continues the process of updating (but not rejecting)
rhetoric and that critics' preoccupation with the Aristotelian unities
may have overshadowed the much greater importance of vraisemblance to this theoretician.

For example, in the *Préface de l'Adone du Marin* (1623), purgation,
not pleasure, is made the aim of poetry and 'pour purger il faut
émouvoir; or comme on ne peut émouvoir sans faire impression,
laquelle impression se fait par moyens et convenables et continués,
et comme d'ailleurs ces romanceries, soit par la qualité, soit par la
quantité de leur matière, en soient entièrement rendues incapables,
on ne peut aussi raisonnablement espérer cette purgation par leur
entremise' (*Opuscules*, pp. 96-7). However, Chapelain does not
follow Aristotle or Heinsius in associating purgation with fear and
pity only. Moreover, it is rather difficult to sense from Chapelain's
words that the author achieves his end of purgation by the construction of his plot although such was in Aristotle's mind the best method
employed by poets. Instead, according to Chapelain's description,
the writer constructs by accumulating means which will make the
reader emerge from his experience moved and purged. It is the difference between unity of action as a plot that achieves the desired
end and unity of action as an assemblage of integrated 'means'
designed each to impress and to move—a distinction of some moment
since the second possibility bears considerable resemblance to the
fashion in which a rhetorician was expected to form his speech.

Admittedly, by condemning the quantity of means in the 'romanceries', Chapelain intimates that he is concerned with unity of action.
At an early point in the *Préface*, he even relegates novels to the
category of non-natural and imperfect subjects because they lack
'ou unité d'action ou unité de personnes agissantes' (p. 76). Yet
when Chapelain comes to discuss *Adone* or the *Odyssey* and to
explain in some detail the kind of plot he admires, it becomes clear
that the two adjectives 'convenables' and 'continués' used to describe the means by which an author impresses and moves state
precisely what Chapelain demands of action: vraisemblance and
simplicity. The action of *Adone* is admirable because it is 'plus
simple qu'intriguée, toute d'amour, et assaisonnée des douces
circonstances de la paix et du sel modéré des facéties' (p. 84). 'Simple'
is meant to contrast with 'confus', used on the following page

to characterize novels. This canon may derive its importance for Chapelain from his source on the different kinds of fable. Heinsius followed Aristotle's division of possible fables into two categories— simple and complex, distinguished by the presence or absence of peripeteia or discovery. Chapelain conceives of three kinds of plot in the manner of Badius and the grammarians:

> la première était appelée des Latins *motoria*, comme celle qui contenait en soi des agitations et de la confusion dans la suite de son sujet, conduites avec art à une fin ou heureuse ou malheureuse, selon que la matière le désirait; la seconde se nommait *stataria*, comme moins agitée et plus tranquille que l'autre, et celle-ci consistait en accidents ordinaires et finissait sans grand attirail, de la sorte que le spectateur se l'était persuadé; la troisième se disait *mixte* comme celle qui tenait de l'une et de l'autre
>
> (*Opuscules*, p. 95).[8]

The difference in concept between Aristotle's simple plot and the *stataria* variety is considerable. By presenting plot as a question of degrees of 'accidents', Chapelain again bypasses the Aristotelian concept of internal coherence and emphasizes his interest in plot as an assemblage of 'means'. Predictably, the emphasis leads back to vraisemblance.

Commenting on the *Odyssey* and Heliodorus' *Histoire éthiopique*, he singles out the fact that both 'ont plus de troubles que la paix n'en reçoit' (p. 82). Their plot is thus unacceptable because it does not reflect the kind of situation which it purports to present. It is in a word, invraisemblable:

> Or cette vraisemblance étant une représentation des choses comme elles doivent avenir, selon que le jugement humain, né et élevé au bien, les prévoit et les détermine; et la vérité se réduisant à elle, non pas elle à la vérité; il n'y a point de doute que la poésie l'ayant pour partage, c'est-à-dire le poète ne traitant que ce qui doit être, et ce qui doit être étant toujours vraisemblable qu'il soit, car ces deux choses se regardent réciproquement, et faisant par icelle un insensible effort sur la fantaisie, en tant qu'elle ne lui apporte rien qui ne se juge pouvoir être facilement ainsi, ce que la vérité même ne fait pas, sinon autant qu'elle est vraisemblable, il n'y a point de doute, dis-je, qu'elle ne soit plutôt crue, ayant pour soi ce qui se fait croire simplement de soi-même, que l'histoire qui y procède plus tyranniquement et qui n'a pour soi que la vérité nue, laquelle ne se peut faire croire sans l'aide et le soulagement d'autrui. Ainsi donc il suffira au poème qu'il soit vraisemblable pour être approuvé à cause de la facile impression que la vraisemblance fait sur l'imagination, laquelle se captive et se laisse mener par ce moyen à l'intention du poète.
>
> (pp. 87-8)

The importance of vraisemblance shines through at every turning. Vraisemblance is superior to truth because it needs no confirmation and makes an easy impression on the mind (and we should remember here the general way in which literature effects purgation according to Chapelain: to purge one must move, to move one must make an impression).

Chapelain's remarks on structure describe the necessary complement to Balzac's view of style. Neither will permit art to do its work outside the confines of their apprehension of the norms of reality. When they read of human events, they demand that the work conform to those norms. They do not sense or do not appreciate to what degree literature might legitimately sacrifice an effort to simulate the tempo or discourse of daily life in order to enhance its message. Thus, little by little, the gulf grows wider between the taste of the humanists and their descendants. Humanist tragedy had regularly placed its moralizing above any effort at such simulation. It created language to embellish its themes and made plot serve their elaboration. No talk of unities was required to overturn such practice, only a feeling to which the novelists, Balzac, and now Chapelain bear witness that literature should reflect and respect the reality portrayed. In *La Poétique* (1639) of Jules de La Mesnardière, we learn how the new importance of vraisemblance influenced the period's views on style, structure, and characterization.

Early in *La Poétique* La Mesnardière rebels at Castelvetro's concept that poetry was created 'pour diuertir' and 'pour diuertir le peuple' (p. H). Certain that poetry must aim rather to calm our passions, the Frenchman asks, 'mais comment a-t'il [Castelvetro] la force de traitter de populaire vn Ouurage maiestueux, qui est proprement la Chronique du renuersement des Empires, & l'histoire des changemés qui sont arriuez dans le Monde par les fautes des Souuerains? Vn Poëme graue & magnifique, qui a pour suiet ordinaire la réuolution des Etats, la recompense des bons Princes, & la punition des méchans?' (p. M) With one significant exception this passage belongs to a line of thinking prompted by the grammarians and perpetuated by the entire sixteenth century. In the phrase 'par les fautes des Souuerains' La Mesnardière joins Balzac in abandoning the concept of fortune in favour of a human explanation of tragedy's catastrophe.

Another sign of the times appears on one of the opening pages of the text proper: 'il ne faut pas que le Poëte s'entremette si fort d'instruire, qu'il ne donne beaucoup de soins au dessein de diuertir. C'est aussi pour cette raison qu'il doit tascher d'acquerir la souueraine politesse, qui est proprement la grace qui touche l'Imagination' (p. 3). This remark is presented even before La Mesnardière gives Aristotle's definition of tragedy. Its key word ('politesse') relates it to such a familiar line of development that it is somewhat surprising to find in an exposition of *La Vrai-semblance Ordinaire* the most traditional discussion of character: 'Vn homme cruel est raui quand il voit de tristes spectacles. . . . Vn Grand Ministre d'Etat sera soigneux, vigilant, courtois & officieux enuers les gens de merite' (pp. 36-7) and so on. It is only when La Mesnardière comes to discuss *Les Sentimens* that we find all the weight of contemporary manners brought to bear. I will give only one example. He can accept that a Prince in love and jealous could blame his beloved, could even confront his rival, but he will not accept 'qu'il traitte inciuilement, quelque sujet qu'il en ait, celle dont il est amoureux, qu'il lui fasse des menaces, ni qu'il l'outrage de parolles. Vn semblable procedé est indigne des grandes Ames' (pp. 249-50). 'Indigne' here seems to me to carry with it every bit as much force as 'vraisemblable' might and the statement is strong enough to show that the canon of 'politesse' as an essential element for giving pleasure was not idly offered.

As applied to style, the canon dispatched with scorn much of the rhetorical trappings already criticized by La Mesnardière's contemporaries and predecessors. Speaking of tragedy's impact on the listener, he states, 'Or elle ne l'instruira point par de longues Moralitez, qui bien qu'elles soient estimables pour la bonté de leur doctrine, ne seroiẽt pas en leur place dans le Poëme Dramatique' (p. 216). *Sententiae* are not banned but they must be used with order and discernment and not in the way of 'quelques Modernes, sous ombre que les Anciens ont abusé de ces beautez' (p. 219). No less significant are La Mesnardière's observations on the incompatibility of rhetorical style and human emotion. They reflect the same thinking Balzac expressed about the Latin poem on St. Peter, but probably derive from certain pages in Heinsius.

In his chapter on *sententia*, Heinsius sketches the tragic poet's stylistic dilemma: 'I would not put thoughts in the mouths of those who have recently known a terrible misfortune as Euripides often does. For [then] they seem to pretend or else be wise. This, however, clashes with emotion, for no one overcome by the force of grief can reason. Without reasoning, however, there can be no thought, as the philosophers know' (p. 154). In La Mesnardière's pages, the solution to this dilemma is simple, categorical, and very characteristic of his fellow theoreticians. If rhetoric in any way detracts from the natural expression of emotion, it must be suppressed: 'rien n'est plus opposé aux Expressions passionnées que *les Sentences morales, les Comparaisons ajustées, & les Conclusions* que l'on tire par des especes d'Argumens' (p. 335). He dismisses *Hecuba* because Euripides 'fait harãguer cette Reine deuant le Roy Agamemnon, auec vn si grand appareil, que les choses qu'elle dit, seroient beaucoup plus conuenables à vn excellent Orateur, qu'à cette Mere infortunee' (p. 378). And, ever faithful to the thinking of the *Essais*, the treatise feels that art may sometimes be best learned from nature, not rhetoric. For a form of speech La Mesnardière calls *Agissante* he writes 'Plus elle imite la Nature, plus elle approche de l'Art' (p. 136). When a lover must convey suffering, La Mesnardière urges 'qu'il cherche des fleurs sur le visage d'vne Amante, & non pas dans la Rhétorique; & qu'il éléue ses desirs sans éleuer son Eloquence' (p. 374).

Respect for the faithful rendering of passion is not easily separated from a fascination with the phenomenon of passion, and, indeed, La Mesnardière demonstrates the same interest in this subject that extends from Montaigne to Balzac. *La Poétique* takes one significant step beyond the usual concern for the transcription of passion, however, and brings it into the realm of structure and motivation.

The treatise's definition of 'Mœurs', for example, supposedly translates Aristotle, whose wording runs: 'Character, as distinguished from thought, reveals "moral purpose" (*proairesis*)—that is, what a dramatic personage will choose or shun in situations where the ground of choice is obscure' (p. 299). Yet La Mesnardière wrote: '*Ces puissantes inclinations qui contraignent la personne de découurir par ses maniéres les choses qu'elle a dans l'Ame, & de paroître ce qu'elle est*' (p. 107). The differences are patent and all the more revealing since Heinsius remained very close to the Greek text, never mentioning anything about the soul or its nature. La Mesnardière may have been influenced by Castelvetro, who also uses 'inclination' when explaining Aristotle's words on character: 'Dice Aristotele, che i costumi sono tali, che dimostrano, quale è la 'nclinatione, & l'elettione dell'huomo, come per cagione d'essempio, i costumi dimostreranno, che altri inclini all'auaritia, & habbia indirizzata la mente sua ad ammassare denari' (pp. 147-8). Despite the common word, the French definition remains significantly different. 'Puissantes', 'contraignent' as well as the idea of revelation ('découurir') are all added.

Seeing character as a strong emotion that betrays our nature brought La Mesnardière to a greater awareness of its role in human events. If he shares with Aristotle the conviction that a complex plot (one containing reversal and discovery) is superior to a simple one, he departs noticeably from Aristotle's discussion to insist that tragedy may have only one reversal. For, although the reversal of fortune can appear sudden and the work of one day, 'il est certain neantmoins que ces effusions de sang qui vangent les Passions des Princes, ont des causes éloignées; & que souuent elles procédent d'ambitions inuetérées, de jalousies furieuses, ou de longs mécontentemens, soit supposez ou veritables, qu'il est malaisé d'enfermer dans vne seule Action, de quelque biais qu'on les y mette' (p. 58). It is remarkable to watch the French theoreticians' continuing unwillingness to discuss unity of action as a phenomenon of logical causality in order to press for other considerations important to them. Chapelain dwelled upon vraisemblance; La Mesnardière argues from the complexity of human emotions. We may feel that a battle is the work of a single day but, in fact, it represents the outcome of much pent-up feeling, too much to be included in one single action. How, then, he says, could a plot contain more than one such complex and devastating reversal. Since it is just such a concatenation of emotions that French Classical tragedy will excel in depicting, we may not take lightly La Mesnardière's words or pass over his quarrel with Castelvetro regarding Meleager's death. For La Mesnardière, 'il n'importe nullement qu'il soit doux ou furieux, passionné ou raisonnable au dernier moment de sa vie: Mais il est tres-important pour faire naistre la Pitié sur les malheurs qui l'enuironnent, de sçauoir s'il tua ses Oncles par colere, par ialousie, ou par quelque autre mouuement qui ait ébloüi sa raison' (p. 186). Again *La Poétique* accentuates the importance of passion and its relationship to structure, a totally different structure from that of humanist tragedy. Whereas the humanists enjoyed those final speeches for their rhetoric, La Mesnardière wants to appreciate the intricacies of character that motivate the action. The moral truths fade into the background and the study of 'l'humain' moves forward. No wonder *La Poétique* decries the confusion of fable and *fabula*: 'La Fable est à bien parler, la Composition du Sujet, ... & non pas comme s'imaginent quelques Poëtes ignorans, l'vne de ces actions ridicules & incroyables des

Dieux de la Metamorphose, & de ceux de l'Iliade, exprimées chez les Latins par le nom de *Fabulæ*' (p. 14).

The Playwrights and their Works. Prefatory and dedicatory remarks by the playwrights yield little to help us chart the movement away from humanist techniques and toward the unities. They do disclose, however, a concern about style. As early as 1596, when introducing the first version of his *Sophonisbe*, Montchrétien appears to have been uneasy about the length of speeches created for his characters: 'Quand a ce que les personnages introduits en la mienne parlent longuemẽt, sans entrerompre le fil de leur discours; sçache que ie ne l'ay fait sans exẽple' (p. 43). Louis Le Jars wrote in 1600 that he had preferred prose for his *Lucelle*, 'S'il est ainsi . . . qu'en la Tragedie ou Comedie on s'efforce de representer les actions humaines au plus pres du naturel . . .' (sig. A2ʳ). Behourt, whose *Esau ou le Chasseur* was probably composed just a few years before *Lucelle*, preserves, he says, all the simplicity of the subject, 'euitãt le plus qu'il m'est possible la trop grande affectation, où plusieurs de ce temps se plaisans trop corrompent toute la naifueté de nostre langue' (p. 5).

Even in the period when regular tragedy was returning to prominence, the playwrights emphasize their choice of style, not technique. Tristan presented *La Mariane* (1636) with: 'Ie ne me suis pas proposé de remplir cét ouurage d'imitations Italiennes, & de pointes recherchées (p. 10). Gombauld translated Tasso's *Aminta* in 1632 and warned his reader: 'Tu ne liras pas non plus icy ces pointes si estudiées & si recherchées, qui sont les delices de nostre siecle' adding, 'il ne faut point tirer de l'esprit ce qui doit venir du cœur' (sig. ẽ2ᵛ). We have heard this sentiment before in Balzac, Heinsius, and La Mesnardière. Gombauld's criticism has special interest because it chooses a specific work to castigate: Théophile's *Pyrame et Thisbé*. Certain reactions attributed to the characters at moments of high emotion are ridiculed and dismissed because 'Cela c'est faire plus du Declamateur que du Poëte . . .' (sig. ẽ3ᵛ). He by contrast has translated a work in which everything is 'fort raisonnable, & fort à propos' (sig. ẽ4ᵛ). Gombauld also praises the structure of *Aminta* but this comes last and without the extended discussion devoted to Théophile and to style.

When we pass from the front material to the text, we find that many French tragedies written between 1630 and 1640 do not seem to reflect any radical transformation in the genre. This impression is due in part to Corneille's genius, which quite outdistances the talent of his contemporaries, and to the strength of a longstanding tradition. The section of Mairet's preface to *La Silvanire* (1631) entitled 'De la tragédie, comédie et tragi-comédie' is, with the exception of the one sentence defining tragi-comedy, a translation into French of the introductory material provided by Badius, paraphrasing Donatus and Diomedes, for his editions of Terence! D'Urfé's dedication of his *La Sylvanire* (1627) to Marie de Médici explains that he is preserving use of rhyme in his play because innovation is highly subject to disapproval. He is less inclined to preserve the *sententiae* of classical drama. The Sages 'nous commendent de nous accomoder au temps, la seuerité de ces premiers hommes estoit telle qu'ils ne pouuoiĕt rien approuuer qui ne fust serieux. . . . Ie croy que maintenant les Roys & les Princes ne se plairoient gueres à n'estre seruis en leurs tables que du bouïllon noir de Sparte' (sig. ĕ2ᵛ). The phrasing leaves open the possibility for some use of *sententiae* and, indeed, they proved as stable an aspect of the genre as the usual five acts.

Similarly, Chevreau's *La Lucresse romaine* (1637) or Scudéry's *La Mort de Caesar* (1636) offer much the same style and material of the earlier tragedies. Bensérade ends his *La Mort d'Achille* (1636) with the contest of Ajax and Ulysses for Achilles' arms and its terrible consequences. Before they fight, we must listen to two speeches, set off in the text by 'HARANGVE D'AIAX' and HARANGVE D'VLISSE'. They run from page 76 to page 88. In Mairet's *Le Marc-Antoine ou La Cléopâtre* (1637) Antoine despairs, assuring his confident Lucile that 'le sort est inconstant' (p. 5) and Lucile responds with the traditional words of encouragement. In the defeated hero we are treated to a portrait in which Antoine admits 'I'ay dormy trop long temps dans le sein des delices, / La peste des vertus, & la source des vices' (p. 55). Yet other notes are also sounded. The playwrights accord us Montaigne's wish and depict the great personages in a more private light. The first scene of *La Mort d'Achille* takes place between Achille and Briseide. Achille calls it himself their 'entretien secret' (p. 5). The conversation turns about the tired theme of a frightening premonition. (Patrocle's ghost has appeared to Achille.) Briseide urges him to be careful but observes 'Achille est redoutable, il est vaillant, mais homme' (p. 3). In humanist tragedy this would mean only that Achille is mortal, like us all. Bensérade may have intended to say no more here but the play in fact develops her words by showing not only the hero's death but also his love for Polixène and the complex emotions created between Achille and Brideide—an aspect of the story entirely passed over by Hardy.[9]

Elsewhere, more fundamental changes appear only to be absorbed by older practices. The opening of Mairet's *Sophonisbe*, for instance, where a furious Syphax confronts his queen, contrasts with the portrait accorded the old king by Montreux and Montchrétien in the excitement generated (instead of pious observations about gods and men) and in the transformation of a traditional example of fortune's reversal into a very jealous, very human individual. Sophonisbe, too, appears in a new light. She loves Massinisse and has attempted to communicate with him. This treasonous gesture only accentuates the hold of love over her. Yet such innovation swiftly passes. Syphax is killed in battle and Act II offers the familiar figure of Sophonisbe, proud queen, enemy of the Romans, hoping for death. If she finally agrees to seek help from the man she was said to love with an invincible passion, it is to please her confident:

> Ce remede, Phenice, est ridicule & vain;
> Il vaut mieux se seruir de celuy de la main,
> Et d'vn coup genereux, digne de mon courage,
> Me ietter dans le port en dépit de l'orage:
> Mais pour vous contenter, ie me force, & veux bien
> Faire vne lascheté qui ne serue de rien.

(p. 31)

Jacques Guicharnaud explains *Sophonisbe's* structure in terms of an effort to turn 'the spectator's attention toward something other than Sophonisbe's guilt' and concludes from the increased appearance of Massinisse that 'the guilty Sophonisbe is replaced by a Massinisse who, in the joy of victory, forgets the Romans...' (p. 217). However, in every retelling of the Sophonisbe story from Livy to Montchrétien Massinisse's dilemma receives as much attention as the fate of the unhappy queen. In fact, if we examine Mairet's work within that tradition, the remarkable element in his play proves to be the initial portrait of Sophonisbe in love, not Massinisse's later prominence. While one version of the story depicted the Numidian hero as eager to claim the bride he had once been promised, none spoke of a prior love in Sophonisbe. It is my own belief that Mairet agreed with La Mesnardière regarding the concatenation of emotions which lies behind sudden events and finding Sophonisbe's second marriage psychologically invraisemblable, determined that she should love Massinisse prior to Syphax' death.[10]

Of greater import to us is Guicharnaud's appreciation of the beginning of Act IV as 'Doubtless one of the most gracious scenes of early French classical tragedy . . .' (p. 213). The scene is between Massinisse and Sophonisbe, who express their joys in loving and being loved. It appears so remarkable because we hear a royal couple speaking in a tragedy, using elevated language, and conveying the impression that they are truly addressing each other, not haranguing the audience. Only the comparable scenes between Pyrame and Thisbé can offer a model for such intimacy and I must confess to believing in the light of Théophile's traditional technique[11] and Gombauld's severe judgment of his style that *Pyrame et Thisbé* captured the French public as we know it did because it was the first play to break through tragedy's conventions to a kind of realism that the period recognized as such. In so doing it paved the way for those moments of intimacy mentioned above and for more thorough revisions of traditional material like Tristan's *Panthée* (1639).

The story of Panthée had already been treated by Billard and Hardy, who recognized an amalgam of so many successful humanist themes in this tale of Cyrus' victory, Abradatas' death, and Panthée's suicide out of love for her incomparable husband. It was the Augustus-Anthony-Cleopatra situation again with certain particular traits of its own. The couple is bound by a similarly all-consuming love. Panthée's death prompts the same admiration from Cyrus that Augustus cannot help feeling before Cleopatra. In addition, Panthée illustrates the theme of chastity since before her suicide she rebuffs one of Cyrus' men who has fallen in love with her.

Billard's treatment gives maximum exposure to Panthée, paragon of virtue and fidelity. She opens his play with praises for her absent husband and fears for her honour. She knows all about Araspe's 'impudique amour / Ennemi de [s]es vœux' (f. 88ʳ). In contrast she describes her ties to Abradatas through the image of the Androgyne, suggesting that the death of one will spell the end of the other. Act II continues the parade of themes. A prince whom Cyrus has just defeated laments his fall from power and seeks to die. His lieutenant begins the usual criticism of such discouragement and they engage in a debate on suicide. The subsequent appearance of Cyrus provides an opposite view of fortune as the Persian tells of his rise from defeat to victory. (The subject and juxtaposition of scenes are strongly reminiscent of Montreux' first act in *Sophonisbe*.) Cyrus mentions Araspe and his passion when discussing the virtues of Panthée: 'Araspe estoit plaisant qui la pensoit contraindre' (f. 93^v). Thus, everyone knows that Panthée would rather die than soil her honour. With the final scene Abradatas makes clear that his love for Panthée is no less great than hers for him. In Act III news of Abradatas' desertion to Cyrus because of Panthée produces a very traditional discussion of the pro's and con's of love and women. In the third scene Panthée sends her husband off to fight for Cyrus. It is hardly a tender farewell. Panthée requests that he show Cyrus:

> que le deuoir [le] porte
> Au mespris de la mort: qu'il n'eust peu s'obliger
> Vn cœur plus genereux, inuincible au danger.
> Qu'un seul Abradatas est digne de Panthee.

(ff. 99^v-100^r)

She reaffirms her love, assures him that she would prefer to die, to see him 'Ensanglanté de coups' than to have him leave the field dishonoured (f. 100^r). The concluding acts underscore the realization by Cyrus' enemy that pride has deceived him and Panthée's suicide upon the body of her dead husband. The work closes with the chorus singing of chaste love and the glory that Panthée has won.

Hardy made certain changes when he composed his play which definitely inspired Tristan. Still Tristan's play creates a quite different effect. I would attribute the difference to the very evolution in style and concepts outlined in this chapter. For, in the main Hardy's innovations lead back to the plot as conceived by his predecessor and not ahead to Tristan.

In typical humanist fashion, Billard presented Araspe's love for Panthée as a given of the story, useful only to accentuate the heroine's untarnished soul. Hardy brings the event into the action. He even creates a dramatic situation by having Cirus (his spelling) place Panthée in the hands of Araspe for protection. 'Ne souffrir qu'on luy tienne vn propos deshonneste', Cirus warns, 'Ie veux que cela soit, au peril de la teste' (I, 109). This gesture closes the first act. As the next act begins, we learn immediately of Araspe's love which is poured out in a long monologue. Panthée arrives and Araspe cannot conceal his feelings. Cirus is informed; he upbraids Araspe and Panthée is so impressed by Cirus' justice that she bids her newly returned husband to fight for this generous victor. At the beginning of Panthée's scene with Abradatas (here called Abradate), Hardy adds a second change: Abradate's sense of jealousy. However, it is swiftly forgotten, just as swiftly as all forget Araspe's indiscretion. These facts point out the danger in placing too much emphasis on Hardy's changes. If he appears motivated by an interest in confrontation and the characters' sentiments, the text does not offer evidence to support such an hypothesis. Araspe's expanded role leads to a rhetorical piece in the florid style of innumerable set pieces written by the humanists; his confrontation with Panthée, to stichomythia:

P. Ne te souuient-il plus du mandement expres
    De ton Roy là dessus, qui te touche si pres?
A. Vn Dieu plus fort que luy me tient sous sa puissance,
    Qui m'absout du peché de desobeïssance.
P. Tu referes vn crime à l'equité des Dieux,
    Vn crime, qui leur est entre tous odieux.
A. Oüy, comme si Iupin chez la troupe celeste,
    Se soucioit beaucoup d'adultere, où d'inceste.

(I, 112)

Abradate's jealousy-inspired questioning of his wife produces nothing more than evidence of Cirus' probity. At the most Hardy proves more concerned than Billard with explaining why Abradate and Panthée come to support Cirus but it is difficult to ignore the fact that in accomplishing his task Hardy returned to the same style and themes important to Billard and to humanists in general.

In his 'Avertissement' Tristan indicates one source of change in his *Panthée*. The preface lauds Mondory's acting and regrets an attack of apoplexy 'dont il n'est pas encore guery parfaitement'. Without this untoward misfortune 'il auroit fait valoir ARASPE aussi bien qu'Herode' (an allusion to Mondory's role in *La Mariane*) (sig. [ẽ3^r]). To give Mondory ample opportunity to reveal his talents, Tristan shows Araspe in three scenes (one a monologue in *stances*) before the confrontation with Panthée and again at the beginning of Act V, where the news of Abradate's death brings new hope.

Araspe's expanded role is not the only important change made by Tristan. Greatly tempered are Cirus' and Panthée's sententious, heavy speeches. Cirus discusses the practical question of how to deal with his foes; Panthée comes to thank him for the kind treatment she has received. Because Cirus relishes the prospect of using her gratitude to enlist her husband's aid, he dares to broach the subject. 'Si le Roy d'Assirie estoit encor viuant, / Ce discours pourroit estre vn propos deceuant' (p. 9), replies Panthée. However, the new ruler is a tyrant, filled with vice. He even attempted to do her harm. 'N'ayant peu m'acquerir par douceur ny par force' (p. 10), she notes, he spread false reports about her conduct.

We need go no further into the text to appreciate how much Tristan's style and characterization reflect the views of his contemporaries. Panthée's remarkable qualities flow from her words just as Le Grand's definition of eloquence suggests they should. She does not need to speak *sententiae* to impress us. Her reactions, her tone are carefully calculated to intimate what Billard and Hardy felt had to be thrust at the audience. The elaborate (and transparent) pains taken by Hardy to justify Panthée's agreement that Abradate should help Cirus, too, disappear before a more natural sequence of events. Tristan employs La Mesnardière's observation that rapid changes in fortune have longstanding explanations. In a single revelation about the Assyrian king we are made to understand the strength of Panthée's virtue and the ease with which she can change sides.

Finally, although Hardy's initial treatment of Araspe and Mondory's acting inspired Tristan to amplify the portrait of this hapless lover, the choice of style was his alone. Here is a sample of Araspe's monologue as conceived by Hardy:

Agité du flambeau d'vne aueugle furie,
Perclus de mouuemens, ma constance perie:
Réduit à n'esperer qu'vn honteux desespoir,
Réduit à desirer ma ruyne, & la voir;
Fut-il onc vn desastre, vn malheur memorable,
A la fiere rigueur de mon sort comparable?
Araspe, pauure Araspe, helas! que n'as-tu pris
Plustost à gouuerner le terrestre pourpris:
Que geolier estably d'vne beauté captiue,
Béauté, ie le diray, la plus belle qui viue,
Tomber en ses liens, t'enferrer de ses fers;
Quels extrêmes tourmens n'ay-ie depuis soufers?
Chagrin, triste, pensif, solitaire, malade
Et de l'âme, & du corps, par sa sorciere œillade;
Œillade qui décoche vn reste de chaleurs
A trauers les nuaux de ses humides pleurs,
Œillade qui sans doute embraseroit le monde,
Si son œil retenoit cette larmeuse bonde:

Œillade qui piteuse vn rocher transiroit,
Que pour prendre les cœurs apostée on diroit:
Œillade qu'vn scadron d'autres beautez diuines,
Mises à nonchaloir, accompagnent voisine.

(I, 109)

In Tristan, Araspe is writing his love verses when Panthée comes upon him and asks to know what he has composed. He consents but first points out,

> puis que l'Eloquence
> A beaucoup d'ornemens qui sont de consequence,
> Afin que ce discours face mieux son effet,
> Ie le vay reciter ainsi que ie l'ay fait.

(p. 33)

The passage would seem to prepare us for what Hardy had already produced. Here is part of what Araspe alludes to:

Ie ne puis me desdire en ce peril extreme,
Ie ne puis le celer, Madame, ie vous ayme,
Et i'ayme mieux mourir adorant vos appas,
Que me rendre immortel ne les adorant pas.
Ie sçay que vostre race aux Astres esleuee
Void sa gloire fameuse en cent marbres grauee,
Et que peu de Heros nous sont representez
Qu'on puisse comparer à ceux dont vous sortez:
Ainsi mon vol hautain attend vn sort funeste,
Ie suis comme Ixion dans le Palais celeste;
N'estant rien qu'vn mortel, i'ose porter les yeux
Dessus vne Beauté qui vient du sang des Dieux.
Mais si de la clemence autant que du visage
Vous ressemblez aux Dieux dont vous estes l'image,
Quelque soudain despit qui vous vienne embraser,
Mon malheur trouuera dequoy vous appaiser.
Vous plaindrez vn effet dont vous estes la cause,
Et direz qu'en faisant ce que le Ciel impose
Par la necessité d'vn arrest tout-puissant,
On peut commettre vn crime & rester innocent.
Helas! quand ie vous veids, ô bon-heur trop fragile!
Ie viuois tout à moy, i'auois l'esprit tranquille,
Et ne me proposois en cest estat heureux
Ny rien de mal-aysé, ny rien de dangereux;
La raison dans mon ame estendoit sa puissance,
Et treuuoit en mes sens beaucoup d'obeïssance.
Mais vos rares beautez ne mirent qu'vn moment
A troubler la douceur de son gouuernement;

Elles veinrent changer tout mon bon-heur en rage,
Mes plaisirs en tourmens, ma bonace en orage.

(pp. 35-4).

It is eloquence of a kind, still relying on mythology, rhetoric, and common conceits of love poetry. Yet it is not eloquence as Hardy or the humanists had understood the term. That heavier, more 'docte' variety had had its day. The public, the playwrights, the century were ready for a new style and a new theatre to depict the segment of reality that belonged inextricably to the new style.

NOTES TO CHAPTER IV

[1] André Lagarde and Laurent Michard, *Les Grands Auteurs français* (Paris: Bordas, 1957), II, 167.

[2] See my *France in the Sixteenth Century* (Englewood Cliffs: Prentice-Hall, 1969), pp. 136-9.

[3] See above, p. 34.

[4] See Desportes' poem to Jean Passerat, 'Tv restois, Passerat, du bon siecle passé / Siecle où les doctes sœurs auoient tant de puissances', in *Recueil des œuvres poetiques de Jan Passerat* (Paris, 1606), sig. Ggl[r]. For Hardy, see his 'Au Lecteur', III, 4, ll. 6-12; for Mlle de Gournay, *L'Ombre*, p. 986; Claude Garnier, *Atteinte contre les impertinences de Théophile, ennemy des bons esprits*, in Frédéric Lachèvre, *Le Procès du poète Théophile de Viau* (Paris, 1909), II, 139. For Hardy's admirer, compare this remark from a liminary piece preceding *Théogène et Cariclée*: 'Ton exemple nous monstre en ce siecle peruers, / Où l'ignorance regne, & le sçauoir succombe . . .' (sig. [ã8r]).

[5] See above, p. 12.

[6] See Chapelain, *Lettres*, I, 156; Balzac to Scudéry, in Gasté, pp. 454-5.

[7] See his *Lettres*, p. 251.

[8] Donatus says simply, 'Comoediae autem motoriae sunt aut statariae aut mixtae: motoriae turbulentae, statariae quietiores, mixtae ex utroque actu consistentes' (Lawton, *Handbook*, p. 12). Badius expands this slightly: 'Comedia omnis aut stataria aut motoria aut mixta est. Stataria dicitur a stando quando actores non nimium discurrunt nec[que] solliciti perturbati aut commoti sunt: nec[que] exclamationibus aut indignationibus sese vexant. Motoria contra dicitur a motu in qua oĩa mouĕtur. Mixta autem dicitur in qua mixtim haec fiunt: ita [quod] nec[que] nimia quies: nec[que] nimia sit commotio' (sig. [ã7v]).

[9] Scudéry's development of the relationship between Dido and Aeneas in his 1637 *Didon* to include their conversations during the hunt (II, 2 and II, 6) offers a similar portrait of intimacy within the older forms of rhetorical discourse.

[10] A second proof of Mairet's concern for such vraisemblance can be found in his presentation of the first meeting of Sophonisba and Massinissa. Montchrétien and Trissino open the exchange with Sophonisba's plea. Mairet postpones introduction of this vital matter in order to lay the foundation for the love

element. Massinissa speaks first, assuring his captive that she will be well treated, that he regrets the misfortune which he has caused her. In response, Sophonisba dwells on his nature, not her plight:

> Assez de Conquerants à force de puissance,
> Rengent les Nations à leur obeyssance;
> Mais fort peu sçauent l'art de vaincre les esprits,
> Et de bien meriter le Sceptre qu'ils ont pris.
> Il n'apparient qu'à vous de faire l'vn & l'autre.

(vv. 798-802)

These verses, part of the thirty-nine spoken in praise of Massinissa, constitute in Mairet those 'sweetest words' which kindle the king's love. Relief, gratitude, and flattery have replaced fierce pride and noble courtesy as the steps which lead to Sophonisba's second marriage and tragedy.

[11] See p. 129.

CONCLUSION

The preceding analysis of conceptual rather than formal changes
in French tragedy will, I hope, stimulate the reader to look again at
the wider context under examination and appreciate the disparity
between the material that has been presented and many ideas about
that context which appear to be taken for granted.

Seeing Jodelle's form in *Cléopâtre captive* as a break with the
medieval past is one such idea. Despite the general acceptance
enjoyed by this theory we have seen how shallow that break was,
how deeply a study of tragedy can immerse us in an aspect of the
sixteenth century that receives little comment in the histories of
French literature. As the Pléiade has risen to a place of exaggerated
prominence, the gnomic literature of adages, apothegms, *dits*,
'histoires tragiques', and other manifestations of a spirit that no
longer moves us has been relegated to an indistinct background. Yet
any short title catalogue of contemporary works or contemporary
libraries would not suggest the same reading tastes that one might
glean from a perusal of the familiar Lagarde et Michard or Castex et
Surer volumes.[1] I have attempted to show how closely related
humanist tragedy is to this neglected side of sixteenth-century
literature and why we would be more faithful to literary trends of the
day if we recognized the continuity of effort from medieval to sixteenth-century literature and equated tragedy with the 'histoires
tragiques', Petrarch's *Trionfi*, or Boccaccio's *De casibus* instead of
with some ill-defined renaissance of classical forms that is then
identified as the foundations of Corneille's theatre.

Miss Doran has observed concerning the comparable period in

England: 'It is not possible to make any clear separation of medieval from classical influence, because much of medievalism itself is classicism transmuted . . . In one of the dominant ideas of early Elizabethan tragedy, the idea that fortune is a goddess not to be trusted, how shall we separate medieval Stoicism from renaissance Senecanism?' (p. 13) Her remarks are no less applicable to France. The humanist movement did introduce new forms, vocabulary, and style to the literati but its most immediate consequence in France seems to have been to provide a greater variety of expression for the older concepts, not a narrowing of techniques. The remarkable spectrum of expression to be found in works entitled 'tragédie' between 1552 and the early seventeenth century is only one glaring example of such variety. The world of those who wrote these tragedies or of those who befriended the playwrights also demonstrates such variety. From the core of humanists like Buchanan and Dorat, we move out not only to the Pléiade but to men like Belleforest, who studied with both, who translated Bandello, the *Sentences illustres* (!) of Cicero, the *Amours de Clitophon et de Leucippe*, and wrote a novel in the pastoral vein which he called *La Pyrénée*. Montreux composed tragedies, novels, pastorals, and translated a book of *Amadis de Gaule*. Bénigne Poissenot wrote a liminary piece for Matthieu's *Clytemnestre* and a volume of *Nouvelles Histoires tragiques*. Are we to conclude that all these men bore divided sensibilities, now romanesque, now didactic, now medieval, now Renaissance? Such conjecture is as useless as an attempt to know whether Laurent de Premierfaict (the same who translated Boccaccio's *De casibus*) rendered the works of Seneca into French with the encyclopedic spirit of Jean de Meung or the humanist enthusiasm of Amyot. The distinctions we see were not necessarily obvious to the sixteenth century. Dorat gladly praised Toutain's translation of the *Agamemnon*, Ronsard's *Franciade*, and the mediocre verses of Blanchon. These several efforts appear so unequal to us, yet if we pay attention to the remarks of Dorat and others, we begin to sense the unifying value of a 'docte' enterprise, the use of *copia*, and the spread of moral truths. Belleforest and Montreux underline this fact when the former admits that he enriched the text of Bandello with 'sentences, . . . harangues, & epistres' (I, 273), the latter, when he composed a novel that resorted continually to letters, speeches, and monologues in order to convey *sententiae* very similar to those employed by Belleforest and humanist tragedy.

From these primary works we again see to what degree erudition and moralizing were clear, recognized goals whereas, ironically, it could be argued that the use of that classical form so important to certain critics derives from a very medieval obedience to source, from slim plot material, but not from any aesthetic consideration at all. Witness the fragility of that regular form, undermined repeatedly by the medieval tradition well into the seventeenth century.

The second concept on which our discussion has some bearing is that of France's return to the rules. Implicit in much of the criticism that accentuates such a 'return' is the view that the Querelle du *Cid* produced a victory for the theoreticians. Descotes states flatly: 'C'est une petite minorité de doctes, soutenue par les Salons, qui a imposé la discipline dramatique, contre le désir profond du grand public' (p. 68). I confess to agreeing with Jules Brody's suggestion that French Classicism needs to be studied by someone who sees it 'as a spirit rather than a system'[2] and hope that the preceding chapters have shown in what ways an analysis of the attitudes that determined the nature of humanist tragedy can direct our attention away from Aristotle and aesthetic systems when we seek to trace a transformation of those attitudes. Moreover, it leads to a realization that greater naturalness in theatre grew important for public and theoreticians alike as the more refined rethought the erudition of the humanists and the courtly world acquired a more widely accepted code of conduct. The dramatists of the 1630's tried to keep pace with these changes, but through practical experiments, not deep involvement in theory. Adam has characterized evolution in tragedy from *Pyrame et Thisbé* to *Horace* as due to 'tâtonnements' ('Sur la première époque', p. 44). It is no secret that the early works by Mairet or Corneille span the diverse genres of the time and that neither they nor their contemporaries exhibited initially any absolute preference for tragedies that observed the rules.

These facts have been long in coming to the surface because accentuating the return to the rules often meant dividing the period into those who accepted and those who opposed regular theatre. That division is often superficial or untrue. Batiffol years ago exploded the idea that Richelieu persecuted Corneille and careful reading of La Mesnardière or Chapelain has revealed among the Aristotelian principles enough amplification and misunderstanding derived from other concerns to make those principles far less important than some would have us believe. Singularly concerned

about what people would accept, they cannot be said to have theo-
rized at an impossible distance from those who applauded the theatre
of the day.

Two prefaces often contrasted because of their approach to
regular tragedy are Ogier's 'Au Lecteur' from the second edition of
Schélandre's *Tyr et Sidon* (1628) and Jean Mairet's preface to *La
Silvanire* (1631). Ogier—the same man who defended Balzac's
letters—is said to represent opposition to the rules and Mairet to
uphold them. In fact, Ogier attacks much more the inconveniences
occasioned by the rules. Because variety is necessary 'pour rendre
la représentation agréable', the author is obliged to place within a
short period of time 'quantité d'accidents et de rencontres qui
probablement ne peuvent être arrivés en si peu d'espace' (p. 51);
the second inconvenience arises from constant recourse to messengers whose *récits* 'font perdre patience à l'auditeur' (p. 52).
Poetry and theatre, he insists, are created to please and entertain.
These aims can be achieved only through affording the audience a
variety of events too great to fall within twenty-four hours.

Here is Mairet's justification for the twenty-four hour rule: 'Il est
croyable avec toute sorte d'apparence qu'ils ont établi cette règle en
faveur de l'imagination de l'auditeur, qui goûte incomparablement
plus de plaisir (et l'expérience le fait voir) à la représentation d'un
sujet disposé de telle sorte que d'un autre qui ne l'est pas; d'autant
que sans aucune peine ou distraction il voit ici les choses comme si
véritablement elles arrivaient devant lui' (p. 68). What strikes is
the common concern for pleasing the spectator and the common
feeling that there exist significant limits to the spectators' patience.
The prefaces diverge primarily at the point where these limits are
defined. Ogier supposes that following the rules will lead automatically to a stretching of these limits; Mairet, that the opposite is true.
The burden of proof fell in time to Ogier, who failed to consider
the possibility of a regular tragedy without messengers and of a plot
capable of satisfying the spectator with a fullness that does not
require innumerable events. Mairet's 'et l'expérience le fait voir'
shows how fully he understood his advantage and the potential of
the rules to please without the inconveniences Ogier could not
separate from them.

Another point of contact between these two men is their attitude
toward the tragedy of the ancients or the Frenchmen who had imitated them. Both intimate in their prefaces that they find classical

plays less than satisfying to modern taste. Ogier specifically calls attention to the difference in taste among nations and attributes the failure of earlier French playwrights to achieve the excellence of the ancients to 'l'ardeur trop violente de vouloir imiter les Anciens' (p. 54). Mairet recognizes that because of the simplicity of classical plays they are 'en quelque façon ennuyeuses' (p. 71). He even admits that a greater variety of effects and incidents would have made these ancient plays more enjoyable to his contemporaries. Mairet's use of the rules depends neither on a blind admiration of the ancients nor on an abstract love of simplicity. He believed that the rules would please the public, that rules and variety were not incompatible. By showing concern for the public and for variety, Mairet departed in no way from the concerns of Ogier. He merely proposed a different solution.

Their open attitude toward antiquity has a long history. Both Peletier and Laudun wrote in treating the subject of imitation that the perfect poet as yet did not exist. They encouraged the novice to outdo his model and to add to it. Montreux felt grateful, but certainly not inferior to the ancients: 'Les anciens ont ietté les premieres pierres, nous les auons liees' (L'Arimène, sig. A2ʳ). Robelin scoffed at those Frenchmen who felt the ancients to be so inimitable that 'pour rēdre leurs escrits plus recōmandables ils les farcissent d'invētions cōceues par les anciēs . . . auec si supersticieuse observation que lon les jugeroit plustost liures traduits' (sig. [H3ᵛ]). La Mesnardière, too, had no mystical appreciation for the ancients: 'S'ils ont failli quelque part, comme sans doute ils l'ont fait, les fautes que nôtre Poëte commettroit en les imitant, n'en seroient pas plus excusables' (p. 219).

These quotations should remind us that the French humanists and Classicists alike refashioned tragedy to conform to the views of their day. Fidelity by the former to a certain rhetorical practice eventually pleased few of the latter. France was making the transition Margeson described in these terms: 'When the nature and intensity of the human experience became a matter of greater concern in the drama than the moral idea, then tragedy became possible' (p. 59). But the process was not simple. Many elements had to be satisfied. Mairet's generation had not lost all respect for rhetoric but now it and form and characterization had to mesh with an enjoyment of variety, an interest in the passions, and above all, a desire to identify with the sentiments and situations portrayed. The eventual victory of the rules signals a two-part realization: the discovery by dramatists that a varied yet unified plot was possible and the recognition by the public that the excesses of the tragi-comedy were not essential for a plot to be exciting. It would be difficult to overemphasize the role of Corneille in developing the necessary dramatic technique and in discovering within the society around him those 'means' which Chapelain saw as necessary to move and to purge. At the same time he was working from new premises about style and audience that his society had begun to formulate, laying well before *Le Cid* the foundation for France's passage from humanism to Classicism.

A final word. I said at the beginning of this study that it was never my intention to rehabilitate the tragedies to be studied and to offer them as misunderstood masterpieces. They are *not* superlative additions to the body of world literature. This fact should not detract, however, from their incomparable value as keys to the period that produced them. Through these works we have seen the importance of the legal class as protectors of humanist aesthetics; we have found conveniently assembled a number of attitudes toward love, kingship, woman, virtue, whose recurrence testifies to their importance for the sixteenth century. We were afforded many occasions to delve into the century's understanding of classical works. On each of these occasions, as with the study of humanist tragedy as a whole, the results were not entirely predictable. Where we had been taught to expect only inferior literature, we discovered a vital aesthetic, consistent with what the period knew about tragedy and about literature's purpose. It may well remain that despite such revelations the modern era, like the seventeenth century, will continue to chafe at the moralizing and the lamentation. That is its privilege. But for those who wish to understand the world of Rabelais and Montaigne this tragedy's faults are its qualities, its fascination, its wealth.

NOTES TO THE CONCLUSION

[1] See, for example, E. Quentin-Bauchart, *La Bibliothèque de Fontainebleau et les livres des derniers Valois à la Bibliothèque Nationale* (1515-1589) (Paris: E. Paul, L. Huard and Guillemin, 1891).

[2] Said in evaluating René Bray's *La Formation de la doctrine classique en France* for the seventeenth-century volume of *A Critical Bibliography of French Literature*, ed. David C. Cabeen and Jules Brody, entry 764.

BIBLIOGRAPHY

I THE PLAYS (including contemporary and modern editions of French and classical works consulted)

Amboise, Adrien d', *Holoferne*. Paris, 1580. B.N. 16° Rés. Yf. 4261.

Les Amoureux Brandons de Franciarque et Callixène. Paris, 1606. B.A. 8° B.L. 14218.

[Baïf, Lazare de, trans.,] *Tragédie de Sophocles intitulée Electra*. Paris, 1537. B.M. 237, i. 37; B.N. 8° Rés. Yb. 1057.

Bardon de Brun, B., *Sainct Jacques*. Limoges, 1596. B.N. 8° Rés. Yf. 3908.

Beaubrueil, Jean de, *Regulus*. Limoges, 1582. B.M. 11737. aa. 7; B.N. 8° Rés. Yf. 3965.

Behourt, Jean, *Esau, ou le chasseur*. Rouen, 1599. B.A. 8° B.L. 14161 (2).

——*Hypsicratée, ou la magnanimité*. Rouen, 1604. B.A. 8° B.L. 14163; B.M. 241. c. 41. (3); B.N. 12° Rés. Yf. 4304.

——*La Polyxène, tragicomédie*. Rouen, 1597. B.A. 8° B.L. 14161 (1); B.M. 241 c. 41. (1); B.N. 12° Yf. 4740.

Bellone, Estienne, *Les Amours de Dalcméon et de Flore*. Rouen, 1621. B.A. GD 8° 5195; B.N. 12° Rés. Yf. 3765.

Belyard, Simon, *Le Guysien*. Troyes, 1592. B.M. 243. f. 7. (1).

Bensérade, I. de, *La Cléopâtre*. Paris, 1636. B.M. 86. a. 6. (1); B.N. 4° Rés. Yf. 213; H.L. *FC6 B4424. B641c.

——*La Mort d'Achille*. Paris, 1637. B.N. 4° Yf. 580; H.L. *FC6 C8147. 643 (B).

Berthrand, Le Sieur de, *La Tragédie de Pryam, Roy de Troye*. Rouen, 1605. B.M. 11736. a. 20.

Bèze, Théodore de, *Abraham sacrifiant*. Ed. Keith Cameron. Geneva: Droz, 1967.

Billard, Claude, *Tragédies*. Paris, 1612. B.M. C. 39. c. 61; B.N. 8° Rés. Yf. 2972; H.L. *FC5 B4935. B612t.

[Bochetel, Guillaume, trans.,] *La Tragédie d'Euripide, nommée Hecuba*. Paris, 1550. B.N. 8° Rés. X. 2535 (incorrectly attributed to Lazare de Baïf); H.L. *FC5 B6313. 544eb.

Bousy, Pierre de, *Méléagre*. Caen, 1582. B.N. 8° Rés. Yf. 4326.

Bretog, Jean. *Tragédie françoise*. Lyons, 1571, rpt. Chartres, 1831.

Brisset, Roland, *Le Premier Livre du théâtre tragique*. Tours, 1590 (contains translations of plays by Seneca and Buchanan).

Buchanan, George, *Baptistes*. In *Opera omnia*, vol. II. Leyden, 1725. B.M. 632. k. 4.

——*Jephthes*. In *Opera omnia*, II. See previous entry.

Chantelouve, François de, *La Tragédie de feu Gaspar de Colligni*. In Pierre L'Estoile, *Journal d'Henri III*, vol. I. The Hague, 1744. B.M. 680. b. 13; B.N. 8° Yf. 6359.

——*Tragédie de Pharaon*. Paris, n. d. B.N. 8° Rés. Yf. 3878.

[Chevalier, Guillaume,] *Philis*. Paris, 1609. B.A. 8° B.L. 14020; B.N. 8° Rés. Ye. 3934.

Chevreau, Urbain, *La Lucresse romaine*. Paris, 1637. B.N. 4° Yf. 492; H.L. *FC6 C4287. 637l.

Chrétien, N., Sieur des Croix, *Les Tragédies de N. Chrestien, sieur des Croix*. Rouen, 1608, B.M. 163. b. 13; B.N. 12° Rés. Yf. 2962-5.

Des Masures, Louis, *Tragédies saintes*. Ed. Charles Comte. Paris: Hachette, 1907.

Du Ryer, Pierre, *Alcionée*. Paris, 1640. B.M. 86. a. 3. (6); B.N. 4° Yf. 662.

Du Souhait, Sieur, *Tragédie de Radégonde, Duchesse de Bourgongne*. Rouen, 1606. B.M. 163. b .46.

Erasmus, D., trans., *Hecuba et Iphigenia in Aulide*. Paris, 1544.

Euripides, *Hecuba*. Trans. Bochetel. See under Bochetel.

——*Hecuba*. Trans. Erasmus. See under Erasmus.

——*Iphigenia in Aulis*. Trans. Erasmus. See under Erasmus.

Euripides, *Théâtre complet*. Trans. Henri Berguin and Georges DuClos. 4 vols. Paris: Garnier-Flammarion, 1965-6.

Faure, Antoine, *Les Gordians et Maximins*. Chambery, 1589. B.A. 4° B.L. 3620; B.N. 4° Rés. p. Yf. 76.

Frischlinus, Nicodemus, *Venus, tragœdia nova*. In *Operum poeticorum*. [Strasbourg,] 1585.

Garnier, Robert, *Œuvres complètes*. Ed. Raymond Lebègue. Texts published to date: *Les Juifves, Bradamante, Poésies diverses*. Paris: Les Belles Lettres, 1949; *La Troade, Antigone*. Paris: Les Belles Lettres, 1952.

——*Porcie*. Paris, 1568. B.N. 8° Rés. Yf. 3949.

——*Les Tragédies de Robert Garnier*. Paris, 1585. B.M. 1073. d. 6; B.N. 12° Rés. Yf. 2959; H.L. *FC5 G1894. B585t. (All quotations from Garnier's tragedies, other than those included in Lebègue's editions of his *Œuvres complètes*, are from this edition.)

Godard, Jean. *La Franciade*. In *Les Œuvres de Jean Godard*, vol. II. Lyons, 1594. B.A. 8° B.L. 12614; B.N. 8° Rés. Ye. 2109; H.L. 38526. 16. 300*.

Gombauld, [Jean Ogier, sieur de, trans.,] *L'Aminte du Tasse*. Paris, 1632.

Grégoire de Hologne, *Gregorii Holonii leodiensis Catherina*, tragœdia de fortissimo. Antwerp, 1556.

——*Gregorii Holonii leodiensis Laurentias*. Antwerp, 1556.

Grévin, Jacques, *César*. In *Théâtre complet*. Ed. Lucien Pinvert. Paris: Garnier, 1922.

Hardy, Alexandre, *Les Chastes et Loyales Amours de Théagène et Cariclée*. Paris, 1623. B.M. 243. c. 6; B.N. 8° Rés. Yf. 4466; H.L. 38587. 24*.

Hardy, Alexandre, *Théâtre*. Ed. E. Stengel. 5 vols. Paris, 1884, rpt. Geneva: Slatkine, 1967.

Heudon, J., *Pyrrhe*. Rouen, 1598. B.A. 8° 12621.

——*S. Clouaud, Roy d'Orléans*. Rouen, 1599. B.A. 8° 12621.

Heyns, Pierre, *Le Miroir des Vefues: Tragédie sacrée d'Holoferne & Judith*. Amsterdam, 1596. B.M. 11737. aaa. 4; B.N. 8° Rés. Yf. 4471.

Le Jeu d'Adam. In *Jeux et Sapience du Moyen Age*. Ed. Albert Pauphilet. Paris: Gallimard, 1951.

Jodelle, Etienne, *Cléopâtre captive*. Ed. Lowell Bryce Ellis. Philadelphia: University of Pennsylvania Press, 1946.

——*Didon se sacrificant*. In *Les Œuvres et Meslanges d'Estienne Jodelle*. Paris, 1574. B.M. 85. e. 3; B.N. 4° Ye. 1037; H.C. *FC5 J5876. B5740.

[La Calprenède, G. de Costes, Sieur de,] *La Mort de Mithridate*. Paris, 1637. B.M. 839. e. 2. (2); B.N. 4° Rés. Yf. 394.

[La Croix, Antoine de,] *Tragi-comédie. L'Argument pris du troisième chapitre de Daniel*. n. p., n. d. B.N. 8° Rés. P. Yc. 1198 (2).

La Péruse, J. de, *La Médée*. Poitiers, 1556. B.A. 4° B.L. 3635.

La Taille, Jacques de, *Alexandre*. Paris, 1573. B.N. 8° Yf. 467; H.L. *FC5 L3405. 573d.

——*Daire*. Paris, 1573. B.N. 8° Yf. 467; H.L. *FC5 L3405. 573d.

La Taille, Jean de, *Saül le furieux*. Ed. A. Werner. In A. Werner, *Jean de La Taille und sein Saül le furieux*. Naumberg: G. Böhme, 1908.

Laudun Daigaliers, Pierre, *Diocletian*. In *Les Poésies de Pierre Laudun Daigaliers*. Paris, 1596. B.A. 8° B.L. 12615; B.N. 12° Rés. Ye. 4284.

——*Horace*. In *Les Poésies de Pierre Laudun Daigaliers*. See previous entry.

Le Breton, Gabriel, *Adonis*. Rouen, 1597. B.N. 12° Yf. 4739.

[Le Coq, Thomas,] *Tragédie représentant l'odieux et sanglant meurtre commis par le maudit Cain*. Paris, n. d. B.N. 8° Rés. Yf. 3876.

Le Jars, Louis, *Lucelle, tragi-comédie en prose françoise* Rouen, 1600. B.N. 12° Yf. 6855.

[Mainfray, Pierre,] *Cyrus triomphant*. Rouen, 1618. B.N. 12° Rés. Yf. 3761.

Mairet, Jean, *Chryseïde et Arimand*. Ed. H.C. Lancaster. Baltimore: Johns Hopkins Press, 1925.

——*Le Marc-Antoine ou La Cléopâtre*. Paris, 1637. B.M. 86. i. 12. (2); B.N. 4° Yf. 497; H.L. *FC6 C8147. 643c (B).

——*La Silvanire*. Paris, 1631. B.M. 86. i. 11; B.N. 4° Yf. 616.

——*La Silvie, tragi-comédie*. Ed. Jules Marsan. Paris: Société nouvelle de librairie et d'édition, 1905.

——*La Sophonisbe*. Ed. Karl Vollmöller. Heilbronn, 1888.

——*La Virginie, tragi-comédie*. Paris, 1635. B.M. 11736. h. 6; B.N. 4° Yf. 226.

Marcé, Rolland de, *Achab*. Paris, 1601. B.A. 8° B.L. 13838.

Marguerite de Navarre, *Comédie de la nativité de Jésus Christ*. Ed. Pierre Jourda. Paris: Boivin, [1939].

Matthieu, Pierre, *Aman*. Lyons, 1589. B.M. 840. a. 9. (2); B.N. 12° Yf. 2058.

——*Clytemnestre*. Lyons, 1589. B.M. 840. a. 9. (3); B.N. 12° Yf. 2059.

——*Esther*. Lyons, 1585. B.A. 8° B.L. 13918; B.N. 12° Rés. Yf. 3890.

——*La Guisade*. Lyons, 1589. B.M. 1073. d. 35; B.N. 8° Rés. Yf. 4534.

Matthieu, Pierre, *Vasthi*. Lyons, 1589. B.M. 840. a. 9. (1); B.N. 12° Yf. 2057.

Mermet, Claude, *La Tragédie de Sophonisbe*. Lyons, 1584 (a translation of Trissino's play).

Le Miracle de la Marquise de la Gaudin. In *Miracles de Notre Dame par personnages*. Ed. Gaston Paris and Ulysse Robert. 8 vols. Paris, 1877. II, 121-70.

Le Mistére du Viel Testament. Ed. Le Baron James de Rothschild. 6 vols. Paris, 1878-91.

Montchrétien, Anthoine de, *Aman*. Ed. George Seiver. Philadelphia: University of Pennsylvania Press, 1939. (The edition reproduces the texts of 1601 and 1604.)

——*David*. Ed. Lancaster E. Dabney. Austin, Texas: University Cooperative Society, 1963. (The edition reproduces the texts of 1601 and 1604.)

——*Les Lacènes*. Ed. Gladys Ethel Calkins. Philadelphia: [University of Pennsylvania Press], 1943. (The edition reproduces the texts of 1601 and 1604.)

——*Sophonisbe*. Ed. Ludwig Fries. Marburg, 1889. (This edition reproduces the texts of 1596, 1603 and 1604.)

——*Tragédies*. Ed. Petit de Julleville. Paris, 1891. (This edition was used for *La Reine d'Écosse* and *Hector*. It reproduces the 1604 text.)

Montreux, Nicolas de, *L'Arimène, ou Berger désespéré, pastorale*. Paris. 1597.

——*Cléopâtre, tragédie*. In *Œuvre de la chasteté*. Paris, 1595. B.M. 4409. aa. 43; B.N. 12° Rés. Y² 1625-26; H.L. *FC5 M7687. 5950.

——*Isabelle, tragédie*. In *Le Quatrième Livre des Bergeries de Juliette*. Paris. 1595. B.N. 12° Y² 7068-69.

——*La Sophonisbe*. Rouen, 1601. B.A. 8° B.L. 14592 (2).

Mont-Sacre, Ollenix du. See Montreux, Nicolas de.

La Mort de Roger, tragédie, qui est la suitte des tragédies de Rhodomont. Troyes, n. d. B.N. 8° Rés. Yf. 4675. (The B.N. catalogue attributes this play to Charles Bauter.)

[Nerée, Richard,] *Le Triomphe de la Ligue*. Leyden, 1607. B.N. 8° Rés. Yf. 3912.

Ouyn, Jacques, *Thobie, tragicomédie*. Rouen, 1606. B.N. 12° Rés. Yf. 2905.

Pageau, Margarit, *Bysathie*. In *Les Premières Œuvres poétiques de Margarit Pageau*. Paris, 1600. B.A. 8° B.L. 8987 Rés.; B.N. 12° Rés. p. Yf. 98.

——*Monime*. In *Les Premieres Œuvres poétiques de Margarit Pageau*. See previous entry.

Percheron, Luc, *Pyrrhe*. Paris, 1845; rpt. Geneva: Slatkine, 1970.

[Perrin, Francois,] *Tragédie de Sichem ravisseur*. Rouen, 1606. B.M. 163. b. 37; B.N. 12° Rés. Yf. 2902.

Philone, M., *Adonias*. Lausanne, 1586. B.A. 8° B.L. 13844; B.N. 8° Rés. m. Yf. 10.

——*Tragédie* [Josias]. Geneva, 1566. B.M. 11408. aaa. 38; B.N. 8° Yf. 6508.

Poullet, Pierard, *Tragédie* [Charite]. Orléans, 1595. B.A. 8° B.L. 13889; B.N. 8° Rés. Yf. 4617.

Prévost, Jean, *Les Tragédies et autres œuvres poétiques de Jean Prévost*. Poitiers, 1618, 13. B.M. 1073. d. 8. (1-3); H.L. 38526. 46. 550*.

Rayssiguier, Le Sieur de, *L'Aminte du Tasse*. Paris, 1632 (a translation).

Rivaudeau, André de, *Aman*. In *Les Œuvres poétiques d'André de Rivaudeau*. Ed. C. Mourain de Sourdeval. Paris, 1859.

Robelin, Jean, *Thébaïde*. Pont-à-Mousson, 1584. B.A. 8° B.L. 14068.

[Roillet, Claude,] *Tragédie françoise de Philanire, femme d'Hypolite.* Paris, 1577. B.N. 8° Rés. p. Yc. 1198 (3).

Romain, Nicolas, *Maurice.* Pont-à-Mousson, 1606. B.A. 8° B.L. 13988.

Rutebeuf, *Le Miracle de Théophile.* In *Jeux et Sapience du Moyen Age.* Ed. Albert Pauphilet. Paris: Gallimard: 1951.

Sainct-Gelays, Melin de, *Tragédie de Sophonisbe.* In *Œuvres complètes de Melin de Sainct-Gelays.* Ed. Prosper Blanchemain. 3 vols. Paris, 1873, III, 161-241 (a free translation of Trissino's play).

Scudéry, Georges de, *Didon.* Paris, 1637. B.N. 4° Yf. 492; H.L. *FC6 A100. B650t7.

——*La Mort de Caesar.* Paris, 1636. B.M. 11737. ff. 35. (6); B.N. 4° Rés. p. Yf. 216 (1); H.L. *FC6 Scu253. 636m.

Seneca, *Senecae tragoediae diligenter recognitae.* Ed. J. Badius. Paris, 1512.

——*Tragédies.* Ed. and trans. Léon Hermann. 2nd ed. Paris: Les Belles Lettres, 1961. (All quotations from Seneca's plays are taken from this edition.)

——*Senecae tragoediae explanatae diligentissime tribus commentariis G. Bernardino Marmita Parmensi, Daniele Gaietano Cremonesi, Iodoco Badio Ascensio.* [Paris], 1514.

——*Tragoediae Senecae cum commento.* Colophon: Impressum Lugduni per Anthoniũ Lambillon & Matinũ Sarazin socios, 1491.

Sophocles, *Electra.* Trans. Lazare de Baïf. See under Baïf.

——*Tragoediae septem.* Ed. Bernardus Quncta. Florence, 1547.

La Sophronie, tragédie françoise. Tirée de Torcato Tasco. Troyes, 1619. B.M. 164. a. 70. (The B.M. catalogue attributes this play to Aymard de Veins.)

Soret, N., *La Céciliade.* Paris, 1606. B.A. 8° B.L. 13884; B.N. 8° Rés. Yf. 3882.

Le Sponsus. Ed. Lucien Paul Thomas. Paris: Presses universitaires de France, 1951.

Terence, *Aphri comicorũ latino[rum] prĩcpis comedie abs Iodoc Badie perq[uam] familiariter post Donatum [et] Guidonẽ Juuenalem in latina lingua cantatissimos exposite.* Lyons, 1517.

Théophile de Viau, *Pyrame et Thisbé.* Ed. J. Hankiss. Strasbourg: Heitz, 1933.

Théophile de Viau [?], *La Tragédie de Pasiphaé.* Paris, 1628; rpt. Paris, 1862. B.M. 11737. a. 37; B.N. 12° Rés. Yf. 4662; H.L. *FC6 T3433. Az627te.

Thierry, Pierre, *David persécuté.* In *Les Œuvres premières du Sieur de Mont-Justin.* Pontoyse, 1600. B.M. 11475. aa. 32.

——*Tragédie de Coriolanus.* In *Les Œuvres premières du Sieur de Mont-Justin.* See previous entry.

Toutain, Charles, *La Tragédie d'Agamemnon.* Paris, 1557 (a translation of Seneca's play).

Tragédie de Jeanne D'Arques, dite la Pucelle d'Orléans. Rouen, 1600 [06?]. B.N. 12° Rés. Yf. 3954.

Tragédie francoise des amours d'Angélique & de Médor. Troyes, n. d. B.N. 8° Rés. Yf. 4673. (The B.N. catalogue attributes this play to Charles Bauter.)

Trissino, G., *La Sophonisbe.* In *Teatro italiano antico,* vol. I. Milan, 1808.

Tristan L'Hermite, François, *Mariane.* Ed. Jacques Madeleine. Paris: Hachette, 1917.

——*Panthée.* Paris, 1639. B.M. 86. i. 4. (2); B.N. 4° Yf. 515; H.L. *FC6 T7388. 639p.

[Troterel, Pierre,] Le Sieur d'Aves, *Tragédie de Sainte Agnès*. Rouen, 1615. B.N. 12° Yf. 6191; H.L. *FC6 T7555 615t.
Urfé, Honoré d', *La Sylvanire*. Paris, 1627. B.N. 8° Ye. 7610.
Virey, Jean de, *La Machabée*. Rouen, 1603. B.N. 12° Rés. Yf. 2904.

II PRIMARY SOURCES (excluding works written for the stage)

Agricola, Nicolaus, *Liber de liberali, et pia institutione iuuentutis*. Ratisbone, 1561.
[Amyot, J., trans.,] *L'Histoire aethiopique d'Heliodorus*. Paris, 1547.
Aphthonius, *Aphthonii praeexercitamenta in veterum aliquot de arte rhetorica traditiones*. Ed. J. Froben. Basel, 1521.
——*Aphthonii sophistae progymnasmata*. London, 1555.
Aristotle, *The Art of Poetry*. Trans. Philip Wheelwright. In *Aristotle*. New York: Odyssey Press, 1951.
——*The 'Art' of Rhetoric*. Ed. and trans. John Henry Freese. Cambridge, Mass.: Harvard University Press, 1959.
——*Poetica d'Aristotele vulgarizzata et sposta per Lodovico Castelvetro*. Basel, 1576.
Arnauld, Antoine and Pierre Nicole, *La Logique ou l'art de penser*. Ed. Pierre Clair and François Girbal. Paris: Presses universitaires de France, 1965.
Bachet, Claude-Gaspar, *Les Epistres d'Ovide traduites en vers françois avec des commentaires*. Bourg-en-Bresse, 1626.
Balzac, Jean-Louis Guez de, *Lettres du Sieur de Balzac*. Paris, 1634.
——*Œuvres*. Ed. L. Moreau. 2 vols. Paris, 1854.
——*Recueil de nouvelles lettres de Monsieur de Balzac*. Paris, 1645.
Bandello, Matteo, *Histoires tragiques, extraites des œuvres italiennes de Bandel & mises en langue françoise. Les six premières par Pierre Boisteau, surnommé Launay, natif de Bretaigne. Les douze suyuans, par François de Belle-forest*. 7 vols. Rouen, 1603-4.
Bary, René, *La Rhétorique françoise*. Paris, 1659.
Birague, Flaminio de, *Les Premières Œuvres poétiques de Flaminio de Birague*. Paris, 1585.
Blanchon, Joachim, *Les Premières Œuvres poétiques de Joachim Blanchon*. Paris, 1583.
Boaystuau, Pierre, *Le Théâtre du monde*. Anvers, 1580.
——trans., Bandello, *Histoires tragiques*. See under Bandello.
Boccaccio, Giovanni, *Amorous Fiammetta*. Trans. B. Giovano del M. Temp. London, 1587.
——*De claris mulieribus*. Bern, 1539.
——*Des nobles malheureux*. [Trans. Laurent de Premierfait.] Paris, 1538.
——*Le Philocope de Messire Jehan Boccacce Florentin, contenât l'histoire de Fleury & Blanchefleur*. Trans. Adrian Sevin. Paris, 1542.
Camus, Jean, *Le Cléoreste*. Lyons, 1626.
Casa, Giovanni [della], *Galatée ou l'art de plaire*. Paris, 1666.
Castelvetro, Lodovico. See under Aristotle, *Poetica*.
Chapelain, Jean, *De la lecture des vieux romans*. Ed. Alphonse Feillet. Paris, 1870.

Chapelain, Jean, *Lettres de Jean Chapelain*. Ed. Ph. Tamizey de Laroque. 2 vols. Paris: Imprimerie nationale, 1880-3.

——*Opuscules critiques*. Ed. Alfred C. Hunter. Paris: Droz, 1936. See also under Searles.

Cicero, *De oratore*. Ed. and trans. E. W. Sutton and H. Rackham. Cambridge, Mass.: Harvard University Press, 1948.

——*De inventione*. Ed. and trans. H. M. Hubbell. Cambridge, Mass.: Harvard University Press, 1959.

——*Orator*. Ed. and trans. H. M. Hubbell. Cambridge, Mass.: Harvard University Press, 1939.

——[?] *Rhetorica ad Herennium*. Ed. and trans. Harry Caplan. Cambridge, Mass.: Harvard University Press, 1954.

Colletet, Guillaume, *L'Art poëtique*. Paris, 1658.

Courcelles, Pierre de, *La Rhétorique de Pierre de Courcelles*. Paris, 1557.

Courtin de Cissé, Jacques, *Les Euvres poétiques de Jacques de Courtin de Cissé*. Paris, 1581.

——trans., *Les Hymnes de Synesse*. Paris, 1581.

Deimier, Pierre, Le Sieur de, *L'Académie de l'art poétique*. Paris, 1610.

Del Rio, Martin Antony, *Syntagma tragœdiæ latinæ*. Paris, 1620.

Du Bellay, Joachim, *La Deffence et illustration de la langue françoyse*. Ed. H. Chamard. 3rd ed. Paris: Didier, 1966.

[Du Perron, Jacques Davy,] *Perroniana et Thuana*. 2nd ed. Cologne, 1669.

[Du Refuge, Eustache,] *Traicté de la Cour*. Rouen, 1627.

Du Souhait, François, *Les Amours de Poliphile et Mellonimphe*. Lyons, 1605.

——*Le Bonheur des sages*. Paris, 1600.

——*Les Pourtraicts des chastes dames*. Lyons, 1600.

Du Vair, Guillaume, 'De l'éloquence françoise'. In *Les Œuvres du Sieur Du Vair*. Paris, 1619.

Erasmus, D., *Adagiorum opus D. Erasmi Roterdami*. Basel, 1526.

——*Ciceronianus*. Trans. Izora Scott. In Izora Scott, *Controversies over the Imitation of Cicero*. 2 parts. New York: Teachers College, Columbia University, 1910, II, 19-130.

——*De civilitate morum puerilium*. Trans. Alcide Bonneau. Paris, 1877.

——*De duplici copia*. See under Erasmus, *On Copia of Words and Ideas*.

——*On Copia of Words and Ideas*. Trans. Donald King and H. David Rix. Milwaukee, Wisc.: Marquette University Press, 1963.

——*The Praise of Folly*. Ed. and trans. John P. Dolan. In *The Essential Erasmus* New York: The New American Library, 1964.

Fabri, Pierre, *Le grant et vray art de Pleine Rhétorique*. Ed. A. Héron. Rouen, 1889.

Faret, Nicholas, *L'Honneste Homme ou l'art de plaire à la cour*. Paris, 1630.

Fontenelle, Bernard Le Bouyer de, *Vie de M. Corneille avec l'histoire du théâtre françois jusqu'à lui*. In *Œuvres de Monsieur de Fontenelle*. 3 vols. Paris, 1766, III, 6-124.

Fouquelin, Antoine, *La Rhétorique françoise*. Paris, 1557.

Gasté, Armand, *La Querelle du Cid, pièces et pamphlets*. Paris, 1898.

Gerzan, François du Soucy, Sieur de, *L'Histoire afriquaine de Cléomède et de Sophonisbe*. Paris, 1627.

H

Gournay, Marie de, *L'Ombre de la Damoiselle de Gournay*. Paris, 1626.

Grenaille, François de, *L'Honneste Garçon*. Paris, 1642.

Grévin, Jacques, 'Brief Discours pour l'intelligence de ce théâtre '. In *Théâtre complet*. Ed. Lucien Pinvert. Paris: Garnier, 1922, pp. 5-10.

[Grosnet, Pierre,] *Les Tragédies de Seneque desquelles sont extraictz plusieurs ēseignemens avthoritez & singulieres sentences tant en latin cōme en francoys tresutilles & prouffitables a vng chascun*. Paris, 1534.

Habanc, V., *Nouvelles Histoires tant tragiques que comiques*. Paris, 1585.

Heinsius, Daniel, *De tragœdiae constitutione*. Leyden, 1643.

Heliodorus, *L'Histoire aethiopoque de Heliodorus*. [Trans. J. Amyot.] Paris, 1547.

Hermogenes, *Rhetoris ad artem oratoriam praeexcitamenta*. Paris, 1540.

Horace, *De arte poetica*. In *Satires, Epistles and Ars poetica*. Ed. and trans. H. Rushton Fairclough. Cambridge, Mass.: Harvard University Press, 1966.

Isocrates, *Trois Liures d'Isocrates*. Trans. Loys le Roy. Paris, 1551.

Jodelle, Etienne, *Les Œuvres & Meslanges d'Estienne Jodelle*. Paris, 1574.

Joseph Juif et Hebrieu [Josephus Flavius], *De Lātiquité Judaïque*. Trans. G. Michel. Paris, 1534.

La Mesnardière, Jules de, *La Poétique de Jules de La Mesnardière*. Paris, 1639.

La Mothe le Vayer, François de, *Œuvres*. 2 vols. Paris, 1654.

La Taille, Jean de, *De l'art de la tragédie*. In A. Werner, *Jean de La Taille und sein Saül le furieux*. Naumberg: G. Böhme, 1908.

Laudun Daigaliers, Pierre de, *L'Art poétique*. Paris, 1598.

Le Roy, Louis, *De la vicissitude ou variété des choses*. Paris, 1577.

——trans., Isocrates. See under Isocrates.

Lipsius, Justus, *Epistolarum selectarum*. Antwerp, 1606.

——*Opera*. 4 vols. Antwerp, 1637.

La Logique de Port Royal. See under Arnauld, Antoine.

Lydgate, John, *Lydgate's Fall of Princes*. Ed. Henry Bergen. 4 vols. Washington, D.C.: The Carnegie Institution of Washington, 1923-7.

Mairet, Jean, 'Préface en forme de discours poétique' [Preface to *La Silvanire*]. In *Corneille critique*. Ed. R. Mantero. Paris: Buchet, Chastel, 1964, pp. 59-75.

Marguerite de Navarre, *L'Heptaméron*. Ed. Michel François. Paris: Garnier, 1950.

Matthieu, Pierre, *Histoire des prosperitez malheureuses d'vne femme cathenoise, grande seneschalle de Naples*. Rouen, 1619.

Melanchthon, Philipp, 'Epistola Phil. Mel. de legendis Tragoediis et Comoediis', in *Opera*. Ed. C. G. Bretschneider. Halle, 1838, vol. 5, 567-72.

[Meslier?], *Histoire véritable des infortunees et tragiques amours d'Hypolite & d'Isabelle, néapolitains*. Rouen, 1593.

Mirandula, Octavianus, *Illustrium poetarum flores*. Paris, 1585.

Montaigne, Michel de, *Essais*. Ed. A. Thibaudet. Paris: Gallimard, 1950.

Montreux, Nicolas de, *Les Amours de Cléandre et Domiphille*. Paris, 1598.

Muret, Marc-Antoine, *Orationes, Epistolae, Hymnique sacri*. Ingolstadt, 1592.

——*Scripta selecta*. Ed. Joseph Frey. 2 vols. Leipzig, 1871.

Ogier, François, *Apologie pour Monsieur de Balzac*. Paris, 1628.

——'Au Lecteur par F.O.P.' [Preface to the second edition of Schélandre's

Tyr et Sidon]. In *Corneille critique*. Ed. R. Montero. Paris: Buchet, Chastel, 1964, pp. 49-58.

[Parfaict, François, and Claude Parfaict,] *Histoire du théatre françois depuis son origine*. 15 vols. Paris, 1745-9.

Pascal, Blaise, *Pensées*. Ed. Ch.-Marc des Granges. Paris: Garnier, 1958.

Pasquier, Etienne, *Les Œuvres d'Estienne Pasquier*. 2 vols. Amsterdam, 1723.

Paul the Deacon, *History of the Langobards*. Trans. William Dudley Foulke. Philadelphia: Longmans, Green, 1907.

Peletier du Mans, Jacques, *L'Art poétique*. Paris, 1555.

Petrarca, Francesco, *Les Triumphes messire francoys petrarque. Translatez de langaige tuscan en frãcois*. Paris, 1514.

Plutarch, *Œuvres*. Trans. Jacques Amyot. 22 vols. Paris, 1783-7. See also under Seyssel.

Poissenot, Benigne, *Nouvelles Histoires tragiques*. Paris, 1585.

Premierfait, Laurent de, trans. *Des nobles malheureux*. See under Boccaccio.

Quintilian, *Institutio oratoria*. Ed. and trans. H. E. Butler. 4 vols. Cambridge, Mass.: Harvard University Press, 1963.

Racan, Honorat de Bueil, marquis de, *Œuvres complètes*. Ed. M. Tenant de Latour. 2 vols. Paris, 1857.

Ramus, Petrus, *Ciceronianus*. Paris, 1557.

Ronsard, Pierre de, *Œuvres complètes*. Ed. Gustave Cohen. Paris: Gallimard, 1950.

Rosset, François de, *Les Histoires tragiques de nostre temps*. 2nd ed. n.p., 1615.

Scaliger, Julius Caesar, *Poetices libri septem*. 4th ed. [Heidelberg,] 1607.

Searles, Colbert, ed., *Catalogue de tous les livres de feu M. Chapelain*. Palo Alto, Stanford U., 1912.

Seyssel, Claude de, trans., *Appian Alexandrin, historien grec*. Paris, 1573. (includes an extract from Plutarch's life of Marc-Anthony, entitled *Le Sixieme Livre des guerres civiles, extraict de Plutarque, en la vie de Marc Antoine*, ff 434^r-450^r).

Sorel, Charles, *Le Berger extravagant*. Rouen, 1639.

Tahureau, Jacques, *Les Dialogues*. Ed. F. Conscience. Paris, 1870.

Tallemant des Réaux, *Historiettes*. Ed. A. Adam. 2 vols. Paris: Gallimard, 1961.

Théophile de Viau, *Œuvres poétiques*. Ed. Jeanne Streicher. 2 vols. Geneva: Droz, 1951-8.

——*Premier Chapitre des fragments d'une histoire comique*. In *Le Procès du poëte Théophile de Viau*. Ed. Frédéric LaChèvre. Paris: Champion, 1909, vol. II, 135-7.

Les Tragiques Amours du braue Lydamas et de la belle Myrtille. Toulouse, 1594.

Vauquelin de la Fresnaye, *L'Art poétique*. Ed. Achille Genty. Paris, 1862.

Vauquelin des Yveteaux, Nicholas, *Œuvres complètes*. Ed. Georges Mongrédien. Paris: A. Picard, 1921.

Virgil, *The Aeneid*. Ed. and trans. H. Rushton Fairclough. 2 vols. Cambridge, Mass.: Harvard University Press, 1960.

III WORKS OF MODERN CRITICISM (Given the impossibility of listing here all the studies available, I have restricted entries to studies quoted in the text and to other works which deal most directly with the attitudes or material analysed above.)

Adam, Antoine, *Histoire de la littérature française au XVIIe siècle*. vol. I Paris: Domat Montchrestien, 1948.
——'Sur la première époque de Corneille', *L'Information littéraire*, II (1950), 43-6.
Austin, R. G., ed., *Aeneidos, Liber quartus*. Oxford: Clarendon Press, 1955.
Banachévitch, Nicolas, *Jean Bastier de la Péruse* (1529-1554). Paris: Presses universitaires de France, 1923.
Batiffol, Louis, 'Richelieu a-t-il persécuté Corneille?' *R.D.M.*, XCIII (1923), 626-57.
Boase, Alan M., *The Fortunes of Montaigne: A History of the Essays in France, 1580-1669*. London: Methuen, 1935.
Borgerhoff, E. B. O., *The Freedom of French Classicism*. Princeton: Princeton University Press, 1950.
Bovet, E., 'La Préface de Chapelain à l'Adonis', in *Aus Romanischen Sprachen und Literaturen. Festschrift Heinrich Morf*. Halle: M. Niemeyer, 1905, pp. 1-52.
Bradbrook, M. C., *Themes and Conventions of Elizabethan Tragedy*. Cambridge, Eng.: Cambridge University Press, 1952.
Bray, René, *La Formation de la doctrine classique en France*. Paris: Université de Paris, Faculté des Lettres, 1927.
Castor, Grahame, *Pléiade Poetics*. Cambridge, Eng.: Cambridge University Press, 1964.
Cave, Terence, *Devotional Poetry in France c. 1570-1613*. London: Cambridge University Press, 1969.
Chamard, Henri, *Histoire de la Pléiade*. 4 vols. Paris: H. Didier, 1939-40.
——*La Tragédie de la Renaissance*. 2 fascicules. Paris: R. Guillon, 1929-30.
Charlton, Henry B., *The Senecan Tradition in Renaissance Tragedy*. Manchester: Manchester University Press, 1946.
Cooper, Lane and Alfred Gudeman, *A Bibliography of the Poetics of Aristotle*. New Haven: Yale University Press, 1928.
Croll, Morris W., *Style, Rhetoric, and Rhythm*. Ed. J. Max Patrick and others. Princeton: Princeton University Press, 1966.
Curtius, Ernst, *European Literature and the Latin Middle Ages*. Trans. W. R. Trask. New York: Pantheon Books, 1953.
Dabney, Lancaster E., *Claude Billard*. Baltimore: Johns Hopkins Press, 1931.
——*French Dramatic Literature in the Reign of Henry IV*. Austin, Texas: The University Cooperative Society, 1952.
——'A Sixteenth Century French Play Based on The *Chastelaine de Vergi*', *M.L.N.*, 48 (1933), 437-43.
Daele, Rose-Marie, *Nicolas de Montreulx*. New York: The Moretus Press, 1946.
Decharme, Paul, *Euripide et l'esprit de son théâtre*. Paris, 1893.
De Jongh, William F. J., *A Bibliography of the Novel and Short Story in French from the Beginning of Printing till 1600*. Albuquerque: University of New Mexico Press, 1944.

Delcourt, Marie, *Etude sur les traductions des tragiques grecs et latins en France depuis la Renaissance.* Brussels, 1925.
——'Jodelle et Plutarque', *Bulletin de l'Association G. Budé*, 42 (1934), 36-52.
Descotes, Maurice, *Le Public de théâtre et son histoire.* Paris: Presses universitaires de France, 1964.
Doran, Madeleine, *Endeavors of Art: A Study of Form in Elizabethan Drama.* Madison: University of Wisconsin Press, 1964.
Doubrovsky, Serge, *Corneille et la dialectique du héros.* Paris: Gallimard, 1963.
Forsyth, Elliott, *La Tragédie française de Jodelle à Corneille: le thème de la vengeance.* Paris: Nizet, 1962.
Friedrich, Hugo, *Montaigne.* Trans. Robert Rovine. Paris: Gallimard, 1968.
Friedrich, Jakob, *Die Didodramen des Dolce, Jodelle und Marlowe.* Kempten, 1888.
Gofflot, L.-V., *Le Théâtre au collège.* Paris: H. Champion, 1907.
Griffiths, Richard, *The Dramatic Technique of Antoine de Montchrestien: Rhetoric and Style in French Renaissance Tragedy.* Oxford: Clarendon Press, 1970.
——'The Influence of Formulary Rhetoric upon French Renaissance Tragedy', *M.L.R.*, 59 (1964), 201-8.
——'Les Sentences et le "but moral" dans les tragédies de Montchrestien', *R.S.H.*, 105 (1962), 5-14.
Guicharnaud, Jacques, 'Beware of happiness: Mairet's *Sophonisbe*', *Y.F.S.*, 38 (1967), 205-21.
Guillaumie, Gaston, *J. L. Guez de Balzac et la prose française.* Paris, 1927.
Harsh, Philip W., *A Handbook of Classical Drama.* Stanford: Stanford University Press, 1944.
Hathaway, Baxter, *The Age of Criticism: The Late Renaissance in Italy.* Ithaca: Cornell University Press, 1962.
Holsboer, S. Wilma, *L'Histoire de la mise en scène dans le théâtre français de 1620 à 1657.* Paris: Droz, 1933.
Jeffery, Brian, *French Renaissance Comedy.* Oxford: Clarendon Press, 1969.
Jondorf, Gillian, *Robert Garnier and the Themes of Political Tragedy in the Sixteenth Century.* Cambridge, Eng.: Cambridge University Press, 1969.
Jourda, Pierre, *Marguerite d'Angoulême.* 2 vols. Paris: H. Champion, 1930.
Katz, Richard, *Ronsard's French Critics: 1585-1828.* Geneva: Droz, 1966.
Kern, Edith G., *The Influence of Heinsius and Vossius upon French Dramatic Theory.* Baltimore: Johns Hopkins Press, 1949.
Kitto, Humphrey D., *Form and Meaning in Drama: A Study of Six Greek Plays and of Hamlet.* London: Methuen, 1956.
——*Greek Tragedy: A Literary Study.* London: Methuen, 1939.
Kohler, Erwin, *Entwicklung des biblischen Dramas des XVI. Jahrhunderts in Frankreich unter dem Einfluss der literarischen Renaissancebewegung.* Leipzig: A. Deichert, 1911.
Lancaster, H. C., *French Dramatic Literature in the Seventeenth Century. Part One (1610-1634).* Baltimore: Johns Hopkins Press, 1929.
——*French Tragi-Comedy: Its Origins and Development from 1552 to 1628.* Baltimore: J. H. Furst, 1907.
——'The Introduction of the Unities into the French Drama of the Seventeenth Century', *M.L.N.*, XLIV (1929), 207-17.

Lancaster, H. C., 'Leading French Tragedies just before the *Cid*', *Modern Philology*, 22 (1924), 375-8.

Lanson, Gustave, 'Les "discours" de Corneille', *R.C.C.*, 9² (1901), 115-22, 219-25, 410-16, 473-9.

——*Esquisse d'une histoire de la tragédie française*. New York: Columbia University Press, 1920.

——'Etudes sur les origines de la tragédie classique en France', *R.H.L.F.*, 10 (1903), 177-231, 413-36.

——'L'Idée de la tragédie en France avant Jodelle', *R.H.L.F.*, 11 (1904), 541-85.

Lantoine, Henri, *Histoire de l'enseignement secondaire en France au XVII*e *et au début du XVIII*e *siècle*. Paris, 1874.

Lawrenson, T. E., *The French Stage in the XVII Century*. Manchester: Manchester University Press, 1957.

Lawton, H. W., *The Classical Tradition and Classicism in France*. Sheffield: University of Sheffield, 1951.

——*Handbook of French Renaissance Dramatic Theory*. Manchester: Manchester University Press, 1949.

——'Sixteenth Century French Tragedy and Catharsis', *Essays presented to C.M. Girdleston*. Newcastle-upon-Tyne: King's College, 1960, pp. 171-80.

Lebègue, Raymond, 'Tableau de la tragédie française de 1573 à 1610', *B.H.R.*, V (1944), 373-93.

——'De la Renaissance au Classicisme: le théâtre baroque en France', *B.H.R.*, II (1942), 161-84.

——*La Tragédie française de la Renaissance*. 2nd ed. Paris: Office de Publicité, 1954.

——*La Tragédie religieuse en France 1514-1573*. Paris: H. Champion, 1929.

——'La Tragédie "shakespearienne" en France au temps de Shakespeare', *R.C.C.*, 38² (1937), 385-404, 621-8, 683-5.

Levi, Anthony, *French Moralists: The Theory of the Passions 1589 to 1649*. Oxford: Oxford University Press, 1964.

Lough, John, *Paris Theatre Audiences in the Seventeenth and Eighteenth Centuries*. London: Oxford University Press, 1957.

Loukovitch, Kosta, *La Tragédie religieuse classique en France*. Paris: Droz, 1933.

Magendie, Maurice, *La Politesse mondaine et les théories de l'honnêteté en France au XVII*e *siècle de 1600 à 1660*. Paris: F. Alcan, 1925.

——*Le Roman français au XVII*e *siecle de l'Astrée au Grand Cyrus*. Paris: Droz, 1932.

Margeson, J. M. R., *The Origins of English Tragedy*. Oxford: Oxford University Press, 1967.

Marsan, Jules, *La Pastorale dramatique en France*. Paris: Hachette, 1905.

Marti, Berthe, 'Seneca's Tragedies, A New Interpretation', *Transactions of the American Philological Association*, 76 (1945), 216-45.

McDonald, Charles Osborne, *The Rhetoric of Tragedy: Form in Stuart Drama*. n.p.: University of Massachusetts Press, 1966.

Mendell, Clarence W., *Our Seneca*. New Haven: Yale University Press, 1941.

Mouflard, Marie-Madeleine, *Robert Garnier 1545-1590*. [I] *La Vie*. La Ferté Bernard: Bellanger, [1961]; [II] *L'Oeuvre*. La Roche-sur-Yon: Imprimerie centrale de l'Ouest, 1963; [III] *Les Sources*. La Roche-sur-Yon: Imprimerie centrale de l'Ouest, 1964.

Mourgues, Odette de, *'L'Hippolyte* de Garnier et l'*Hippolytus* de Sénèque', *The French Renaissance and its Heritage*. Ed. D. R. Haggis. London: Methuen, 1968, pp. 191-202.

Mysing, Oscar, *Robert Garnier und die antike Tragödie*. Leipzig, 1891.

Nadal, Octave, 'La Scène française d'Alexandre Hardy à Corneille', *Le Préclassicisme français*. Ed. Jean Tortel. Paris: Les Cahiers du Sud, 1952, pp. 208-17.

Nolhac, Pierre de, 'La Bibliothèque d'un humaniste au XVIᵉ siècle: livres annotés par Muret', *Ecole française de Rome*, III (1883), 202-38.

Ong, Walter J., 'Fouquelin's French Rhetoric and the Ramist Vernacular Tradition', *Studies in Philology*, 51 (1954), 127-42.

Payen, Fernand, *Le Barreau et la langue française*. Paris: Grasset, 1939.

Putnam, Michael C. J., *The Poetry of the Aeneid*. Cambridge, Mass.: Harvard University Press, 1965.

Ratel, Simonne, 'La Cour de la Reine Marguerite', *R.S.S.*, XI (1924), 1-29, 193-207; XII (1925), 1-43.

Reese, Helen Reese, *La Mesnardière's Poétique* (1639): *Sources and Dramatic Theories*. Baltimore: Johns Hopkins Press, 1937.

Reynier, Gustave, *Le Roman sentimental avant l'Astrée*. Paris: A. Colin, 1908.

Rigal, Eugène, *Alexandre Hardy*. Paris, 1889.

——*De l'établissement de la tragédie en France*. Paris, 1892.

——*Le Théâtre français avant la période classique*. Paris: Hachette, 1901.

Rousset, Jean, *La Littérature de l'âge baroque en France*. Paris: Corti, 1953.

Sayce, R. A., 'The Use of the Term Baroque in French Literary History', *Comparative Literature*, 10 (1958), 246-53.

Schérer, Jacques, *La Dramaturgie classique en France*. Paris: Nizet, 1951.

Schimberg, André, *L'Education morale dans les collèges de la Compagnie de Jésus en France sous l'ancien régime*. Paris: H. Champion, 1913.

Scott, Izora, *Controversies over the Imitation of Cicero*. 2 parts. New York: Teachers College, Columbia University, 1910.

Stabler, Arthur Phillips, 'The *Histoires Tragiques* of François de Belleforest', Diss. University of Virginia, 1958.

Sturel, René, 'Essai sur les traductions du théâtre grec en français avant 1550', *R.H.L.F.*, XX (1913), 280-96, 637-66.

Sutcliffe, Frank, E., *Guez de Balzac et son temps: littérature et politique*. Paris: Nizet, 1959.

Valency, Maurice, *The Flower and the Castle*. New York: MacMillan, 1963.

van Roosbroeck, Gustave L., 'Corneille's Early Friends and Surroundings', *Modern Philology*, 18 (1920), 361-81.

——*The Genesis of Corneille's Mélite*. Vinton, Iowa: Kruse Publishing Co., n.d.

——'Preciosity in Corneille's Early Plays', *Philological Quarterly*, 6 (1927), 19-31.

Verrall, Arthur W., *Euripides The Rationalist*. Cambridge, Eng.: Cambridge University Press, 1913.

Webster, T. B. L., *The Tragedies of Euripides*. London: Methuen, 1967.

Weinberg, Bernard, 'Badius Ascensius and the Transmission of Medieval Literary Criticism', *Romance Philology*, 9 (1955-6), 209-16.
——*Critical Prefaces of the French Renaissance*. Evanston: Northwestern University Press, 1950.
——'From Aristotle to Pseudo-Aristotle', *Comparative Literature*, 5 (1953), 97-104.
——*A History of Literary Criticism in the Italian Renaissance*. 2 vols. Chicago: University of Chicago Press, 1961.
——'Scaliger Versus Aristotle on Poetics', *Modern Philology*, 39 (1942), 337-60.
——'The Sources of Grévin's Ideas on Comedy and Tragedy', *Modern Philology*, 45 (1947), 46-53.
Wells, Henry W., 'Senecan Influence on Elizabethan Tragedy: A Re-Estimation', *Shakespeare Association Bulletin*, 19 (1944), 71-84.
Wiley, William L., *The Early Public Theatre in France*. Cambridge, Mass.: Harvard University Press, 1960.
Yates, Frances A., 'Some New Light on "L'Ecossaise" of Antoine de Montchrétien', *M.L.R.*, 22 (1927), 285-97.

INDEX